SCRIBES AND SCHOLARS

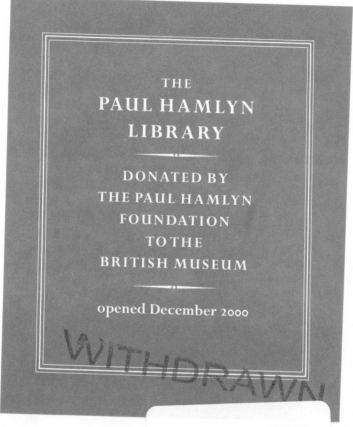

091.2 REY

SCRIBES
AND SCHOLARS

A Guide to the Transmission
of Greek and Latin Literature

BY

L. D. REYNOLDS

Fellow and Tutor of Brasenose College, Oxford

AND

N. G. WILSON

Fellow and Tutor of Lincoln College, Oxford

SECOND EDITION
REVISED AND ENLARGED

CLARENDON PRESS · OXFORD

Oxford University Press, Ely House, London W.1

GLASGOW NEW YORK TORONTO MELBOURNE WELLINGTON
CAPE TOWN IBADAN NAIROBI DAR ES SALAAM LUSAKA ADDIS ABABA
DELHI BOMBAY CALCUTTA MADRAS KARACHI LAHORE DACCA
KUALA LUMPUR SINGAPORE HONG KONG TOKYO

CASEBOUND ISBN 0 19 814371 0

PAPERBACK ISBN 0 19 814372 9

© *Oxford University Press 1968, 1974*

FIRST EDITION 1968
SECOND EDITION 1974
REPRINTED 1975

Printed in Great Britain by
Butler & Tanner Ltd, Frome and London

PREFACE

This book is designed as a simple introduction for beginners to a field of classical studies which generally remains little known or understood despite its importance and intrinsic interest. In schools and universities students read Greek and Latin authors in editions equipped with an apparatus criticus, but they are too often un-acquainted with the historical facts which make such an apparatus necessary, and are at a loss to evaluate the information that it gives. There are few works in English to which they can be referred, and a short guide is needed, especially one which can be read by those whose linguistic and historical knowledge is limited.

We have attempted to outline the processes by which Greek and Latin literature have been preserved, describing the dangers to which texts were exposed in the age of the manuscript book, and showing to what extent ancient and medieval readers or scholars were concerned to preserve or transmit classical texts. The history of texts cannot be separated from the history of education and scholarship, which also bulk large in these pages. On the other hand, matters of pure palaeography receive attention only if they are of direct importance for transmission.

The book is intended in the first place for students of Greek and Latin, but the theme handled is so inextricably connected with the cultural history of the Middle Ages and Renaissance that we think our account may be useful to anyone concerned with these periods. We also hope that students of biblical scholarship may find something of interest.

Reasons of space have compelled us to compress the material to the utmost and to omit some topics which we should have liked to treat, such as the general history of scholarship since the Renaissance. In addition it has sometimes been necessary to make a simplified statement of points that the expert reader will regard as complicated and controversial. Detailed footnotes, apart from increasing the price of the book, seemed out of keeping with the character of such an introductory work, but in general we have tried to indicate the primary sources in brackets in the main body of the text. The shelf-marks of manuscripts, often abbreviated and perhaps unfamiliar to the reader, are expanded and to some extent explained in the *index codicum*. Our major debts to the work of others are indicated in the Bibliography. Technical terms are explained where necessary, not in a separate glossary, and the reader who wishes to refer back to the explanation may find it through the index.

We should like to record here our gratitude to Professor R. G. Austin, Dr. R. W. Hunt, Mr. E. J. Kenney, Professor H. Lloyd-Jones, Professor Sir Roger Mynors and Mr. D. C. C. Young for much valuable advice and assistance. We should also like to thank the British and foreign libraries indicated in the notes to the plates for their permission to reproduce photographs of manuscripts in their possession.

June 1967   L.D.R.
                                                               N.G.W.

PREFACE TO THE SECOND EDITION

In preparing this new edition we have attempted to retain the principal feature of the original, a readable text unencumbered by a heavy apparatus of learning, and at the same time to meet the criticism that the absence of notes might make it difficult for readers to pursue any topic of special interest to them. We did not wish to go to the length of documenting all our statements with footnotes and hope that the addition of short notes to each chapter, largely bibliographical in character, will achieve a satisfactory compromise.

A new chapter, necessarily very selective, has been added in order to carry our survey down to the modern period. We have also made a number of additions and corrections to the original text and brought details up to date. We have profited a great deal from the kindness of friends and reviewers, and from the particular circumstance that the book has been subjected to the expert and critical eye of those responsible for the Italian and French editions. Much of the new material was prepared in the first instance for a French translation about to be published by Les Éditions du Seuil and we owe a special debt to M. Pierre Petitmengin of the École Normale Supérieure, whose acute suggestions have enabled us to make many improvements in both detail and substance.

December 1973

L.D.R.
N.G.W.

CONTENTS

A*

1. ANTIQUITY

I. ANCIENT BOOKS

A description of the processes by which classical literature has been transmitted from the ancient world to the present day may conveniently begin with a brief outline of the origin and growth of trade in books. In Greece of the pre-classical age literature preceded literacy. The nucleus of the Homeric poems was handed down through several centuries during which the use of writing appears to have been completely lost; and in the latter part of the eighth century, when the Phoenician alphabet was adapted for the writing of Greek, the tradition of oral literary composition was still strong, with the result that it was not immediately thought necessary to commit the Homeric poems to writing. According to a tradition frequently repeated in antiquity the first written text of the epics was prepared at Athens in the middle of the sixth century by order of Pisistratus. This account, though not above suspicion, is plausible; but it does not follow that copies of the text of Homer began to circulate in any considerable numbers, for Pisistratus' object was in all probability to ensure the existence of an official copy of the poems to be recited at the festival of the Panathenaea. The habit of reading epic poetry instead of hearing it recited will not have been created overnight, and books remained something of a rarity until well into the fifth century. On the other hand the growth of forms of literature which do not depend on oral composition ensured that from the seventh century onwards there was a need for authors to put their works in writing, even if only one copy was made for the purpose of reference; thus Heraclitus is said to have deposited his famous treatise in a temple, and perhaps for this reason it survived to be read by Aristotle in the middle of the fourth century (Diog. Laert. 9.6). The multiplication and circulation of copies was probably extremely limited, and it may be conjectured that the first works to reach even a modest public were either the writings of the Ionian philosophers and historians or those of the sophists. There must also have been a certain demand for copies of the poetic texts that formed the basis of school education. It is not until the middle of the fifth century or a little later that a book trade can be said to have existed in Greece: we find references to a part of the Athenian market where books can be bought (Eupolis fr. 304K), and Socrates is represented by Plato as saying in his *Apology* (26) that anyone can buy Anaxagoras' works for a drachma in the orchestra. All details of the trade, however, remain unknown.

Of the appearance of the books that were produced in classical Greece not much can be said with certainty. The number of books or fragments surviving from the fourth century is so tiny that it would not be reasonable to regard them as a representative sample. The general statements that follow are therefore based primarily on Hellenistic material, but it may be inferred with some plausibility that they are true also for the classical period. An attempt will be made to show how the physical differences between ancient and modern books affected the ancient reader in his relation to literary texts.

The form of the book was a roll, on one side of which the text was written in a series of columns. The reader would unroll it gradually, using one hand to hold the part that he had already seen, which was rolled up; but the result of this process was to reverse the coil, so that the whole book had to be unrolled again before the next reader could use it. The inconvenience of this book-form is obvious, especially when it is remembered that some rolls were of considerable length; one of the longest surviving (P. Oxy. 843) contained when complete the whole of Plato's *Symposium* and must have been about twenty-two feet long. Another disadvantage was that the material of which it was composed was by no means strong, and damage easily ensued. It is not difficult to imagine that an ancient reader faced with the need to verify a quotation or check a reference would rely if possible on his memory of the passage rather than go to the trouble of unwinding the roll and perhaps thereby accelerating the process of wear and tear. This would certainly account for the fact that when one ancient author quotes another there is so often a substantial difference between the two versions.

The standard writing material was papyrus (Plate I), prepared by cutting thin strips from the fibrous pith of a reed that grew

freely in the Nile delta; in the first century A.D. there were also
minor centres of production in Syria and near Babylon. Two
layers of these strips, one laid at right angles over the other, were
pressed together to form sheets (Pliny, *N.H.* 13.68ff.). The sheets
could then be glued together in a long row to make a roll. Many
sizes of sheet were made, but the average book allowed a column of
text between eight and ten inches high, containing between
twenty-five and forty-five lines. As there was only one large source
of supply the book trade was presumably exposed to fluctuations
arising from war or a desire by the producers to exploit their
virtual monopoly. Some such difficulty is implied by Herodotus'
remark (5.58) that when writing material was in short supply the
Ionians had used sheep and goats' skins as a substitute. In resorting
to this expedient they seem to have followed the practice of their
Oriental neighbours. But leather as a writing material compared
unfavourably with papyrus, and was no doubt used only in
emergency. In the Hellenistic period, if Varro can be trusted (cf.
Pliny, *N.H.* 13.70), the Egyptian government placed an embargo
on the export of papyrus, which seems to have stimulated the
search for an acceptable alternative. At Pergamum a process was
devised for treating animal skins to give a better writing surface
than leather, the result being what is now called parchment
(otherwise known as vellum); the word owes part of its etymology
to the name Pergamum, and the derivation can be seen more
clearly from the Italian form *pergamena*. But if this tradition is
true the experiment was at first short-lived; one must assume that
the Egyptian embargo was soon removed, for it is not until the
early centuries of the Christian era that parchment comes into
common use for books; early examples are fragments of Euripides'
Cretans (P. Berol. 13217) and Demosthenes *On the false embassy*
(Brit. Mus. Add. 34473 = P. Lit. Lond. 127).

To what extent the supply and price of papyrus hindered or encouraged its use in Greece is impossible to say. But when employed for the production of a book it was almost invariably
covered with writing on one side only. The form of the book made
this necessary, since a text written on the back of a roll would have
been very easily rubbed away, and perhaps the surface of the
papyrus contributed to the formation of this convention, since

scribes always preferred to use first the side on which the fibres ran horizontally. On rare occasions we hear of rolls written on both sides (Juvenal 1.6, Pliny, *Epp.* 3.5.17), but such books were exceptional. A shortage of writing material did, however, sometimes cause a literary text to be written on the reverse across the fibres: a famous example is the manuscript of Euripides' *Hypsipyle* (P. Oxy. 852). It is important to note in this connection that the quantity of text carried by an ancient book was very small: the copy of Plato's *Symposium* mentioned above, though very large by ancient standards, contained a text which does not occupy more than about seventy printed pages.

Finally it should be emphasized that the text as arranged on the papyrus was much harder for the reader to interpret than in any modern book. Punctuation was never more than rudimentary. Texts were written without word-division, and it was not until the middle ages that a real effort was made to alter this convention in Greek or Latin texts. The system of accentuation, which might have compensated for this difficulty in Greek, was not invented until the Hellenistic period, and for a long time after its invention it was not universally used; here again it is not until the early middle ages that the writing of accents becomes normal practice. In dramatic texts throughout antiquity changes of speaker were not indicated with the precision now thought necessary; it was enough to write a horizontal stroke at the beginning of a line, or two points one above the other, like the modern English colon, for changes elsewhere; the names of the characters were frequently omitted. The inaccuracy of this method, and the state of confusion to which texts were soon reduced by it, may be seen from the condition of the papyri containing Menanders' *Dyscolus* and *Sicyonius*. Another and perhaps even stranger feature of books in the pre-Hellenistic period is that lyric verse was written as if it were prose; the fourth-century papyrus of Timotheus (P. Berol. 9875) is an instance, and even without this valuable document the fact could have been inferred from the statement that Aristophanes of Byzantium (c. 257–180 B.C.) devised the traditional colometry which makes clear the metrical units of the poetry (Dion. Hal., *de comp. verb.* 156, 221). It is to be noted that the difficulties facing the reader of an ancient book were equally troublesome to the man who wished to transcribe his own copy. The risk of misinterpretation and consequent corruption of the text in this period is not to be underestimated. It is certain that a high proportion of serious corruptions in classical texts go back to this period and were already widely current in the books that eventually entered the library of the Museum at Alexandria.

II. THE LIBRARY OF THE MUSEUM AND HELLENISTIC SCHOLARSHIP

The increase of the book trade made it possible for private individuals to form libraries. Even if the tradition that sixth-century tyrants such as Pisistratus and Polycrates of Samos possessed large collections of books is discounted (Athenaeus 1.3a), it is clear that by the end of the fifth century private libraries existed; Aristophanes pokes fun at Euripides for drawing heavily on literary sources in composing his tragedies (*Frogs* 943), and his own work, being full of parody and allusion, must have depended to some extent on a personal book collection.

There is no trace of any general library maintained at the public expense at Athens, but it is likely that official copies of plays performed at the leading festivals such as the Dionysia were kept in the public record office. Pseudo-Plutarch (*Lives of the ten orators* 841f) ascribes to the orator Lycurgus (c. 390–324 B.C.) a proposal to keep official copies in this way, but the need would probably have arisen earlier. We know that after the original performance plays were revived from time to time. New copies of the text must have been needed for the actors, and if they had been obliged to obtain these by a process of transcription from private copies it would be surprising that such a complete range of plays survived into the Hellenistic age.

The advance of education and science in the fourth century made it only a matter of time before academic institutions with their own libraries were founded. It is not surprising to find Strabo reporting (13.1.54) that Aristotle built up a large collection of books, no doubt representing the wide diversity of interests in the Lyceum. This collection and that of the Academy were the models emulated shortly afterwards by the king of Egypt when establishing the famous library at Alexandria (Diog. Laert. 4.1, 5.51).

The main interests of the Lyceum were scientific and philosophical, but literary studies were not neglected. Aristotle himself wrote on problems of interpretation in Homer besides his well-known *Poetics* and *Rhetoric*; and in connection with the latter there is some evidence that he and his successors were interested in the study of Demosthenes' speeches.

Of much greater significance were the literary studies undertaken at the Museum in Alexandria. This was formally, as the name implies, a temple in honour of the Muses presided over by a priest. It was in fact the centre of a literary and scientific community, and it is essential not to underestimate this last aspect of it; the librarian Eratosthenes (c. 295–c. 214 B.C.), though a literary man, was also a scientist who achieved fame for his attempts to measure the circumference of the earth, and it is probable that other distinguished Alexandrian scientists were members. The Museum was maintained at the expense of the king, and the members of it had study rooms and a hall in which they dined together. They also received a stipend from the royal purse. It has been observed that there is a superficial resemblance between this institution and an Oxford or Cambridge college, but the analogy breaks down in one important respect: there is no evidence that the scholars of the Museum gave regular instruction to students. The community was probably set up by Ptolemy Philadelphus c. 280 B.C., and it soon won a reputation, perhaps arousing jealousy through the lavishness of its arrangements, for we find the satirist Timon of Phlius writing of it c. 230 B.C. 'in populous Egypt they fatten up many bookish pedants who quarrel unceasingly in the Muses' bird-cage' (Athenaeus 1.22d).

An essential part of this foundation, housed in the same complex of buildings or in the near neighbourhood, was the famous library. It seems that some steps had been taken already in the previous reign by the first Ptolemy to set up a library, by inviting Demetrius of Phalerum, the eminent pupil of Theophrastus, to come to Alexandria for the purpose c. 295 B.C. The library grew rapidly. The number of volumes is variously estimated by the ancient sources, but owing to the inaccuracy with which all large figures given by classical authors are transmitted it is difficult to calculate the true figure. If we accept as true the tradition that in the third

century the library contained 200,000 or 490,000 volumes (Eusebius, *Praep. Evang.* 350b, Tzetzes, *prolegomena de comoedia*),
allowance must be made for the fact that a single roll would contain no more than a Platonic dialogue of moderate length or an
Attic play. There is also no means of knowing to what extent the
libraries made it their policy to stock duplicate copies. But
despite this uncertainty it is beyond doubt that great efforts were
made to form a complete collection of Greek literature, and there
are anecdotes which throw light on the spirit in which the business
of the library was conducted. The king is said to have been determined to obtain an accurate text of Attic tragedy, and persuaded
the Athenians to lend him the official copy from the public record
office. The Athenians asked for a deposit of fifteen talents as
security for the return of the texts, but having once obtained these
the Egyptian authorities decided to keep them and forfeit their
deposit (Galen 17(1).607). We also learn from Galen that in their
anxiety to complete their collection the librarians were frequently
deceived into purchasing forgeries of rare texts (15.105).

The task of the librarians in reducing to order the mass of books
flowing into the Museum was enormous. The principle of arrangement in the library is not known, but one indication of the vast
labours involved is that Callimachus, who was not himself chief
librarian, compiled a kind of bibliographical guide to all branches
of Greek literature, which occupied one hundred and twenty books
(the *Pinakes*, frr. 429–53). Owing to the conditions of ancient book
production the librarians faced certain problems that do not
trouble their modern counterparts. Texts copied by hand are
quickly liable to corruption; to make an accurate copy of even a
short text is a harder task than is generally realized by those who
have not had to do it. In addition to this pre-Hellenistic books gave
no help to the reader in any difficulty. Consequently there must
have been numerous passages where the author's meaning could
no longer be discerned, and many others in which various copies of
texts reaching the Museum showed serious discrepancies. The
incentive that this gave to the librarians to put the text in order led
to a great advance in learning and scholarly methods. It is no
coincidence that five of the first six librarians (Zenodotus, Apollonius Rhodius, Eratosthenes, Aristophanes, and Aristarchus) were

among the most famous literary men of their day, and it is in no small measure due to the success of their methods that classical Greek texts have come down to us in a state that is reasonably free from corruption.

In one case we can see clearly the influence which the scholars of the Museum exercised on the state of texts in common circulation. Of the many fragments of ancient copies of Homer a modest proportion are as early as the third century B.C. The text in these papyri is rather different from that now generally printed, and there are numerous lines added or omitted. But within a short time this type of text disappeared from circulation. This suggests that the scholars had not merely determined what the text of Homer should be, but succeeded in imposing this text as standard, either allowing it to be transcribed from a master copy placed at the disposal of the public, or alternatively employing a number of professional scribes to prepare copies for the book market. Discrepancies in the text of authors other than Homer were probably less serious, but not enough early papyri are preserved for us to form a judgement; it is a reasonable assumption that the Alexandrians did what was necessary to prepare a standard text of all authors commonly read by the educated public.

After the standardization of texts the next feature of Alexandrian scholarship that merits attention is the development of a number of aids to the reader. The first step was to ensure that fifth-century books coming from Attica, some of which must have been written in the old alphabet, were all transliterated into the normal Greek spelling of the Ionic alphabet. Until 403 B.C. Athens had officially used the older alphabet in which the letter epsilon represented the .vowels epsilon, epsilon-iota and eta; similarly omicron was used for omicron, omicron-upsilon and omega. The drawbacks of this script need no comment, and already before the end of the fifth century the more accurate Ionic alphabet was being used for some Athenian inscriptions on stone: probably the same was true of Athenian books. Nevertheless it is certain that some texts reaching the Alexandrian library were in the old script, for we find Aristarchus explaining a difficulty in Pindar as due to misinterpretation of the old alphabet; he tells us that at *Nemeans* 1.24 an adjective which appears to be in the nominative singular (ἐςλός) is incorrect for metrical reasons and must be understood as the accusative plural (ἐςλούς) (cf. schol. ad loc.). Another point at which the critics showed their awareness of the old alphabet was Aristophanes, *Birds* 66. It is important to note that the adoption of the Ionic alphabet for early Attic texts has been recognized as the norm since the Alexandrian period. In contrast to the procedure used for editing texts in all other literatures there has never been an attempt to restore the original orthography of the authors in its entirety.

A second aid for readers was an improvement in the method of punctuation and the invention of the system of accentuation, both commonly ascribed to Aristophanes of Byzantium. In a text lacking word-division the addition of a few accents gave the reader a substantial help, and it is rather strange that they did not immediately come to be regarded as indispensable to a written text. But though they were sometimes written over words that would otherwise have been difficult or ambiguous, in general it is hard to see what principle determines their addition in ancient books, and they were not regularly added until the beginning of the tenth century.

Although these improvements in the outward appearance of literary texts had significant and lasting results, they were of far less importance than the advances in scholarly method made by members of the Museum. The need to establish the text of Homer and the other classical authors inspired scholars to define and apply the principles of literary scholarship more systematically than had been attempted before. Discussion of difficult passages led not merely to the production of a reliable text of the authors in question, but to commentaries in which the problems were discussed and interpretations offered. There had previously been some isolated works devoted to Homer; Aristotle had written on problems in the text, and much earlier Theagenes of Rhegium (c. 525 B.C.), perhaps spurred by Xenophanes' attacks on the immorality of the Homeric gods, had attempted to remove this embarrassing weakness of the poems by resorting to allegorical interpretation. But now a mass of critical literature was produced for the first time. Some of it was highly specialized; for instance Zenodotus apparently wrote a life of Homer and a treatise on the length of time required for the action of the *Iliad*. Aristophanes wrote on grammatical regularity (περὶ ἀναλογίας) and compiled corrections and supplements to the bibliographical guide to Greek literature that Callimachus had composed. Work of this character was not confined to Homer; we hear of monographs on the characters of comedy by Hypsicrates and on the myths of tragedy by Thersagoras (P. Oxy. 2192). These explanatory works were in all cases written as separate texts independent of the work that they illustrated; apart from brief and rudimentary notes commentary on an author was not at this date added to the margin of a text, but occupied another book. In the case of Homer especially, and less frequently in lyric poetry, drama, Demosthenes, and Plato, a number of conventional signs were put into the margin of the text to indicate that the passage was interesting in some way, for instance corrupt or spurious, and that the reader would find comment on the point in the explanatory monograph. Although very little survives from this class of literature in its original form, there is one famous example in the papyrus of part of a work by the later scholar Didymus (1st cent. B.C.) on Demosthenes (P. Berol. 9780). But in general our knowledge of these works comes from fragments of them that have been incorporated into the later form of commentary known as scholia; these are regularly transmitted in the margins of medieval manuscripts, and more will be said of their history below.

We come now to a brief discussion of the critical signs and the commentaries. The first and most important sign was the *obelos*, a horizontal stroke placed in the margin just to the left of a verse. It was used already by Zenodotus, and indicated that the verse was spurious. Some other signs of less importance and frequency seem to have been devised by Aristophanes. The final development of the system as applied to Homer was made by Aristarchus, who produced complete editions of both *Iliad* and *Odyssey*. He used six signs: apart from the *obelos* we find the *diplē* >, which indicated any noteworthy point of language or content; the dotted *diplē* (περιεςτιγμένη) ⪈ referred to a verse where Aristarchus differed in his text from Zenodotus; the *asteriskos* ※ marked a verse incorrectly repeated in another passage; the *asteriskos* in conjunction with the *obelos* marked the interpolation of verses from another passage; and finally the *antisigma* ⊃ marked passages in which the order of the lines had been disturbed (Plates I and II).

It is natural that a complicated system of this kind, which had the drawback that the reader wishing to discover a scholar's reasons for placing a sign at any given point had to consult another book, commended itself to scholarly readers only. No more than a tiny proportion of the surviving papyri, about fifteen of more than six hundred, display them. In the medieval manuscripts of the tenth century and later they are usually omitted; but there is one famous and important exception to this rule, the tenth-century Venetian manuscript of the *Iliad* (Marc. gr. 454), which preserves a vast collection of marginal scholia. As the commentary on an author was written in the margins by this date, and not in a separate book, there was perhaps less incentive to transcribe the signs; but fortunately the scribe of the Venice manuscript was determined to copy what he found in his exemplar without omission. Consequently the book shows a great number of the conventional signs, and it is by far the most complete and reliable source of our knowledge of this feature of the work carried out by the Alexandrians. It does not, however, always agree exactly in the use of the signs at the points where it can be compared with a papyrus, and there are signs which are not linked with a corresponding note in the scholia.

Though the Homer commentaries of Aristarchus and his colleagues are lost, enough of them can be reconstructed from the extant scholia, which are more copious than those on any other Greek author, to allow us to form a good judgement of the scholarly methods of the time. It is clear that many copies of the Homeric text reached the Museum from widely different sources; the scholia refer to texts coming from such places as Massilia, Sinope, and Argos. These were sifted and evaluated by the scholars, but it is not clear which text, if any, was taken to be the most authoritative. The procedure which made the Alexandrians notorious was their readiness to condemn lines as spurious (ἀθετεῖν, ἀθέτηϲιϲ). Their reasons for doing so, though possessing a certain specious logic, generally fail to convince the modern reader. One ground frequently alleged was undignified language or conduct (ἀπρέπεια). The first passage of the *Iliad* which was condemned in this way will serve as an example. At the opening of book I (29–31) Agamemnon, when refusing to release Chryseis, says to her father the priest: 'I will not set her free; no, sooner shall old age overtake her in my palace at Argos, far from her home, where she shall work the loom and serve my bed'. The lines are obelized in the Venice manuscript, and the ancient commentary on them reads as follows: 'the lines are athetized because they weaken the force of the meaning and the threatening tone . . . it is also improper for Agamemnon to make such remarks'. Another typical instance occurs at *Iliad* 3.423–6, where Zenodotus rejected the lines on the ground that it is unbecoming for the goddess Aphrodite to carry a seat for Helen. And naturally all passages that tended to show the gods in an unflattering light were an easy target for critics of this frame of mind; hence there were some who athetized the affair between Ares and Aphrodite in *Odyssey* VIII.

Scholars capable of treating a text so drastically, especially in their willingness to condemn lines as spurious for inadequate reasons, might have done great damage to the text. But fortunately for subsequent generations of readers the Alexandrians avoided the temptation to incorporate all their proposed alterations into the text itself and were content to note proposals in their commentaries; but for this restraint our text of Homer would have been seriously disfigured. It is interesting to note that most of their proposals did not commend themselves sufficiently to the ancient reader to become part of the ordinary text in circulation; this of course is not necessarily to be taken as evidence of the superior judgement of the reading public in antiquity, which may scarcely have given any thought to such matters. A count of the emendations made by the Alexandrians has shown that of the 413 alterations proposed by Zenodotus only 6 are found as readings in all our papyri and manuscripts, and only a further 34 in a majority of them, whereas 240 are never so found. Of the 83 emendations that can be ascribed to Aristophanes only one found universal approval, and 6 others appear in a majority of witnesses to the text, while 42 are never found in the text. Aristarchus was more influential, but even his suggestions were not readily accepted; out of 874 readings 80 are universally found, 160 occur in the majority of texts, and 132 in the scholia only.

It would be wrong to end this account of the Alexandrians without mentioning some more favourable specimens of their criticism. Certain parts of their work were of a high enough standard to be of permanent value. Their attempts to identify verses or passages of dubious authenticity were not always based on weak reasoning. They were suspicious of *Iliad* X, the story of Dolon, and had doubtless recognized that it was different in style from the rest of the *Iliad* and loosely attached to the narrative. In Odysseus' descent to the underworld in *Odyssey* XI Aristarchus noticed that lines 568–626 did not belong to the main thread of the story. Perhaps most interesting was the observation by Aristarchus and Aristophanes that the *Odyssey* ought to end at 23.296. Modern scholars might prefer to avoid condemning these passages as spurious and to regard them instead as products of a later stage of composition than the main body of the text; but this does not detract from the merit of the critics' observations.

Another matter for which the ancients, especially Aristarchus, deserve praise is the development of the critical principle that the best guide to an author's usage is the corpus of his own writings, and therefore difficulties ought to be explained wherever possible by reference to other passages in the same author (Ὅμηρον ἐξ Ὁμήρου σαφηνίζειν). This notion underlies many notes in the scholia which state that a given word or expression is more typically Homeric than the alternative possible reading. The principle was naturally liable to abuse if employed by a critic of mediocre intelligence, as happened all too often; for it might be taken to imply that if a literary text contains an expression that is both unique and difficult it must be modified in order to agree with the author's general practice. Such an extreme interpretation of the rule could have led to disastrous results, and it is greatly to the credit of Aristarchus that he appears to have devised a complementary principle, that there are many words or expressions in Homer which occur only once but should be accepted as genuine and left standing in the text (cf. schol. A on *Iliad* 3. 54). Problems which require the correct application of these principles still cause great difficulty to critics of the present day.

Finally it should be made clear that though the critics concerned themselves mainly with notes of a linguistic or antiquarian character, they were not blind to the literary merits of the poetry, and occasionally offer an apt comment on a fine passage. An example may be taken from the famous episode in *Iliad* VI, where Hector takes his leave of Andromache and Astyanax, and the poet describes how the child is frightened at the sight of the plume on his father's helmet. The critics commented: 'these verses are so full of descriptive power that the reader does not simply hear the sound of them but sees the scene before him; the poet took this scene from everyday life and copied it with supreme success'. Shortly afterwards comes the comment: 'while representing everyday life with such success the poet does not in the least destroy the stately tone appropriate to epic' (cf. schol. T on *Iliad* 6.467, 474, from MS. Burney 86 in the British Museum).

Most of this account of Alexandrian scholarship has been concerned with the text of Homer because of the copious evidence available. But it is certain that Alexandrian work on other authors was of great importance, and a few facts may be briefly enumerated. The text of tragedy was established, probably by reference to the Athenian official copy, as was mentioned above. The colometry of the lyric passages was devised by Aristophanes of Byzantium, so that they were no longer written out as if they were prose. A number of treatises on various aspects of the plays were written, and Aristophanes is credited with the authorship of the arguments outlining the plot prefixed to the plays; it is generally held, however, that the arguments now surviving are either not his work or have been considerably altered in the course of time. Marginal signs to guide the reader were much more sparingly used than in editions of Homer. The commonest was probably the letter chi, which indicated a point of interest in much the same way as the *diplē* in the Homeric text; this sign is mentioned in the scholia and occasionally is found in a medieval manuscript. A specially interesting feature of Alexandrian work on tragedy is the detection of lines altered or added by actors, generally in the plays of Euripides, who was more popular than the other dramatists. These interpolations are probably quite numerous, but it is not easy in every case to be absolutely certain that the line or lines in question are not original; and if they are clearly late, it may be obscure whether they should be attributed to Hellenistic actors (or more strictly producers) or to later interpolators. The scholia, however, which depend ultimately on Hellenistic work, do designate some lines as actors' interpolations. At *Medea* 85–8 the scholiast accuses the actors of misunderstanding the proper punctuation of 85 and altering the text in consequence; he adds rightly that 87 is superfluous, and its origin is not far to seek. At *Orestes* 1366–8 the chorus announce that one of the Phrygians is about to come out onto the stage through the front door of the palace, whereas in 1369–71 the Phrygian says that he jumped down off the roof. According to the scholia the original stage direction required the actor to make the jump, but this was regarded as dangerous, and so the actor descended by the back of the scenery and came out through the front door. In an effort to disguise this change 1366–8 were composed. Though these lines are needed in order to give a proper introduction to the new character and are linguistically blameless, they can be used to put us on the track of a more extensive interpolation.

Other Alexandrian works that should not go without mention are the editions of comedy, Pindar and the lyric poets. Here too the colometry had to be determined, and at one point we can see how Aristophanes rightly used it to show that a phrase which did not correspond metrically with the antistrophe should be deleted from the text (schol. on Pindar, *Olympians* 2.48). The task of editing comedy was undertaken in the same way as that of tragedy. We do not know what copies of the text were taken as the basis of the edition, but the rich collection of material contained in the surviving scholia to Aristophanes shows that his plays were studied with energy and enthusiasm.

III. OTHER HELLENISTIC WORK

The great age of Alexandrian work occurred in the third and second centuries; in the early part of the period the Museum was unrivalled. After a time, however, the rulers of Pergamum decided to challenge this position by founding a library of their own. The scheme is primarily associated with the name of king Eumenes II (197–159 B.C.): vast buildings were erected, and excavation by German archaeologists in the last century brought to light some sections of the library. Much less is known of the Pergamene library than of the Alexandrian. The librarians clearly undertook bibliographical studies on a large scale, and literary men found it useful to consult their work along with that of the Alexandrians (Athenaeus 8.336d, Dion. Hal., *de Dinarcho* 1). But the Pergamene scholars are not credited with editions of the classical authors and appear to have confined themselves to short monographs on specific points, sometimes directly in controversy with the Alexandrians. Their interests were not exclusively literary; Polemon (c. 220–160 B.C.), though he collected examples of parody, was first and foremost a student of topography and inscriptions; these important topics of historical scholarship had both remained outside the usual range of studies undertaken in the Museum. The most famous name linked with Pergamum is that of Crates (c. 200–c. 140 B.C.). He is known to have worked on Homer; some of his proposals for emending the text are preserved in the scholia, and he paid special attention to geography in Homer, attempting to reconcile it with Stoic views on the subject. He was also the first Greek to give lectures on literary subjects in Rome (see p. 19).

The Stoics gave a good deal of attention to literature. To them an important part of interpreting Homer was the application of allegorical explanations, and one of their treatises on this by a certain Heraclitus has survived. Apart from Homeric studies they dealt with grammar and linguistics, elaborating a fuller terminology than had previously existed. But the first formal Greek grammar was by Dionysius Thrax (c. 170–c. 90 B.C.); he appears to have been just old enough to have been a pupil of Aristarchus, but is not to be counted as an Alexandrian in the full sense, since his teaching was done largely in Rhodes. His grammar begins with a definition of the parts of the subject, the last of which, described by the author as the noblest of all, is the criticism of poetry. He then goes on to deal with parts of speech, declensions and conjugations, but matters of syntax and style are not discussed. This brief guide enjoyed a lasting vogue, as is attested by the volume of commentary upon it written by later grammarians. It was the basis of Greek grammars until comparatively modern times, and had the distinction of being translated into Syriac and Armenian in late antiquity.

The best Alexandrian work had now been completed; the decline of the school was brought about by the action of Ptolemy Euergetes II, who instituted a persecution of Greek literary men (c. 145–4 B.C.); among others Dionysius Thrax, who had begun his career in Alexandria, went into exile. The only eminent figure in the remaining part of the Hellenistic age is Didymus (1st cent. B.C.). He achieved notoriety in the ancient world through the bulk of his writings (but the story that 4,000 books came from his pen must be an exaggeration, even if it is assumed that many of these may not have been any longer than modern pamphlets). His name is mentioned frequently in scholia, and it is clear that his work extended over the whole range of classical poetry. As far as can be judged from the fragmentary nature of the evidence his activity was not so much composition of original commentaries as compilation from the already huge mass of critical work, and he is important because his compilations were evidently one of the main sources of material used by the later scholars who drew up the scholia in their present form. One book of his whose influence can be traced in extant works is his collection of rare or difficult words from tragedy (τραγικαὶ λέξεις); from this source derive a number of entries in the later dictionaries such as Hesychius. Didymus is also important for his work on prose authors; he commented on Thucydides and the orators, and the only substantial passage from his writings that is still preserved is part of a monograph on Demosthenes (P. Berol. 9780). This book when complete contained notes on speeches IX–XI and XIII. It confirms the usual view of Didymus as a compiler without any great originality or independence of mind; there are many quotations from sources otherwise lost, such as Philochorus and Theopompus, whereas Didymus' own contribution is very small. He goes so far as to record without comment a report that speech XI is a compilation of Demosthenic topics put together by Anaximenes of Lampsacus; yet this view, whether correct or not, demands discussion from any commentator. Not all interesting passages are discussed, but this kind of monograph was often less comprehensive in scope than its modern counterpart would be. On the other hand it is a welcome surprise to find that the commentary, instead of being confined to matters of linguistic interest or of value only to teachers of rhetoric, deals with chronological problems and historical interpretation.

IV. BOOKS AND SCHOLARSHIP IN THE ROMAN REPUBLIC

Although written records may have existed from very early times, Latin literature did not begin until the third century B.C. Inspired by Greek example, it was probably committed from its first beginnings to the form of book which had long been standard in the Greek world, the papyrus roll. By the middle of the second century Rome had a considerable body of literature of her own, poetry and plays and prose, and the growth of such a sophisticated literary and philosophical society as the Scipionic circle implies that books circulated freely within a limited class of Roman society. A century later, when Cicero and Varro were at their peak, the world of books had become very much a part of the world of the educated Roman.

Little is known about the ways in which Latin literature was handed down during the first two hundred years of its life. In the days when there was no organized machinery for the multiplication and circulation of books, no established libraries to preserve them, and before scholarship had begun to take a critical interest in their contents, the channels of transmission must have been casual and hazardous. Some works fared better than others. The national epics of Naevius and Ennius enjoyed a special status and received some scholarly attention at a comparatively early date. Prose was probably less fortunate. The one work of Cato which has been transmitted to us directly, his *De agri cultura*, appears to have been mangled and modernized through frequent and uncontrolled copying. There seems to have been no corpus of his speeches available in Cicero's day; Cicero protests against the neglect into which they have fallen (*Brutus* 65f.) and says that he had managed to gather together more than 150 of them. Dramatic texts had their own particular hazards, as we can see clearly in the case of Plautus. His plays were written for performance, bought by the magistrate or his agent, and transmitted initially as stage copies. We know from the prologue to the *Casina* that the plays were revived from time to time, and a subsequent restaging would mean that the script was cut, padded out, recast, or modernized to suit the taste of the producer or the audience. There are still traces of this early tampering with the text in our manuscripts; the different versions of the last scene of the *Poenulus* are an obvious example. Plautus' popularity was so great that he readily attracted spurious accretions and we are told (Gellius 3.3.11) that at one time no less than 130 plays were circulating under his name. Terence's plays enjoyed a more sheltered transmission, but some manuscripts preserve an alternative ending of the *Andria* which may go back to an early date.

This period of fluid transmission may account for many of the corruptions in these texts. In one place Varro has preserved for us (*L.L.*7.81) the authentic description of the shifty Ballio sidling through the door (*Pseud.* 955):

> ut transvorsus, non provorsus cedit, quasi cancer solet.

An attempt to get rid of the archaic *provorsus* produced the flat version of the line presented by both the surviving recensions of the text, the Ambrosian palimpsest (A) and the remaining manuscripts (P):

> non prorsus, verum ex transverso cedit, quasi cancer solet.

But in the *Miles Gloriosus* (24) A preserves the Plautine *epityra estur insanum bene* ('his cheese and olive spread is madly good eating') while both P and Varro (*L.L.* 7.86) read *insane*. In general the text of Plautus seems to have suffered surprisingly little since the days of Varro. The survival of what we have of early Latin literature is largely due, in the first instance, to the renewed interest which was taken in these writers during the last century of the Republic, and the comparative soundness of their texts we owe in part to the work of the early Roman grammarians.

According to Suetonius, the study of grammar was first introduced into Rome by the Homeric scholar Crates of Mallos. Crates came to Rome on a diplomatic mission, probably in 168 B.C., broke his leg in a sewer and turned his enforced convalescence to good use by giving lectures on poetry. The gradual infiltration of Hellenistic culture was doubtless governed by more complex factors than the breaking of a bone, but we must be thankful to Suetonius for turning his colourful spotlight onto a point in time when the Romans, who by the death of Ennius had a well-established literary tradition of their own, were ready to take an academic interest in their literature and language. He names two grammarians of this early period, C. Octavius Lampadio and Q. Vargunteius. Lampadio worked on the *Punic War* of Naevius and may have been interested in Ennius too, but the evidence is suspect: a copy of the *Annals* thought to have been corrected by Lampadio himself was still extant in the second century A.D. (Gellius 18.5.11). Vargunteius is reported to have given well-attended lectures on the *Annals*. Outside professional circles, a strong preoccupation with literary and linguistic matters is apparent in the poetry of Accius and Lucilius.

But the first of the great Roman grammarians was L. Aelius Stilo, of whom our ancient authorities speak with the highest respect. A firm and perhaps significant date in his life is the year 100 B.C., when he followed Metellus Numidicus into exile at Rhodes. It has been plausibly conjectured that he may have acquired his knowledge of Alexandrian scholarship there, from Aristarchus' own pupil Dionysius Thrax. At all events, Aelius is the first scholar who is recorded as having employed at Rome the conventional critical signs of the Alexandrians. The evidence for this is found in a remarkable document known as the *Anecdoton Parisinum*. This tract, preserved in a manuscript written at Monte Cassino towards the end of the eighth century (Paris lat. 7530), describes the critical signs used by Aristarchus and his successors. It almost certainly derives, with similar accounts, from the lost *De notis* of Suetonius. An important sentence reads (when some of the names have been conjecturally restored):

His solis [*sc.* notis] in adnotationibus Ennii Lucilii et historicorum [= writers of comedy?] usi sunt Varro Servius Aelius aeque et postremo Probus, qui illas in Vergilio et Horatio et Lucretio apposuit, ut Homero Aristarchus.

The name Aelius is not in doubt, and his interest in Plautus and the elucidation of archaic texts would naturally involve him in scholarship of the Alexandrian type. Although Plautus is no substitute for Homer, the nature of his text and the circumstances of its transmission presented problems similar to those which had exercised Hellenistic scholars and for which their critical methods had an obvious relevance. Plautus' text needed to be standardized: there were a mass of spurious plays, and the genuine ones contained later accretions and interpolations and varied considerably from copy to copy. The production of a list of the genuine plays had already exercised Accius; Stilo occupied himself with the problem, as did others, and pronounced twenty-five to be genuine. His son-in-law Servius Claudius was certainly interested in detecting interpolations, for Cicero speaks of his skill in saying 'hic versus Plauti non est, hic est' (*Fam.* 9.16.4). Aelius had a great influence on his pupil Varro (116–27 B.C.). Varro was a polymath, with a special interest in literary history, drama, and linguistics. He seems to have played a decisive part in selecting which plays of Plautus should be passed on to posterity as the genuine article. Although he accepted others as authentic, Varro singled out twenty-one plays as being unquestionably Plautine and this canon, known as the *fabulae Varronianae*, must coincide with the twenty-one plays which have come down to us. The establishment of the text of these early writers involved other questions of textual criticism besides authenticity, and Varro's awareness of routine problems is clear from his definition of *emendatio* as *recorrectio errorum qui per scripturam dictionemve fiunt* (fr. 236F).

Another activity for which there was ample scope was the interpretation of obsolete or difficult words. Evidence for this activity abounds in Varro and in what poor remains we have of the first Latin lexicon, the important and influential *De significatu verborum* of the Augustan grammarian Verrius Flaccus. This survives, partly in the abbreviated version made by Pompeius Festus, partly in the still more jejune epitome of Festus made by Paul the Deacon in the eighth century, with scattered references elsewhere. For instance, the *Nervolaria* of Plautus contained a trenchant description of decrepit prostitutes:

scrattae, scruppedae (?), strittabillae, sordidae.

These ladies were already encrusted with learning by Varro's time: he quotes (*L.L.* 7.65) the views of three different writers on the second word. Since the interpretations of these difficult words were often written between the lines of one's copy (as Varro himself testifies, *L.L.* 7.107), they could easily win a place in the text or give rise to doublets. For instance, at *Epidicus* 620 the P recension offers the reading *gravastellus* ('little old man'), while A has *ravistellus* ('little man with grey hair'); both variants were known to Festus and so go back at least to Augustan times. At *Miles Gloriosus* 1180 we have three variants, all ancient: the authentic reading is *exfafillato bracchio* ('uncovered'), preserved by P and attested by ancient authorities; but *expapillato* ('bared to the breast') can be traced back to antiquity; and A appears to offer a third variant (*expalliolato*), which must be at least as old as A itself (5th cent.).

The expansion of literature and scholarship in the late Republic was accompanied by important developments of a practical nature, and it is not surprising that during this period we first hear of plans for a public library at Rome and of the existence of more organized facilities for publishing books. There were already large private libraries. Greek books in particular had flowed in as part of the *praeda belli* and Lucullus' library, open to those who wished to use it, was famed. Cicero took enormous trouble to build up a fine collection of books; he received much help and advice from his friend Atticus and was fortunate to inherit the library of the scholar Servius Claudius. But it was Caesar who first planned a large public library. He commissioned Varro (among whose many works was a *De bibliothecis*) to collect books for it, but the plan was not realized: the first public library at Rome was founded in the Atrium Libertatis by C. Asinius Pollio in 39 B.C.

We hear nothing of a book trade at Rome before the time of Cicero. Then the booksellers and copyists (both initially called *librarii*) carried on an active trade, but do not seem to have met the high standards of a discriminating author, for Cicero complains of the poor quality of their work (*Q.f.* 3.4.5, 5.6). It was perhaps to fill this gap that Atticus, who had lived for a long time in Greece and had experience of a well-established book trade, put his staff of trained *librarii* at the service of his friends. It is not easy to see whether Atticus is at any given moment obliging Cicero as a friend or in a more professional capacity, but it is clear that Cicero could depend on him to provide all the services of a high-class publisher. Atticus would carefully revise a work for him, criticize points of style or content, discuss the advisability of publication or the suitability of a title, hold private readings of the new book, send out complimentary copies, organize its distribution. His standards of execution were of the highest and his name a guarantee of quality.

From the exchange of letters between Cicero and Atticus we can get a good idea of the casual and fluid nature of publication in the ancient world. There was no copyright or royalty (hence the importance of literary patronage) and private circulation could easily pass by degrees into full-scale publication; an author could incorporate changes into a published text by asking his friends to alter their copies, but other copies would remain unaltered. Cicero drastically reshaped his *Academica* when Atticus was in the process of having copies made and consoled him for the effort wasted with the promise of a superior version. But copies of the first draft were in existence; both 'editions' survived, and we have a more substantial part of the first than of the second. Cicero also protests that his *Oratio in Clodium et Curionem*, of which fragments have survived in some scholia, was published without his consent. In the *Orator* (29) he had incorrectly attributed some lines of Aristophanes to Eupolis and asked Atticus to rectify the mistake quickly in all copies. In this case he succeeded in correcting the tradition which has come down to us, but he was not so lucky when in the *Republic* (2.8) he wished to alter *Phliuntii* (as he had wrongly called the inhabitants of Phlius) to *Phliasii*; the sole manuscript of the work which has survived still has *Phliuntii*, and it is the modern editor who makes the change which Cicero requested.

V. DEVELOPMENTS UNDER THE EARLY EMPIRE

By the end of the Roman Republic the institutions and processes which govern and guard the transmission of the written word were already in existence, and under Augustus and his successors they were refined and consolidated. The book trade flourished and we soon hear of the names of established booksellers: Horace speaks of the Sosii, later Quintilian and Martial tell of Tryphon, Atrectus, and others. By the time of the Younger Seneca book collecting had become a form of extravagant ostentation. Augustus founded two public libraries, one in 28 B.C. in the Temple of Apollo on the Palatine, the other, not long afterwards, in the Campus Martius.

Thereafter libraries were a common form of both private and imperial munificence, in Rome and the provinces; one of the most famed and lasting was the Bibliotheca Ulpia founded by Trajan, which long survived the disasters of fire and strife and was still standing in the fifth century. Given an enlightened emperor, patronage could foster scholarship as well as literature: under Augustus Hyginus was appointed Palatine librarian and Verrius Flaccus was made tutor to the imperial children. It was during this period that school education too took the form which it was to keep for centuries and, with the state taking an increasing interest in education, it became standardized throughout the Roman world.

Secondary education at Rome was provided by the *grammaticus* and this largely consisted of the careful reading and detailed interpretation of poetry. Prose was more the concern of the *rhetor*, but their provinces to a certain extent overlapped. An important development was begun sometime after 26 B.C. by Q. Caecilius Epirota, a freedman of Atticus, who instituted in the school which he had opened the practice of studying Vergil and other modern writers. Vergil's entry into the normal school curriculum may have been at the expense of Ennius. From now on a successful poet, a Horace or an Ovid, saw his works passing into the school syllabus before he was decently dead and this continued until the archaizing reaction at the end of the first century interrupted the process and froze the canon of classical authors. Although poets like Horace and Lucan continued to be read in the schools, two poets were studied above all others, Vergil and, more surprisingly, Terence; in prose Cicero and Sallust occupied a similarly pre-eminent position.

The intense and minute study which was devoted to commonly read authors by expert and inexpert alike could affect their text for both good and ill. The large demand for popular works and those in the school curriculum might be expected to have flooded the market with poor copies and, while the close attention of scholars and grammarians would tend to safeguard the purity of the text, it is unfortunately only too apparent that scholars at all periods and with the best intentions have the power to deprave as well as to emend a text which passes through their hands. On the whole, neither the ill effects of popularization nor the interference of pedants appear to have muddied the main stream of our textual traditions nearly as much as might have been feared, but there is interesting evidence of some early corruption in standard authors. As early as the sixties Seneca (*Epist.* 94.28) quotes one of the unfinished lines of the *Aeneid, audentis fortuna iuvat* (10.284), with the supplement *piger ipse sibi obstat.* The gnomic quality of the half-line and the inviting vacuum which it left to be filled might so easily have generated a proverb that it is going too far to assume that Seneca actually used an interpolated copy of Vergil, but there is no doubt that those who wished to improve the national epic were already at work. Livy offers a clearer case. Quintilian, writing about thirty years after Seneca, tells us (9.4.74) that the preface to Livy's history began with the dactylic opening *facturusne operae pretium sim,* and that this should be preferred to the corrupt version current in his day. We owe the stylistic nicety of Livy's opening words, with their epic ring, to Quintilian, for all the manuscripts of the Nicomachean family, on which we depend at this point, read *facturusne sim operae pretium.* In the next century Gellius complains (20.6.14) that Sallust's *maiores vestrum* (*Cat.* 33.2) had been corrupted to *maiores vestri,* and the surviving manuscripts show that his complaint was justified. In the case of such authors it was never too soon for the textual critic to ply his trade.

The great Augustan scholar Verrius Flaccus still devoted his attention to the early writers, but his contemporary Julius Hyginus, a man of wide learning, wrote a work on Vergil which included observations on his text. He would read *sensus . . . amaror* for *sensu . . amaro* at *Georgics* 2.247 on the alleged authority of a manuscript *ex domo atque ex familia Vergilii* (Gellius 1.21); in *Aeneid* 12.120 he would emend *velati lino* to *velati limo* (*limus* being a sacrificial apron), more plausibly perhaps, but it is difficult not to conclude that Hyginus was more interested in improving Vergil than Vergil's text. Remmius Palaemon, an influential grammarian, continued to put the emphasis on modern authors, and Asconius, who stands out amongst ancient commentators for his good sense and integrity, wrote on Cicero, Vergil and Sallust. But of the scholars of the first century the most famous in his own day and in later ages was M. Valerius Probus of Beirut. His dates fall somewhere between A.D. 20–105 and his period of scholarly activity probably belongs to the closing decades of the century. He is a controversial figure, for our information about him is scanty and easily exaggerated. Such facts as we have about his life come from Suetonius (*De gramm.* 24). He tells us that Probus, disappointed in his hopes of military promotion, turned to the study of the old authors whom he had learned to admire at school in the provinces and who were now out of fashion at Rome. He gathered together a large number of texts and went through them in accordance with Alexandrian methods, providing aids to the reader and adding critical signs in the margin: *multaque exemplaria contracta emendare ac distinguere et adnotare curavit.* He did not set himself up as a teacher, but had a few followers with whom he would very occasionally read texts; he published only a few short pieces, but left behind a fair-sized *silva observationum sermonis antiqui.* His use of the tools of Alexandrian criticism is attested by the *Anecdoton Parisinum* (see p. 20): he is credited with the use of certain *notae* (the *asteriscus, asteriscus cum obelo, diplē*) and his employment of others is stated or implied in later commentaries; he is said to have worked specifically on Vergil, Horace, and Lucretius. Traces of his activity, some perhaps apocryphal, are found in later commentators, Servius and Donatus, and in Gellius. For instance, at *Aen* 1.44 he wished to emend *pectore* to *tempore*; at 8.406 he found the expression *coniugis infusus gremio* unbecoming and read *infusum*; at 10.173 he put a comma after *trecentos*; at 10.539 he would replace *armis* by *albis*; in Terence's *Adelphi* he assigned the words *quid festinas, mi Geta* (323) to Sostrata; in Sallust's *Catiline* (5.4: *satis eloquentiae, sapientiae parum*) he wished to foist upon Sallust the word *loquentia.* Little of this inspires confidence. It is not certain that he collated manuscripts, but he may have had access to at least one authoritative text: he claimed that his knowledge of Vergil's use of *i* and *e* in such accusatives as *urbes/urbis* and *turrem/turrim* was based on a manuscript corrected by Vergil's own hand (Gellius 13.21.1–8). It is difficult to assess his influence on our textual traditions. Probus has been such a convenient peg upon which to hang flimsy reconstructions of the early history of a number of texts that he has been credited with authoritative editions of Vergil, Terence, Horace, Lucretius, Plautus, Persius, and Sallust. Evidence of his work on Vergil and Terence is found in Servius and Donatus and others, and we have a couple of isolated references to an interest in Plautus and Sallust. A life of Persius exists which claims to have been taken *de commentario Probi Valeri*. Of his alleged editions of Horace, Lucretius, and Plautus we have nothing but conjecture. Copies which he had corrected doubtless circulated in antiquity, some of his written work was available, and the views which he had expressed in his informal seminars, handed down by word of mouth, were accessible to a later generation, as Gellius demonstrates. Such a legacy would account for the evidence; much more is needed to demonstrate a series of authoritative editions shaping the main streams of transmission. At all events, there is little trace of Probus' known corrections and emendations in our extant manuscripts. This is reassuring evidence of the strong respect which the Romans had for the authentic text. Our tradition of Vergil shows how little the scholarly work which grew around an author need affect his text.

VI. ARCHAISM IN THE SECOND CENTURY

The marked decline in creative literature which set in during the second century was accompanied by a widespread academic interest in the writers of the past. In particular, there was a resurgence of enthusiasm for the early writers of Rome. The beginnings of this archaistic revival can be seen in Probus; it was encouraged by Hadrian, and its influence can be traced in the works of Fronto, Gellius, and Apuleius. This cult of the archaic, besides producing the most baroque effects in the prose of the period, ensured that the writers of the early Republic— Ennius, Plautus, Cato, and lesser figures as well—were taken down from the shelves and studied with passionate interest. To this revival we owe much of our knowledge of these early writers. Their chances of ultimate survival were slim; their language was too archaic and obscure for them to survive the narrowing interests and declining literacy of the ages to come, and, with some notable exceptions, they lived on only in the fragments and gossip preserved by Gellius or one of the later collectors of words and facts.

We can glean from the pages of the *Attic Nights* of Aulus Gellius a remarkable picture of the antiquarian book trade in the second century A.D. He tells us that he saw on sale in a bookshop at Rome an ancient Latin version of the *Annals* of Fabius Pictor (5.4.1), and relates how one of his teachers, in order to look up a word, procured at immense pains and expense an old manuscript of Ennius' *Annals* 'almost certainly corrected by Lampadio himself' (18.5.11). Valuable finds could still be made in the libraries of Rome and the provinces: at Rome he found a rare work by Aelius Stilo (16.8.2), at Patras a venerable copy of Livius Andronicus (18.9.5), at Tibur a manuscript of the Sullan historian Claudius Quadrigarius (9.14.3). One of his friends had a Vergil *mirandae vetustatis, emptum in Sigillariis xx aureis* (2.3.5), quite a find to make, if the story be true, at a Christmas fair. Fronto corroborates this antiquarian's paradise when he speaks of the high price and prestige attached in his day to manuscripts of Cato, Ennius, Cicero, and other Republican writers, when they had been written by such men as Lampadio and Aelius Stilo, edited by Tiro, or copied by Atticus or Nepos (*Ad M. Caes.* 1.7.4). It is tempting to think that the venerability of the books still to be found at this period has been exaggerated by commercial guile or the enthusiasm of the collector, and there seems little doubt that some of the more recherché items were expensive and egregious fakes; but the important features of the situation remain even if some of the details are suspect, the continued availability of Republican writings, the value attached to old authors and old manuscripts, and the keenness of scholars to hunt these out, sometimes merely in the hope of recovering an authentic reading. The practice of consulting other manuscripts in order to improve one's own copy must have happened at all times, but is only sporadically documented. The earliest evidence for anything on the scale of a recension goes back to this period and concerns the activity of Statilius Maximus, a known Ciceronian scholar of the late second or early third century. In a manuscript of Cicero's speeches discovered in 1417 (see p. 122) the second speech *De lege agraria* begins with a note which has travelled down with the text and takes us back so many centuries: *Statilius Maximus rursum emendavi ad Tyronem et Laecanianum et Domitium et alios veteres III. oratio XXIIII.* The general sense is clear: Statilius corrected the text with reference to a number of manuscripts, including one which claimed to go back to Tiro.

VII. THE COMPENDIUM AND THE COMMENTARY

The intellectual decline which had begun in the second century was accelerated by the economic breakdown and political chaos of the third, and no major literary figures emerged until the age of Claudian. Many of the works produced during this period, though they may be dreary in themselves, are important for the history of classical texts. Some are important because they ensured the continuance of the classical tradition through the Middle Ages, when the great works of literature were either not available or unsuited to the needs and capacities of the time; some are still of value, because their sources have been lost or mutilated. Among these was the compendium. Florus had written an abridgement of Roman history in the reign of Hadrian and an epitomized Livy was known before that. These were followed in the third century by Justinus' epitome of the Augustan writer Pompeius Trogus, and in the fourth by the abbreviated histories of Eutropius, Aurelius Victor, and others unnamed. Some of these were widely read in ages which could not assimilate the rich fare of Livy and had lost the works of Tacitus. Already in the late third century the emperor Tacitus (275–6) is alleged to have ordered that the works of his namesake be copied ten times a year, *ne lectorum incuria deperiret* (*Hist. Aug.* 27.10.3). This story is almost certainly a fabrication of the late fourth century, but it is *ben trovato*. Apart from the political disasters of the third century, which must have taken their toll, the prominent absence of any real literature strongly suggests that the preservation and transmission of the literary heritage may likewise have suffered from neglect and misunderstanding. In other fields we have Festus' epitome of Verrius Flaccus and Solinus' plundering of Pliny and Mela. The period which produced so many potted handbooks was also the great age of the commentator and scholiast, of whom the best known are Acro and Porphyrio on Horace and the two great scholars of the fourth century, Aelius Donatus and Servius; Donatus wrote on Terence and Vergil, Servius contributed to the great Vergilian commentary which bears his name. Donatus was also the author of two grammars, the *Ars Minor* and *Maior*, which, together with the *Institutiones grammaticae* of Priscian (6th cent.), provided the Middle Ages with their textbooks on grammar.

Two other compilations should be mentioned here in view of their significance for a later age, the *De compendiosa doctrina* of Nonius Marcellus, of uncertain date, and the *De nuptiis Philologiae* of Martianus Capella, written in the first part of the fifth century. The first is a dictionary, still valuable in that it contains many quotations from works now lost; the author appears to have excerpted two tragedies of Ennius himself. The *De nuptiis* is an allegorical treatise on the seven liberal arts, which appear as bridesmaids at the wedding of Mercury and Philology. By the late fourth century the liberal arts had been standardized as grammar, rhetoric, dialectic, arithmetic, music, geometry, and astronomy. The canonical seven were handed on to the Middle Ages and became, in theory, the basis of medieval education. In time they split into two groups, the *trivium* (grammar, rhetoric, dialectic) and the *quadrivium* (arithmetic, music, geometry, astronomy), an elementary and a more advanced course.

The grammars and compilations of late antiquity served a double purpose, for the quotations which they used to illustrate a word or fact provided the men of the Middle Ages with what was at times the sum of their knowledge of ancient literature, and allowed them to give their writings a veneer of learning which was pathetically at variance with the narrowness of their classical reading.

VIII. FROM ROLL TO CODEX

Between the second and fourth centuries a development took place which is of the utmost significance for the history of the book and therefore for the transmission of classical texts in general. This was the gradual disappearance of the roll in favour of the codex, that is to say the adoption of a book with essentially the same appearance as the one we use today.

Down to the second century A.D. the standard vehicle for all literary texts had been the papyrus roll, but from the earliest times an alternative medium had existed in the writing tablet, which consisted of a number of wax-coated boards fastened together with a thong or clasp. These were used throughout antiquity for letters, school-exercises, rough notes, and other casual purposes.

The Romans extended their scope by using them for legal documents and took the important step of replacing the wooden tablets with parchment leaves. These parchment notebooks (*membranae*) were in use by the end of the Republic, but it took a long time for them to achieve the status of books.

The first mention of literary works being published in parchment codices is found in Martial, in a number of poems written during the years 84-6. He emphasizes their compactness, their handiness for the traveller, and tells the reader the name of the shop where such novelties can be bought (1.2.7-8). Although there is one surviving fragment of a parchment codex in Latin written about A.D. 100 (the anonymous *De Bellis Macedonicis*, P. Lit. Lond. 121), the pocket editions which Martial was at pains to advertise were not a success. The codex did not come into use for pagan literature until the second century; but it rapidly gained ground in the third, and triumphed in the fourth. It could be made of either papyrus or parchment, but it was the parchment codex which eventually won the day. Although a papyrus roll might last as long as 300 years (Galen 18(2).630), the average life would be shorter, and parchment was a much more durable material; in time its toughness was to prove a vital factor in the survival of classical literature. The impulse to change the format of the book must have come from the early Christians; for while the pagan codex was a rarity in the second century, the codex form was already universal for biblical texts.

The advantages of the codex over the roll were many: it was handier, more capacious, easier to consult. Reference was made still easier by numbering the pages, and the addition of a list of contents guarded against forged interpolations and other interference with the text. These were important considerations in the days when much of life revolved around the authoritative texts of the Scriptures and the Code. The importance of the codex for religion and law is obvious. It had a relevance for literary texts too: a book which could hold the contents of several rolls meant that a corpus of related texts or what was considered the best of an author's work could be put under one cover, and this was attractive to an age which was inclined to trim its intellectual heritage to a manageable form.

The change from roll to codex involved the gradual but whole-sale transference of ancient literature from one form to another. This was the first major bottle-neck through which classical litera-ture had to pass. It must have been somewhat reduced in the process, but the losses are not easily specified or assessed. There was the danger that little-read works would not be transferred to codex form, and in time their rolls would perish. A voluminous author, if some of his rolls were not available at a critical moment, might never recover his missing books.

Since some of the earliest surviving books of antiquity are parch-ment codices of the fourth century, it may be appropriate to mention at this point the separate question of the main scripts used in Roman times for the production of books. These were Square Capitals, Rustic Capitals, Uncial, and Half-uncial. Square Capitals survive in only a few imposing manuscripts of Vergil and seem to have been reserved for *de luxe* editions. The main book-hand of the classical period was the Rustic Capital (Plate IX), more fluid than the square variety and written with the superficial negligence which has given it its name. The earliest specimen which we can date is a fragment of a poem on the battle of Actium (Naples, P. Herc. 817), written between the event it describes (31 B.C.) and the destruction of Herculaneum (A.D. 79), where it was found. This hand continued in much the same form down to the early sixth century; famous manuscripts in this script are the codex Bembinus of Terence (Vat. lat. 3226) and the great codices of Vergil, the Mediceus, Palatinus, and Romanus. A handsome rounded script, Uncial, emerged as a fully developed hand in the fourth century and lasted until the ninth. An early example is the Vatican palimpsest of the *De republica* (Vat. lat. 5757 of the late 4th or early 5th cent., Plate X); one of the finest is the fifth-century Puteanus of Livy's third decade (Paris lat. 5730, Plate XI). The admixture of minuscule forms led to mixed forms of Uncial, in particular Half-uncial. There are a number of classical texts written in this script, mainly papyri, but it was predominantly used for Christian writings.

IX. PAGANISM AND CHRISTIANITY IN THE FOURTH CENTURY

The fourth century witnessed the final clash between Christianity and paganism. In 312 the first Christian emperor Constantine dramatically reversed the policy of his predecessor Diocletian by allowing the Christians freedom of worship, and within the space of a few decades they had taken the war into the pagan camp. The climax of the struggle found expression in the dignified debate which took place in 384 between Ambrose, then bishop of Milan and coming to the height of his power, and Q. Aurelius Symmachus, the pagan writer and administrator, who made a moving plea for the restitution of the Altar of Victory which had been removed from the Curia. In 394 the leader of the last pagan resistance, Virius Nicomachus Flavianus, was defeated by Theodosius and committed suicide in the old tradition. At the centre of the pagan opposition in the West were the Roman senators, who recaptured for a time the spirit of their ancestors and rallied to the defence of their traditions and heritage.

A vivid and sympathetic memorial to this movement is still extant in Macrobius' *Saturnalia*. The relevance of this learned symposium lies in the setting and *dramatis personae*. In the year 384, on the occasion of the Saturnalia, a number of cultivated upper-class Romans meet on successive days in the houses of Vettius Agorius Praetextatus, Virius Nicomachus Flavianus, and Symmachus, and have much learned talk about religion, history, philology, and in particular their great pagan poet Vergil. Among those present are other known opponents of Christianity. Servius is there as a representative of professional scholarship, a little over-awed by the company. We know Praetextatus had died in 384, Flavianus in 394; Macrobius has nostalgically recreated the great pagan society of the past as a framework for his learned compilation and we see its members, before their world had crumbled around them, discussing the minutiae of Roman life and literature with the sophisticated learning of the great Romans of the Republic.

But these men have left their own memorial, modest but effective, in the notes, generally called subscriptions, which are attached to a number of Latin texts. The production of correct texts of the Latin authors, if only with the modest aim of having a readable text on one's shelf, happened all the time. But the subscriptions suggest that there was a sudden increase in this activity towards the end of the fourth century and the intensification of the process was in origin a facet of the pagan revival. Fortunately it outlived paganism: the great Roman families of late antiquity carried on the tradition, and the descendants of the Symmachi and Nicomachi and others, pagan and Christian alike, continued to guard their national heritage as wave after wave of barbarians poured into the Empire.

Fortunately the triumph of Christianity did not remove the need for readable texts of the pagan authors. Christians who were hostile to pagan literature found themselves in an acute dilemma. It was clearly ill suited to be the basic stuff of Christian education. The poets were polytheistic and the tales they told about their gods, and particularly about the father of them all, were usually devoid of edification or downright immoral; Roman rhetoric, though it could be useful if employed in the right cause, encouraged glibness in speech and argument out of keeping with simple piety; even the philosophers, who had so much to offer to the Christian thinker, also contained much that was inimical to religious faith and the Christian way of life; the magnitude of the pagan achievement in all spheres of human activity, of which its written as well as its material remains were a constant reminder, might tend to sap confidence in new values and institutions. On the other hand, the enormous debt which Christians owed to the classical heritage and the extent to which they could still benefit from it was obvious even at times when the tension between the two cultures was at its highest. Just as Ambrose in his *De officiis ministrorum* was able to produce an influential manual of Christian ethic by reworking the basically Stoic content of Cicero's *De officiis*, so Augustine, writing at a time when he was least sympathetic to secular letters, in his *De doctrina Christiana* successfully adapted classical Roman rhetoric and in particular the theory of the three styles as elaborated by Cicero in the *Orator* to the needs of the Christian preacher. The agony of the dilemma which faced the orthodox Christian nurtured in the pagan schools is in human terms most dramatically reflected in Jerome as he runs through the gamut of conscience and renunciation, temptation and compromise. The last was inevitable. In general it was recognized that pagan literature could be plundered with profit provided that due caution was observed and the end justified the means. Jerome uses the analogy of the captive woman in Deuteronomy (21 : 10–13) who may be taken to wife and made a true Israelite when she has had her head shaved and her nails pared (*Epist*. 70.2). Augustine sanctions the use of secular learning by likening it to the despoiling of the Egyptians (*De doctrina* 2.60). Although the Christian attitude to pagan learning remained complex and fluid and generalization is dangerous, these two simple parables did echo through the ages and provided a handy justification for those who wished to have the best of both worlds. For the moment practical necessity had the last word: the old Roman system of education continued, for the simple reason that there was no alternative. Christian writings were not suitable for the school syllabus, the basic textbooks were all pagan, and in any case the ordinary cultivated Roman had few qualms about the traditional education; the obligations of polite society and his own highly developed sense of style made it difficult for him to turn over to the less sophisticated diet of Christian literature. The Roman educational system, authors and gods and all, continued until the monastic and episcopal schools were able to replace it with an education which, however much it owed to the traditional system, was essentially Christian in direction and purpose.

X. THE SUBSCRIPTIONS

The subscriptions provide a series of fascinating testimonies to the interest evinced in late antiquity in classical literature and its preservation. These notes, originally appended at the end of a work or the books of a work, have sometimes been copied from manuscript to manuscript along with the text. But the scribe might easily omit them, and the survival of so many is an indication of the extent of the activity. The work which Praetextatus did on the correction of texts is recorded in his epitaph (Dessau, *ILS* 1259, 8–12), but there is no trace of it in any surviving manuscripts, though the family tradition continued into the sixth century: the Vettius Agorius Basilius Mavortius who worked on the text of Horace sometime after 527 must have been a member of the same family. One of the few subscriptions with a claim to be original is that found in the codex Mediceus of Vergil (Laur. 39.1, Plate IX), where Asterius, consul in 494, records that he had corrected and punctuated the text.

The subscriptions begin towards the end of the fourth century and continue into the sixth. They vary from the simple *Iulius Celsus Constantinus v.c. legi* (Caesar's *Gallic War*) to a more detailed statement giving the date, place, and circumstances of the revision. As often as not the writer turns out to be an administrator, or even an army officer, rather than a professional scholar. In some cases the amateur corrector sought expert help or had access to another manuscript, in others he confesses, with a *cri de cœur*, that he has worked *sine exemplario* or *prout potui sine magistro*.

Among the earliest is the subscription attached to Apuleius' *Golden Ass*:

Ego Sallustius legi et emendavi Romae felix, Olibrio et Probino v.c. conss., in foro Martis controversiam declamans oratori Endelechio. Rursus Constantinopoli recognovi Caesario et Attico conss.

This is an interesting document which goes back to the pagan revival. The years in question are 395 and 397 and the Sallustius who carried out the revision would be a member of the family closely connected with Symmachus. The work was carried out under the eye of Endelechius in the forum of Augustus, which, with the neighbouring forum of Trajan, accommodated schools of rhetoric and grammar. One of the three families of Martial manuscripts goes back to an ancient recension which was corrected by Torquatus Gennadius in 401, also in the forum of Augustus, and the imperial fora remained as intellectual centres down to the end of the ancient world.

The most celebrated series of subscriptions are those found in various books of the first decade of Livy:

Nicomachus Flavianus v.c. III praef. urbi emendavi apud Hennam.
Nicomachus Dexter v.c. emendavi ad exemplum parentis mei Clementiani.
Victorianus v.c. emendabam domnis Symmachis.

The Nicomachean recension of Livy's first decade was a colla-
borative effort on the part of the related families of the Nicomachi
and Symmachi, who had the ambitious project of editing the
whole of Livy. Nicomachus Flavianus is the son of the pagan
leader, Nicomachus Dexter is his grandson; Victorianus, who is
here helping the Symmachi, edited one of the works of the elder
Flavianus. Part of the work of revision was done at the villa of the
Nicomachi at Enna in Sicily.

The continuation of this tradition can be seen in the subscription
to Macrobius' commentary on Cicero's *Somnium Scipionis*:

Aurelius Memmius Symmachus v.c. emendabam vel distinguebam
meum [*sc*. exemplar] Ravennae cum Macrobio Plotino Eudoxio v.c.

Here the great-grandson of the Symmachus who appears in the
Saturnalia is seen correcting another work by Macrobius, and
helping him is a grandson of the author himself. The chain
extends to the very threshold of the Middle Ages, for this Symmachus, consul in 485, was the father-in-law of Boethius.

2. THE GREEK EAST

I. SCHOLARSHIP AND LITERATURE UNDER THE ROMAN
EMPIRE

In the early centuries of the Roman empire intellectual life in the
Greek provinces was in a state of decline. Despite the existence of
institutions of higher education such as the schools of philosophy
and oratory at Athens, Rhodes, and elsewhere, there were few
outstanding achievements in literature or scholarship. The
Museum at Alexandria still existed; although the end of independent government in Egypt brought to a close the royal
patronage of scholarship, the situation was soon restored, for we
find Strabo reporting (17.1.8) that the Roman emperor now supported the Museum, and there are explicit references to scholars
entitled to its privileges. But notable works of scholarship do not
seem to have been produced. Only the library continued to render
service as a leading collection of material for the scholarly public;
the tradition that Caesar was accidentally responsible for its
destruction during his visit to Egypt (48–47 B.C.) has been widely
accepted, but the sources are not entirely in agreement as to the
extent of the damage, and it seems likely that no more than a
section of the library was burnt, or that the deficiencies were made
good by Antony, who was said to have transferred the Pergamene
library to Alexandria (Plutarch, *Antony* 58); total destruction is
also difficult to reconcile with the fact that Strabo apparently did
his geographical research in Alexandria. Literary work is harder to
trace. In the Augustan age Aristonicus did further selection of the
Homeric commentaries, and Tryphon studied and classified figures
of speech (the treatise which now passes under his name has been
revised by later redactors). During the reign of Tiberius there
are again signs of some activity; Theon commented on various
poetic texts, especially Hellenistic, such as Theocritus, Apollonius
Rhodius, and Callimachus; a scrap of his notes on Pindar's
Pythians has recently come to light (P. Oxy. 2536). Apion prepared
a glossary to Homer that is quoted by Hesychius and Eustathius
(a little of it survives in P. Rylands 26). Heliodorus wrote a com-

mentary on the metres of Aristophanes, parts of which are found
in the extant scholia. But as far as we can see none of these works
was outstanding as an advance in scholarly method or critical
principles. Much the same is true of the second and third centuries,
except that the grammarians Apollonius Dyscolus and his son
Herodian were important in their own field, and some of their
works survive independently of the scholia. Apollonius was the
first grammarian to write on syntax in something approaching the
modern sense of the term; the name Dyscolus is said to have been
given to him owing to the difficulty of his subject-matter. Among
other things he characterized the Greek perfect tense as a description of a present state; also he showed clearly for the first time the
difference implied by the use of present and aorist in moods other
than the indicative. In both these matters he made an advance on
the Stoic theorists, who had already managed to develop a useful
terminology for the tenses.

The decline of scholarship and criticism does not need to be
explained purely as part of the general decline of the time. There
was another more tangible influence at work. Though school
education included the reading of Homer and the other poets,
especially tragedy and comedy, there was increasing emphasis on
the study of rhetoric. As a result a large number of handbooks on
oratory were written, and the Attic orators, in particular Demosthenes, received more attention than before. Interest was to some
extent diverted from the poets. A more fundamental change in
education may have been connected with the fact that the poverty
of Greece and her evident inferiority to Rome in all spheres easily
bred a nostalgic admiration for the achievements of the classical
period; if men could no longer perform acts worthy of the great
days of old, they might at least attempt to rival them in literary
style. The growth of this feeling can be traced as early as the
reign of Augustus, and it became especially prominent in the
second century A.D. By this time the Greek language had under-
gone considerable changes, as can be seen from a comparison of the
classical language with that of the New Testament or the letters
and documents among the papyri. A desire to write in classical
style at once created a need for manuals of instruction, and the
energy of men with literary tastes was turned to the writing of these

textbooks. Dictionaries composed by Aelius Dionysius and Pausanias under Hadrian (117–38) have survived in fragments; we have also complete works by Pollux and Phrynichus dating from the reigns of Marcus Aurelius (161–80) and Commodus (180–92). These books all gave guidance to the would-be writer of classical Attic prose; in general they listed words or constructions current in everyday use which a writer might be tempted to employ, and then added the correct classical idiom. Any cultured person who interlarded his prose with modern expressions not found in the great Athenian writers was considered to have spoiled his style seriously and to have made a shameful display of ignorance and bad taste; this emerges quite clearly from the dedicatory letter which Phrynichus prefixed to his *Ecloge* and in the heading to the work. These experts in classical Attic did not always agree in their recommendations, nor were they equally strict in the construction of the rules they propounded. Some, such as Phrynichus, failed to appreciate the distinction between poetic and prose diction, and recommended usages which are found only in Greek tragedy; this made them unreliable guides for the school or university student. A certain degree of controversy arose among them. One issue was whether a single occurrence of a word in a classical author justified its usage, and three times in the *Ecloge* (206, 258, 400) we find Phrynichus stating that he is not satisfied to recommend words in this category, since he wishes to follow the well-established and common usage of Attic authors. Controversy also arose when incorrect instructions were given by a purist; there is a work by the so-called 'Anti-Atticist' showing that a number of prohibited expressions could be traced in Athenian texts earlier than c. 200 B.C.

Although the fashion was artificial in the extreme and had undesirable effects on literary compositions of every kind, the practice of Atticism lasted a very long time; it was the governing principle for all literary men not merely under the Roman empire but right to the end of the Byzantine period. The Byzantines may as a rule have been less successful in their imitation of ancient models than the writers of the Second Sophistic age such as Lucian and Aristides, but there is no doubt that their aims were identical, since lexica of Attic diction were composed by later scholars, for example Photius in the ninth century and Thomas Magister in the fourteenth; and as late as the fifteenth century we find the historian Critobulus writing an account of the fall of Constantinople to the Turks in 1453 in a style which is clearly intended as an imitation of Thucydides. Stylistic archaism on this scale has no parallel except perhaps in China, where it is still possible for Mao Tse Tung to think it worth writing lyrics in the style of eighth-century poets like Li Po.

Atticism had another important and less unfortunate consequence. The requirement to use only Attic diction of the best period ensured that in schools the classics of Athenian literature continued to be read as part of the regular curriculum, and this in turn meant that new copies of the text of major works were being steadily produced in sufficient numbers to guarantee the survival of most of them; only Menander was an exception. Even when the Eastern empire was at its lowest ebb the tradition of reading classical literature in the schools was never quite obliterated.

Close linguistic study of Attic texts led to other results. The occurrence of non-Attic words in a text supposed to come from the classical period might rouse suspicions as to its authenticity; and in fact we find Phrynichus remarking that the speech *Against Neaera* in the Demosthenic corpus is to be regarded as spurious partly on account of its impure language (*Ecloge* 203). But the minute linguistic observations of the schools were not entirely beneficial. They had the effect of instilling the forms and inflections of the Attic dialect so deeply that, when an educated man was transcribing a text, he tended to replace forms drawn from other dialects by the Attic forms which he knew so well. This is clear in works which contain Doric dialect, such as the lyrics of tragedy or Theocritus' *Idylls*; in many parts of the text original Doric forms have been eliminated by successive generations of copyists. The text of Xenophon has suffered in the same way. Phrynichus tells us (*Ecloge* 71) that Xenophon departed from his native Attic dialect by writing the word for 'smell' as *odmē* instead of *osmē*; similarly Photius in his *Lexicon* says that Xenophon used the poetic form of the word for 'dawn', *ēōs*, instead of the Attic *hĕōs*; but in both these cases the surviving manuscripts of

Xenophon regularly show the normal Attic forms. Here too the influence of the scribes is clear.

II. THE CHRISTIAN CHURCH AND CLASSICAL STUDIES

The effects of the growth of the Christian Church upon education and literary studies must now be considered. In earlier antiquity religious toleration had been the rule rather than the exception, and adherents of many different faiths had lived peacefully side by side, but the animosity with which Christians and pagans regarded each other brought about a substantial and permanent change. Many influential clergy disliked equally the unbelievers and the classical Greek literature which they studied with enthusiasm, and so the members of Christian communities were advised not to read such books. If this attitude had been adopted by all the clergy it would in due course, as the new religion became universal by the fifth century, have imposed an effective censorship on classical literature; as it is there can be little doubt that one of the major reasons for the loss of classical texts is that most Christians were not interested in reading them, and hence not enough new copies of the texts were made to ensure their survival in an age of war and destruction. But the literary merit of the classical authors was sufficient to tempt some Christians to read them, particularly as there were, at least in the early period, comparatively few Christian literary classics which could be recommended as an acceptable substitute for the traditional texts studied at school. Allegorical interpretation might be used to make certain passages inoffensive to Christian taste. Another important consideration was the need to make Christianity appeal to the well-educated pagan, and one means to this end was the demonstration that some of the important concepts of the new faith could be discussed in terms borrowed from the classical philosophers, especially the Stoics and Plato. The fusion of Greek and Christian thought in Justin and Clement exemplifies this attitude.

Early church fathers of the highest authority were content that Christians should read some pagan texts during their education. When Saint Gregory Thaumaturgus attended Origen's school at Caesarea in 233–8 he found his master encouraging pupils to read classical literature, and especially the philosophers; only those authors who denied the existence of a deity or a divine providence were to be avoided (Migne, *PG* 10.1088A, 1093A). It should be noted that Origen's willingness to learn from pagan culture extended to the realm of textual criticism. The interpretation of the Old Testament had become a matter of controversy, since the Septuagint was at variance with some other early Greek versions, and difficulty arose if precise interpretation of a passage was required. Origen adapted the system of marginal signs used by the Alexandrian critics to the Old Testament; an obelus marked a passage found in the Greek but not in the Hebrew, and an asterisk passages in which the Hebrew agreed with translations other than the Septuagint. In his *Hexapla* Origen went further and devised a method of presenting the Hebrew text and the translations in parallel columns. The successive columns were the original Hebrew, the Hebrew in Greek letters, the Greek translations of Aquila, Symmachus, the Septuagint, and Theodotion. The resulting book, a cumbrous anticipation of a modern apparatus criticus, must have been enormous, and no doubt partly for that reason it has not come down to us in its original form, except that fragments of a five-column version omitting the text in Hebrew characters survive as the lower script in a Milan palimpsest (Ambros. S.P. 11.251, *olim* O. 39 sup.).

The outlook of the fathers of the fourth century was no less liberal. Saint Basil wrote a short treatise advising the young on the best method of profiting from Greek literature (Homily 22), and Saint Gregory of Nazianzus criticized the majority of Christians for their complete rejection of pagan works, some of which he believed to be useful (*PG* 36.508B). There was in general no attempt to alter the school curriculum by banishing the classical authors. For a brief period Julian's persecution of the Christians in 362 tempted Apollinaris (c. 310–90) to construct a totally Christian curriculum, for which he and his father composed a long poem in Homeric style on the antiquities of the Jews and a paraphrase of the Psalms, also in hexameters. But the persecution soon ended, and pagan and Christian continued to use the same educational system without serious polemic or controversy. Some professors of rhetoric were Christians, but they did not exclude pagans from their classes: in the fourth century at Athens the Christian

Prohaeresius won the admiration of his staunchly pagan student Eunapius. Similarly at Gaza in the early sixth century the leading figures Procopius and Choricius pursued classical and Christian studies together.

The major classical texts, which had a firm position in the curriculum, were read by believer and unbeliever alike; but the survival of other texts was immediately put in danger when the new religion became universal, since the mass of the public, after the completion of their education, had no further interest in reading pagan books. It is sometimes asserted that the Church formally imposed a censorship and burnt pagan books as a matter of policy. The policy, if it ever existed as such, took a long time to have its intended effect; in the seventh century the poems of Sappho were still being read in Egypt (P. Berol. 5006). Occasionally there is a report of the burning of pagan books; Jovian in 363–4 is said to have burnt a library assembled at Antioch by his predecessor Julian (*Suda*, s.v. Iobianos). But this was an isolated case of vindictiveness: such destructive fervour was usually reserved for the works of fellow Christians who had deviated into heresy, and several ceremonial bonfires of unorthodox books are recorded in the fourth and fifth centuries.

The attitude of the church remained substantially unaltered throughout the Byzantine age. Classical authors maintained their place in the schools. Eminent members of the higher clergy figure among the most competent students of classical Greek at all times. There is no reliable evidence for censorship. A famous statement by the humanist Petrus Alcyonius (1486–1527), to the effect that the ecclesiastical authorities caused the texts of pagan poets to be burnt, is not supported by any other evidence. The numerous authors he mentions in this connection had probably been lost through other causes by the end of the Dark Ages. The Byzantine church was only concerned to destroy books by heretics; for instance in 1117, when the metropolitan Eustratius of Nicaea was examining arguments against the views of the Armenian church, he discovered works by Saint Cyril that appeared to contain heretical tendencies, and when copies of these works by Cyril began to circulate he brought the matter before the authorities, who ordered that all copies should be sent within forty days to

Santa Sophia to be destroyed. Again in 1140 it came to the ear of the patriarch that a monk's heretical works were being circulated; after a search three copies were found and burnt. On the other hand no case has yet come to light in which the Church took similar measures against a classical text; even the works of the detested apostate Julian survived.

III. THE EARLY BYZANTINE PERIOD

While the general condition of the ancient world declined rapidly higher education in the Eastern part of the empire was more flourishing than ever before. Schools can be traced at Alexandria, Antioch, Athens, Beirut, Constantinople, and Gaza; they were in effect the universities of the ancient world. They varied in character and importance: at Alexandria Aristotle was one of the main topics of study; the chief subject at Beirut was law. The need for such institutions was created by a vast increase in the Roman civil service in the fourth century. The government required administrators of liberal education and good prose style, as the emperor Constantius stated explicitly in 357 in an edict preserved in the Theodosian code (14.1.1). The study of classical poetry and oratory continued in the schools as before; special attention was given to cultivating Attic prose style, and for this purpose a number of rhetorical tricks of style had to be mastered. The works of the early Atticist writers of the second century A.D. such as Lucian and Aristides were regarded as models no less deserving of imitation than the classics of ancient Athens; this equal valuation of Attic and Atticist lasted right through the Byzantine period. Literary education seems to have held its own for some time against the claims of more practical disciplines; but at the end of the fourth century we find Libanius, the head of a famous literary school, complaining that students are being attracted to the study of law and Latin, which were also of obvious benefit to potential civil servants (*Autobiography* 214 and 234). One by one the schools declined or closed, until by the middle of the sixth century only Constantinople and Alexandria remained: Justinian himself had closed the philosophical school at Athens in 529, and the other cities had been much reduced by war or natural disasters.

The emphasis on rhetoric and Atticism did not encourage much scholarship in the modern sense of the term. One achievement, however, which may belong to this period, is the redaction of ancient commentaries into the form of scholia now placed in the margins of a text instead of occupying a separate book (Plates II and III). In particular there is reason to believe that work on Demosthenes and the other orators was carried out in the school at Gaza. The task was essentially one of compilation and selection, requiring intelligence in the choice of material selected from previous exegetical works; but in practice the scholia to all authors are marred by stupid or irrelevant notes. The date of this activity is usually placed in the fourth or fifth centuries, but it remains uncertain, since the identity of the compilers cannot be established. The idea of entering copious scholia in the margins of a text may have arisen at any time after the codex became the normal form of book; yet copious marginal scholia are not commonly found until the ninth century.

In this connection it should perhaps be mentioned that Procopius of Gaza (c. 460–c. 530) is supposed to have invented a form of literature that bears some resemblance to scholia, namely the catena, a running commentary on a book of the Bible which puts together the opinions of several previous interpreters, frequently with verbatim quotations of their arguments. This invention marked a new stage of biblical studies; but whether the catena is to be regarded as a forerunner of classical scholia or as an imitation of them is a question that has not yet been answered.

The last feature of this period which merits discussion is the progressive narrowing of the range of literature normally read. After the third century it becomes more and more uncommon to find any educated man showing knowledge of the texts that have not come down to the modern world. To explain this fact Wilamowitz formulated the theory that in the second or third century a school syllabus was selected by a prominent schoolmaster, and this became so influential that all schools adopted it. With the general decline of culture and impoverishment of the empire no texts outside this range were read and copied often enough to be guaranteed survival. To take an example: seven plays by Aeschylus and seven by Sophocles were selected, and because of this no others have come down to us; nine or ten plays of Euripides were chosen for reading in school, but in this case a lucky chance led to the survival of a single manuscript containing a number of other plays. Though the theory has much attraction there is reason to think that it presents too schematic a view of the history of texts. An initial objection is that there is no positive evidence as to the identity of the schoolmaster in question. One possible candidate would be Eugenius, who in the fifth century wrote on the colometry of fifteen plays. If this figure is correct it hints already at a selection of nine plays from Euripides and three from each of the other dramatists; but the reduction of the set books to the number of three is more probably a feature of the revised curriculum of late Byzantine schools. However, when so much remains unknown, it would be wrong to lay emphasis on our ignorance of the origin of the selection. More important is the reading of texts outside the syllabus in late antiquity; there are fifth-century fragments of Euripides' *Phaethon* and *Melanippe Desmotis*, and seventh-century fragments of Sappho and Callimachus, and three of the four documents in question come from the country districts of Egypt, where a taste for reading the less common pagan texts might have been expected to die out at a rather earlier date. By contrast Menander was still being read in the school at Gaza in the sixth century, but did not survive into the middle ages. Last and most important, it is clear that not all the losses of ancient literature took place so early. In the ninth century Photius was able to read a large number of books that have subsequently disappeared and are known to us from no source except his own account of them. For these reasons it is perhaps best to abandon the idea that a conscious act of selection by an individual was a primary factor in determining the survival of texts.

By the latter part of the sixth century the decline of learning and culture was serious. The imperial university at Constantinople, refounded by Theodosius II c. 425, and a new clerical academy under the direction of the patriarchate, were the only major educational institutions in the main part of the empire; the school at Alexandria continued, but rather in isolation. The exhausted condition of the empire did nothing to encourage learning, and before any recovery could take place matters were made worse by the religious controversy over icon-worship. For some three centuries there is little record of education and the study of the classics. The iconoclasts were not finally defeated until 843, when a Church council formally restored the traditional practices of image worship. Very few manuscripts of any kind remain from this period, and there is little external evidence about classical studies. The only works of the epoch which deserve mention are those of Choeroboscus, a lecturer in grammar at the seminary in Constantinople, and the *Canons* of Theognostus, a lengthy work on orthography from the early ninth century; owing to the change in the pronunciation of Greek, spelling was as much an obstacle to schoolchildren as it is in England today.

IV. GREEK TEXTS IN THE ORIENT

Here a brief digression is needed in order to mention a rather neglected chapter in the history of transmission, the significance of translations of Greek texts into Oriental languages. At some point during late antiquity Greek texts began to be translated into Syriac, activity being centred in the towns of Nisibis and Edessa. The lands of the eastern Mediterranean are commonly believed to have been bilingual under the Roman empire. But this view is exaggerated, and the mass of the population probably spoke little or no Greek. When the authoress of the *Peregrinatio Aetheriae*, a very early account of pilgrimage, visited the Holy Land about 400, she noted that at church services the officiating priest conducted the liturgy in Greek, and an assistant immediately gave the Syriac version of what he had just said (ch. 47). The Church could only achieve its purposes by use of the vernacular.

Probably the first text to be translated was the New Testament, followed shortly by a range of patristic works. The earliest manuscripts of these versions go back to the fourth and fifth centuries, and it is well known that they are of value to theologians. It comes as a surprise, however, to find that other forms of Greek literature were translated. The schools of Nisibis and Edessa are known to have prepared versions of Aristotle, and a section of Theophrastus' *Meteorology* survives in Syriac alone. Philosophy and science were not the only concerns of the Syrians. They translated some Lucian and the grammar of Dionysius Thrax, as if attempting to give their pupils the benefits of a Greek literary education in translation.

These latter translations are not of any great value to the modern scholar interested in establishing the correct form of the Greek text; it sometimes happens that the Syriac, instead of helping to correct the Greek, has to be corrected from it.

Arabic versions of classical texts are perhaps more numerous than their Syriac counterparts and certainly better known; this may be due to the accident of survival. The stimulus to make these translations seems to have come purely from a desire to use the best handbooks of science and philosophy available, and it is unlikely that a translation of the Bible preceded that of classical texts. As a rule the translations were made from an existing Syriac version, and so allowance must be made for two stages at which the inaccuracy of a translator could mar the expression of the original. When an Arabic version exists side by side with the Greek tradition one cannot assume as a matter of course that it will substantially help in determining the Greek text. Yet a famous example will show that utter pessimism is unjustified. In Aristotle's *Poetics* the Arabic text, though exceptionally difficult to understand, offers a few readings which the editor must accept and several more which he must consider seriously, a reasonable harvest if the brevity of the treatise is borne in mind. That the *Poetics* should have been translated is a cause of some surprise at first sight; but the explanation of both the Syriac and Arabic renderings may be simply that all the writings of 'the master of those who know' were held to be important enough to justify translation. For the most part, however, it was science and philosophy that interested the Arabs. Plato, Aristotle, and Theophrastus were much studied. The mathematicians received special attention; the version of Apollonius of Perga *On conic sections* is important because several books of it have been lost in the Greek; the same is true of Philo of Byzantium's *Mechanics* and works by Archimedes and Hero of Alexandria. The medical writings of Hippocrates, Galen, and Dioscorides were closely investigated. By no means all the versions that are attested have yet been found in Arabic manuscripts; we know of many of them only from references to them in medieval Arabic encyclopedias. But since the study of Arabic manuscripts still has much progress to make there is hope that more versions will be recovered.

What has been said above about the general quality of the translations needs to be qualified in one respect. It is clear that in the ninth century there was one translator whose scholarly attainments were at least equal to those of his contemporaries in Byzantium. Hunain ibn Ishaq (809–73) was competent in Arabic, Persian, Greek, and Syriac, the last apparently being his mother tongue. He began his work as a translator at the age of seventeen, and if his command of languages was already good at that age it seems that he must have grown up in a multilingual community. He appears to have lived in Baghdad, where he founded a school of translators, and he refers to meetings in that city at which Christians gathered to read their ancient literature. Though he does not make it clear whether this reading was of originals or Syriac versions, he does say that Greek communities, perhaps using monasteries as focal points, preserved the use of the language, and that it was possible to find Greek manuscripts all over the Islamic world. He himself searched for them in Mesopotamia, Syria, Palestine, and Egypt. In a letter to a friend who had asked for a detailed list with indications of content of all Greek medical works known to him Hunain gives a long account of his method of work. He writes at length about Galen, and considers particularly which texts have been translated into Syriac only and which into Arabic also, who the translator was, to whom the work was dedicated, and where Greek manuscripts might be found of works not yet translated. His comments on his predecessors are revealing. He frequently claims that they were incompetent in linguistic knowledge, or were certainly working from damaged or illegible manuscripts, a hindrance which Hunain himself had to face from time to time. In such cases he collates the faulty existing version against as many Greek manuscripts as he can find and produces a revised rendering. The quantity of Greek books that he had access to and their damaged condition are emphasized more than once. It is possible that the scrupulous consideration and comparison of divergent texts was a technique that he learnt at least in part from Galen, who employs much the same methods in handling the difficult text of the Hippocratic corpus. Such merit as Arabic versions possess may well be due to the scholarship of Hunain and his associates.

One other language should be mentioned. Translation into Armenian probably began for the purposes of the Church as it did in Syria. The Armenian version of the Bible is one of the most celebrated. In the field of patristic literature some works by Philo have come down to us in the Armenian alone, and the same is true of part of Eusebius' *Chronicon*. As to classical texts, the translations of Plato and Dionysius Thrax are mentioned in another context (see pp. 16, 53). An intriguing and tantalizing report suggests that other Greek books of purely literary and secular character were translated; apart from a number of historians there is mention of unnamed works by Callimachus. An account of the plot of Euripides' *Peliades* comes from an Armenian source.

V. THE RENAISSANCE OF THE NINTH CENTURY

The first real achievements of Byzantine scholarship belong to the middle of the ninth century. There were men of outstanding ability who were able to exercise their powers to the best advantage in the more peaceful condition of the empire. In 863 the assistant emperor Bardas revived the imperial university, which had disappeared in the turmoil of the preceding centuries, by founding a school in the capital under the direction of Leo, a philosopher and mathematician of distinction; other professors appointed at the same time were Theodore the geometrician, Theodegius the astronomer, and Cometas the literary scholar; the last of these may have specialized in rhetoric and Atticism, but he also prepared a recension of Homer. Leo's scholarly temperament can be seen from an episode during his residence on the island of Andros. He met a learned man who gave him some tuition in rhetoric, philosophy, and arithmetic; this made him wish to pursue the subjects further and he crossed over to the mainland in order to search for books in monastic libraries. His motive is characteristic of the changed atmosphere in Byzantium; during the Iconoclastic era emperors like Leo the Armenian had hunted for books merely in order to find texts which could lend them support in theological controversy.

The revival of learning coincided with, and was perhaps assisted by, certain changes in the appearance and production of manuscripts. Hitherto the standard script of books had been the uncial character, which had reached its fully developed form as early as the fourth century, and had changed surprisingly little in the course of centuries. Despite its impressive appearance it had the serious disadvantage that it was slow to write and so large that the quantity of text on each page was strictly limited. When the cheaper writing material of the ancient world ceased to be readily available, as the papyrus plantations were either exhausted or used mainly by the Arabs after their conquest of Egypt in 641, the demand for parchment must have increased sharply; even in an age which was not much interested in literature, theological and liturgical texts were required and the needs of the civil service had to be satisfied. To meet this difficulty it appears that the expedient was devised of adapting for use in books the script that had been current for some time in official circles for letters, documents, accounts, and the like; the modern technical term for the revised script is minuscule. It occupied far less space on the page and could be written at high speed by a practised scribe. The first dated example belongs to the year 835, and is known as the Uspensky Gospels (Leningrad gr. 219). As the script of this book is by no means immature or primitive, the adoption of this style should probably be dated at least half a century earlier. The place of its origin is not known for certain, but there are some grounds for thinking that it was popularized by members of the important Stoudios monastery in the capital, which was a well-known centre of book production at a later date. Gradually the uncial hand was abandoned, and by the end of the tenth century it was no longer used except for a few special liturgical books. The new script facilitated the copying of texts by making more economical use of parchment, and not long afterwards the situation was improved by another invention. In 751 the Arabs had taken some Chinese prisoners of war at Samarkand and learnt from them the process of paper-making. Soon Arab production in the East and in Spain reached substantial proportions, and in due course it was exported to Byzantium. Hostilities between the two empires may have had an unfavourable effect on the trade, but there is no doubt that paper came to be widely used in Byzantium, and it seems to have been used in the imperial archives from the middle of the eleventh century.

The transliteration of old uncial books into the new script was energetically undertaken by the scholars of the ninth century. It is largely owing to their activity that Greek literature can still be read, for the text of almost all authors depends ultimately on one or more books written in minuscule script at this date or shortly after, from which all later copies are derived; the quantity of literature that is available to us from the papyri and the uncial manuscripts is only a small proportion of the whole. In the process of transliteration mistakes were sometimes made, especially by misreading letters that were similar in the uncial script and therefore easily confused. At many points in Greek texts there are errors common to all the extant manuscripts which appear to derive from the same source, and this source is usually taken to be a ninth-century copy. A further assumption generally made is that one minuscule copy was made from one uncial copy. The uncial book was then discarded, and the minuscule book became the source of all further copies. The theory has a certain a priori justification on two grounds, since the task of transliteration from a script that was becoming less and less familiar would not be willingly undertaken more often than was absolutely necessary, and there is at least some likelihood that after the destruction of the previous centuries many texts survived in one copy only. But these arguments do not amount to proof, and there are cases which can only be explained by more complicated hypotheses. In the tradition of Plato one manuscript (Vienna, supp. gr. 39) differs greatly from all others in its errors, and it is difficult to believe it derived from the same ninth-century exemplar; it may derive from the transliteration of a different uncial book, so that at least two old books would seem to have survived the Dark Ages. A confirmation of this is that when a Greek text has been translated into an Oriental language at an early date, perhaps the fifth century, the readings which are characteristic of the Oriental translation may occur also in a small group of the Greek manuscripts. This is true of the Armenian version of some of Plato's dialogues, the Arabic version of Aristotle's *Poetics*, and, if the example of a patristic text may be admitted here, of the Syriac translation of Saint Gregory of Nyssa's *De virginitate*. Another argument pointing in the same direction can be drawn from the difficulty which arises in the study of the manuscripts of some texts that were very frequently read during the Middle Ages, such as the Euripidean plays included in the school curriculum. Here the relation of the manuscripts cannot be established precisely by the usual method, since they do not fall into groups that coincide regularly in error. This situation presupposes that medieval scholars and schoolmasters frequently compared their own copy of the text with others and made alterations or added variant readings above the line; this process is known as contamination. In such cases it may be that more than one copy survived the Dark Ages to be transcribed, so that two or more transliterations took place; alternatively, only one transliteration was made but this copy was deposited in some central place where it was consulted by interested readers and received as marginal additions the variant readings that had been found in other copies. It is easy to imagine, though there is no external evidence for the assumption, that such deposits of semi-official copies took place in the library of the academy set up by Bardas. It is also possible that similar copies existed in the patriarchal academy, for there is a manuscript of Plato's *Laws* (Vat. gr. 1) written in the early tenth century with marginal variants added in the next century by a scholar who refers to these additional readings as coming from 'the patriarch's book'; unfortunately we cannot be sure whether this was a private copy or part of the library in the seminary.

The Bardas university was founded under favourable conditions, and was probably the centre of a lively group of scholars concerned to recover and disseminate classical texts of many different kinds. Yet it does not seem to have had the influence that might have been expected, for there is very little reference to it at later dates. Its professors are completely overshadowed by their contemporary Photius (c. 810–91), a man of remarkable attainments who is perhaps as important for his position in the Church and the affairs of the government as for his devoted encouragement of learning. Twice he held the patriarchal throne of Constantinople (858–67, 877–86), and in these years some of the negotiations which led to schism between the Eastern and Roman churches took place; it is only one of the consequences of this schism that efforts to obtain assistance for the weakened empire of the fourteenth and fifteenth centuries were seriously impeded by the estrangement of the two churches. For our purpose, however, the most interesting phase of Photius' life is the time before his sudden and rapid elevation to the patriarchate (he was still a layman until a week before the appointment). As a young man he had always been a keen student of a wide range of subjects, and from an early age succeeded in leading two different careers simultaneously. Jealousy and spite gave rise to a tradition that, rather like Faust, he achieved his knowledge by making a bargain with a Jewish magician, giving up his Christian faith in return for success, learning, and riches. He was much in favour at the court, and occupied positions of trust in the circle of the emperor; but apart from this he conducted a kind of private literary club. In 855 he was appointed to an embassy with the task of negotiating an exchange of prisoners of war with the Arab government. Before going on the long and dangerous journey Photius wrote, as an offering and consolation to his brother Tarasius, a summary of books that may have been read or discussed at the gatherings of his circle, especially those which Tarasius himself had not been able to attend. The resulting work, known as the *Bibliotheca* (alternatively *Muriobiblos*), is a fascinating production, in which Photius shows himself the inventor of the book-review. In 280 sections which vary in length from a single sentence to several pages Photius summarizes and comments on a wide selection of pagan and Christian texts (the proportions are nearly equal, and 122 sections deal with secular texts). He claims to have compiled it from memory, but it is generally regarded as a revised version of the notes he had made in the course of his reading in the last twenty years. It is not arranged according to any plan. Photius claims that the order of the authors reviewed is that in which they occurred to him, and he had not the time to be more systematic. Its value to the modern scholar is that Photius summarizes many books that are now lost: that applies for example to some twenty of the thirty-three historians he discusses. Much can be learnt of the interests of a prominent Byzantine figure of the time: in the secular texts historians are most numerous, but among others there are orators, novelists, and compilers of Atticist dictionaries. The latter are significant, for they show the author's concern with stylistic considerations, which is also shown by his frequent brief characterizations of the style of an author; the desire to write and appreciate a good Attic style was never far from the thoughts of Byzantine literati. The breadth of Photius' interests is enormous. That a pious man and future patriarch should bother to read the Greek novelists is surprising; he enjoyed them linguistically, but could not bring himself to be favourable to their contents. It is also notable that he read anti-Christian tracts; this is incidentally a strong argument against the notion that the ecclesiastical authorities attempted to impose a censorship. Philosophy is not well represented in the *Bibliotheca*, but there is evidence of his knowledge in this field elsewhere in his works. The most serious limitation of taste shown in the book is the absence of poetry. One wonders whether in this respect it is a true record of Photius' own reading. It is a possible but not certain inference that classical poetry was not yet a subject of interest in intellectual circles; the fact that surviving manuscripts of the poets are not datable earlier than c. 925 may be relevant here. Cometas' interest in Homer mentioned above is not a serious objection to this view, since the epics enjoyed an inviolable position in the school curriculum which put them in a class apart from all other poetry.

Photius' only other work deserving mention here is his *Lexicon*, the first complete copy of which was discovered in 1959 in a remote monastery in Macedonia. It is a typical work of its class, valuable for its brief quotations of classical texts not now available. The purpose was to amalgamate and revise various existing books of the same kind; in the *Bibliotheca* Photius remarks how useful such a book would be. In his Atticism he was moderate and willingly admitted words from poetic sources if they seemed the most expressive means of conveying a notion. These quotations from the poets do not imply a reading of the full text, but were probably drawn as such from his sources. Besides this lexicon he was partly responsible for the compilation of at least one other, and he further shows his stylistic pedantry by correcting the usage of friends' letters.

The sudden appearance of so distinguished a person after the obscurity that had previously reigned is remarkable; it is all the more strange that nothing is known of the identity of his tutors, nor of the sources from which he was able to acquire knowledge of so many rare texts. From this time onwards, as a result of the

activity in Photius' salon and in the new university, there is a
practically continuous tradition of classical studies in Byzantium.
Literary texts were copied regularly and more technical works,
especially mathematical and medical, were much studied, not
least because they were still in general the best textbooks available. The first major result of these new stimuli to scholarship can
be seen in Arethas (c. 860–c. 935), who became archbishop of
Caesarea in Cappadocia; again it is a churchman who shows great
interest in learning.

Whereas Photius' own books do not survive, or at least have not
been identified, several volumes from the library of Arethas still
exist, and copies derived from other lost volumes are known, so
that a good picture of his collection can be obtained. The preserved
volumes are masterpieces of calligraphy on fine quality parchment,
and it happens that the prices of some of them were recorded by
the original owner. For his Euclid (D'Orville 301, A.D. 888) he paid
14 gold pieces; the cost of his Plato, a thicker volume of larger
format (E. D. Clarke 39, A.D. 895, Plate III), was 21 pieces. In
relation to contemporary incomes such prices are an indication of
the high cost of a book; civil service salaries started at 72 gold
pieces per annum, and might rise in exceptional circumstances to
3,500. Book collecting was not a hobby for men of modest means.

Arethas commissioned books from professional scribes, in the
main monks of monasteries which accepted regular orders on a
commercial basis, and he then wrote a large amount of commentary in the margins in his own hand (Plate III). Though he was not
a critic of great power or originality these marginal commentaries are valuable because they were drawn from good sources;
the notes in his copies of Plato and Lucian are examples of this.
Surviving volumes of his library include Plato, Euclid, Aristotle's
Organon, Aristides, Lucian, and some Christian writers. Others
that can be inferred from various evidence are Pausanias, Dio
Chrysostom, and Marcus Aurelius; the last of these was probably
the exemplar which ensured the further survival of this text.
Once again there is an absence of interest in poetry, while Atticist
writers are well represented; but Arethas evidently differs from
Photius by showing no taste for historical writing.

The sources of Arethas' collection are unknown. The copies of

Plato and Euclid were acquired while he was a deacon. At this date he was probably living in the capital, where copies of most authors must have been readily available for some time. For rarer texts it may have been necessary to look further afield, but we do not possess any information about the book trade that throws light on Arethas' acquisitions. However, since a historian of c. 800, George Syncellus, refers to old and valuable books coming from Caesarea in Cappadocia, one may speculate that when Arethas arrived in his archbishopric he made some discoveries there.

VI. THE LATER BYZANTINE PERIOD

With the death of Arethas some time in the thirties of the tenth century a new period begins, in which eminent scholars and bibliophiles are much more difficult to identify. Some stimulus to learning was given by the activity of the erudite emperor Constantine VII Porphyrogenitus (913–59). During a long period of enforced semi-retirement he compiled various manuals of statecraft which survive partially. These took the form of encyclopedic compilations based on a very wide range of historical sources, and as such are of some importance to classical scholars, since many of the texts do not survive elsewhere. This great activity of Constantine was doubtless not carried out by him single-handed, but nothing is known of the collaborators. Shortly afterwards, perhaps in the reign of John Tzimisces (969–76), the collaboration of scholars resulted in a work which is of value for much the same reason as the works of Constantine; this is the *Suda*, less correctly known as Suidas (as if it were a proper name), which might be best described as a combination of dictionary and elementary encyclopedia. It has articles on a great number of classical personages and topics, and despite a certain amount of dubious or erroneous material transmits much useful information. Some of its sources can be traced; among those most frequently used are the text and scholia to Aristophanes, for which the *Suda* is in effect a fairly important witness. However, it is the lost sources, some not now easily identifiable, which give it its value. Though the intelligence of the authors cannot be rated very high, their work does mark some advance, in so far as it is considerably more than a lexicon of Attic diction and is one of the earliest books with a claim to the title of encyclopedia, and perhaps the earliest encyclopedia to have alphabetical arrangement.

It should not be assumed that because individual scholars of this date remain unknown, the impetus given to literary studies by Photius had entirely ceased to have effect. Extant manuscripts of classical texts make it clear that even in the early tenth century the reading of classical poetry other than Homer had begun; the earliest copies of Theognis (Paris supp. gr. 388) and Musaeus (Barocci 50) almost certainly belong to this date. Several other poetic texts were being read by the middle of the century or a little later, and in fact some of the most valuable of all surviving manuscripts are the result of this activity; one may give as instances the text of the Greek Anthology, sometimes known as the *Palatine Anthology*, which serves to distinguish it from the anthology later composed by Planudes (Heidelberg gr. 23 + Paris supp. gr. 384); the Venice *Iliad* (Marc. gr. 454, Plate II), the importance of which is even greater for the scholia than for the text; the Ravenna Aristophanes, which is the only medieval manuscript to contain all eleven plays (Ravenna gr. 429); Laur. 32.9, which besides being the only medieval copy of all seven plays of Aeschylus is also of fundamental importance for the texts of Sophocles and Apollonius Rhodius. Prose authors were not neglected, and we can instance the leading manuscript of Polybius, written by the monk Ephraem, probably in 947 (Vat. gr. 124), and two copies of Demosthenes (Paris gr. 2935 and Laur. 59.9). These three codices were written by scribes whose hands can be identified elsewhere, and thus we can form some impression of the range of books written by a single scribe, even if they were often commissioned works and hence not representative of the scribes' own interests. Ephraem can be identified as the scribe of three other books: Venice, Marc. gr. 201, Aristotle's *Organon*, A.D. 954; Athos, Lavra 184, *Acts* and *Epistles*, undated; Athos, Vatopedi 747, Gospels, A.D. 948. The Paris Demosthenes was mainly written by the scribe of the Plato mentioned earlier (Vat. gr. 1), while the other Demosthenes is probably in the same hand as the Ravenna MS. of Aristophanes. Many manuscripts of classical authors written at various dates in the Byzantine period can be connected in this way by identification of the scribe's hand. Though the surviving books may not be more than a small proportion of those copied, the number of possible identifications does suggest that the copying of ancient texts was in the hands of quite a small group of scholars, schoolmasters, and professional scribes.

Classical learning and education continued in the eleventh century much as before. The major change of this epoch consisted of a reorganization of the imperial university; whether this was provoked by a decline in the institution in the form that Bardas had given it is unknown, but the new arrangement included the setting up of a faculty of law and another of philosophy. The changes were made under the aegis of the emperor Constantine IX Monomachus in 1045. The law school does not concern us here, except to note that its foundation antedates by some years that of the famous faculty at Bologna, from which modern law faculties ultimately derive their origin. The philosophical school, which also gave instruction in grammar, rhetoric and literary subjects, was under the direction of Michael Psellus (1018–78), much the most versatile man of his generation, who distinguished himself as civil servant, senior adviser to several emperors, historian, and academic philosopher. His literary output attests his wide reading of the classics, but his intellectual interests were rather more in philosophy, and his eminence as a lecturer and teacher led to a renewed interest in Plato and to a lesser extent Aristotle. The fortunes of the school were not entirely favourable. For reasons which seem to have been political rather than intellectual, the school's teachers fell into disfavour at the court, and Psellus himself had to retire to a monastery for a time; but he returned to important positions in due course, and it is likely that the school continued its work.

A further revival of philosophy, this time with Aristotle as the main author for study, can perhaps be traced to the early twelfth century. Anna Comnena, the princess who was forced to live in the seclusion of a monastery and composed a famous *History*, was connected with two scholars who wrote commentaries on Aristotle, Eustratius of Nicaea and Michael of Ephesus. The most interesting fact about this activity is that their treatises are devoted largely to the *Politics* and the zoological works; these texts had not yet been supplied with commentaries, despite the enormous amount of study of Aristotle that had taken place in the ancient world and early Byzantine period. It rather looks as if Anna may have noticed this gap and decided to commission the necessary commentaries.

From the twelfth century onwards the story can be carried forward once more by reference to outstanding individuals. Undoubtedly the most eminent figure in the scholarship of this age was Eustathius (fl. c. 1160–92), who after being a teacher of rhetoric in one of the leading institutions of the capital was appointed to the archbishopric of Thessalonica in 1175. During his teaching career in the capital he must be assumed to have accomplished most of his scholarly work. The libraries of Constantinople no doubt held treasures not yet exploited by men of learning, and one may suspect that Eustathius did not entirely relish the promotion which removed him to another city; though important, Thessalonica does not seem to have been at that date a centre of intellectual life. His interest in classics did not prevent him from taking his clerical duties seriously, and we still possess a treatise by him on the reform of the monastic life; among other things it shows that most monks had no interest in books or learning and were unworthy of their vows, and the bibliophile in Eustathius comes out in an anecdote he tells of an abbot who sold a beautiful calligraphic copy of Saint Gregory Nazianzen because his monastery had no use for it. This section of the tract serves to remind us that the tradition of learning was alien to the spirit of many members of the Church, however much high prelates set an example by their display of deep learning. Eustathius himself knew a number of texts that have since been lost and would be useful to us if still preserved. This is apparent partly from his use of otherwise unknown sources in his commentaries and partly from a quotation he gives of a few lines of Sophocles' *Antigone*; here he refers to 'good copies' (ἀκριβῆ ἀντίγραφα) which give the full text of lines 1165–8, whereas all the manuscripts of Sophocles now reduce the passage to incoherence by omitting one of the lines. Eustathius had evidently noted the unsatisfactory state of the text and compared other copies until he found one with the right text. It seems quite likely, to judge from a remark in his introduction to Pindar, that he read more of his *Epinicia* than we possess today.

His major works were his commentaries on classical authors.
What he wrote on Pindar does not survive except for the introduction, and of his notes to Aristophanes no more is known than
minute fragments preserved in late manuscripts. But we have his
notes to Dionysius Periegetes, a late poet of little merit who wrote
an account of geography in about 1,000 hexameters; these verses
have come down to us in so many manuscripts that they must be
presumed to have served as the textbook of geography in Byzantine schools. More important and much more voluminous are his
commentaries on Homer; that on the *Iliad* fills about 1,400 large
pages of print in the Leipzig edition of 1827–30. Both these commentaries are essentially compilations, with very little that has
been contributed by Eustathius himself. The scale of the commentary, especially that on Homer, is enormous; the discussion of
the first line of the *Iliad* runs to 10 pages, and if even a modest
proportion of this was ever used by a teacher in the Byzantine
classroom, the result must have been to confuse the pupil by a
mass of learning of dubious relevance and at the same time to
prevent him reading through the text at a pace sufficient to yield
some enjoyment. Eustathius is fond of allegorical interpretations,
and criticizes Aristarchus for not adopting them. The work is useful
to the modern scholar occasionally, but only because of those
qualities which made it unduly cumbersome for the author's contemporaries; as far as relevance is concerned it is no advance on
the average standard of commentary produced in the ancient
world.

Two of Eustathius' lesser contemporaries deserve mention.
John Tzetzes (c. 1110–80) was not in holy orders but appears to
have run a school in Constantinople. Apart from some letters
which reveal a good deal about his personality and day-to-day life
his writings include commentaries on three plays of Aristophanes,
Hesiod, and part of Homer. He is inferior to Eustathius in knowledge and intelligence, and is quite unjustifiably conceited about
his own attainments: it is not easy to respect the man who in the
middle of a note on Aristophanes (*Plutus* 677) states that he would
not lengthen his explanation but for the fact that there is a good
deal of space left on the present page of his book. Nevertheless the
allusions in his letters show his wide reading, and we know that he

attended meetings at which interpretations of classical texts were discussed; more information about this philological club would be very welcome. Like Eustathius he too had read some books that we no longer have, including some Callimachus and Hipponax. The same is true of Michael Choniates (otherwise known as Acominatus), a somewhat younger man who corresponded with Eustathius and like him was elevated to a bishopric at some distance from the capital, in this case Athens. In his letters he bemoans his fate; to have the use of the undamaged Parthenon as his cathedral was no compensation for the loss of educated society, and his congregations of ignorant peasants were incapable of appreciating the beauties of his high-flown Atticist sermons. But he was the proud owner of one very rare book no longer extant, the *Hecale* of Callimachus, and delighted in quoting from it in his letters. He and Tzetzes are the latest Byzantines of whom we can say with certainty that they could read more classical poetry than we can.

The reason for this lies in an event of the utmost importance which Michael Choniates lived to see, the capture and sack of Constantinople by the Fourth Crusade in 1204. Great damage was done, and there is little doubt that libraries suffered severely. For the historian of literature this sack of the city was a greater disaster than the more famous one of 1453. In 1204 the rare texts mentioned in the previous paragraph were destroyed; at any rate there is no trace of them when the seat of government was restored to Constantinople in 1261 after the fall of the Latin kingdom. If the events of 1204 had not taken place these texts might well have found their way to the West through the agency of the numerous Italian visitors and book collectors who went to Greece and brought back manuscripts. By the time that the city fell into the hands of the Turks little remained to be discovered by the collectors; the only substantial and well-attested loss is recorded in the statement of Constantine Lascaris that a complete copy of the *Universal History* by Diodorus Siculus was destroyed by the Turks.

While the capital was occupied by the Franks and most of Greece was parcelled out among Western barons, the Byzantine administration dragged out a precarious existence at Nicaea, preserving the empire's possessions in Asia Minor. Despite the drastic reduction in the wealth and power of the empire this period of exile in Nicaea was by no means one of the worst for literary studies. The emperors John Vatatzes and Theodore Ducas Lascaris were concerned to promote schools and libraries and eventually built up quite a tradition of secondary education. Little is known in detail, since very few manuscripts can be identified as having been written in the Nicaean empire, but it seems clear that poets and orators were studied, and some of Theodore's own letters display cultivated and scholarly attitudes. Other scholarly work was done by the monk Nicephorus Blemmydes (c. 1197–c. 1272), who wrote on many topics, including logic, physics, and geography, and made a journey to parts of the old empire now under Latin control in search of books that could not be found in Asia Minor. This is one of the few short periods in which literary studies flourished outside the capital. It is also possible that the thirteenth century was an age of considerable culture in the outlying Byzantine province in the heel of Italy; Sicily and the extreme south of Italy were largely Greek in speech during the Middle Ages, and a good deal is known of the numerous Greek monasteries there. The part of this territory most closely in contact with Constantinople was the district of Otranto, where there was a famous monastery of Saint Nicholas that maintained a school and a large library. A number of books written there and in the neighbouring towns of Nardò and Gallipoli do suggest a reasonably flourishing state of school education; there are copies of Homer, Hesiod, and Aristotle safely attributable to these centres, and a number of other books, including some lexica, may have been written there. But there is no trace of any advanced scholarship or any attempt to write commentaries on classical authors.

The Latin kingdoms in Constantinople and Greece were brought to an end in 1261, and the Greek emperors reigned once again from their traditional capital; but their empire was reduced in size and power, being gradually whittled away by the invasions of the Turks on the eastern side and the encroachment of Italian trading states such as Genoa and Venice in Greece and the islands; mercenaries hired to assist the empire often did more harm than good, as for instance a band of Catalans who did an immense amount of damage before setting up a small independent state in

Athens. Nevertheless the late thirteenth and early fourteenth centuries saw some of the best Byzantine work on classical texts. Though little is known of the leading institutions of the capital, there appear to have been several schools in Constantinople and Thessalonica, presided over by men of learning. In an account of this brevity there is not room to describe more than two of them. The first is the monk Maximus Planudes (c. 1255–1305), who worked in the capital and achieved much in a rather short life. Besides running a school for a time he was sent on a diplomatic mission to Venice, and either before or during this acquired a good working knowledge of Latin, an exceptionally rare attainment in Byzantium (otherwise it appears to have been confined to a few lawyers and interpreters). He read widely in Latin, evidently with considerable interest, for he prepared a large number of translations, among which figure Augustine, Boethius, Macrobius and very remarkably Ovid's *Heroides*, *Metamorphoses*, and amatory works. Not all these translations have yet been printed, but it has been plausibly suggested that those of the theological works might yet prove useful as an introduction for Greek theologians to the Latin fathers; the conservatism of the Greek literary language is such that Planudes' versions could be printed with little change, but the more serious obstacle, the Greek refusal to be reconciled to the Western Church, has remained essentially unaltered until the present day. The first contact between Byzantium and the West for purposes other than trade agreements or religious disputation had no immediate result; but in the next century the monk Demetrius Cydones continued the task of translation with some works of Aquinas, and a traffic of ideas moving in the opposite direction was begun by the Italians who came to Constantinople to learn Greek. Of more practical and immediate importance was Planudes' study of Greek texts. He is generally thought to have been responsible for the production of a large volume (preserved in Florence as Laur. 32.16) containing a collection of classical poetry, which includes school authors and others such as Nonnus. But his interests were far from being confined to the usual range of school texts; we find him searching for Plutarch's works, of which he compiled a catalogue, and he drew up a revised version of the Greek Anthology which includes quite a

number of epigrams that do not occur in the Palatine manuscript;
of this latter work his autograph is now in Venice (Marc. gr. 481).
His method of dealing with Greek texts was not always such as to
commend him to modern editors; in one case, the didactic poem on
astronomy by Aratus (c. 315–c. 240 B.C.), which was probably used
as a textbook on astronomy if the subject was taught in school,
Planudes could not resist the temptation to revise some parts of the
text which were factually inaccurate. Instead of simply recording
in a commentary the advances in knowledge, he replaced lines
481–96, 501–6, and 515–24 by passages of his own composition
(Plate VI). Further information about his interests can be gleaned
from his letters. He mentions manuscripts of the abstruse mathematical writer Diophantus, and we know that he was interested in
other scientific authors such as Ptolemy and Euclid; he also wrote
a pamphlet about the introduction of Arabic numerals (in general
the Greeks still used the cumbrous alphabetic system of numerals).
Another feature of his letters worthy of mention is that he frequently requests one of his correspondents who lives in Asia Minor
to obtain for him some parchment, and is irritated when his friend
can do no better than find him some asses' skins. The shortage of
writing material experienced by one working in or near the capital
is very surprising. It may be worth noting in passing that though
he had been employed by the emperor on an embassy and was
clearly a scholar of distinction, there is no sign that he ever obtained imperial patronage or support for his scholarly work, and
this is generally true of Byzantine scholars with the partial exception of those working under the kingdom of Nicaea.

Rather less catholic in his tastes but no less important as a
scholar than Planudes was Demetrius Triclinius, a schoolmaster
who is known to have lived in Thessalonica c. 1305–20. His work
on the standard poetic texts of the curriculum can be traced
partly through autographs that survive and partly in the numerous
later books which contain commentaries headed by his name
(Plate VII). His chief claim to a place of honour in the history of
scholarship is that he was the first Byzantine to have a grasp of the
metres of classical poetry and to exploit his knowledge. All his
predecessors had either virtually ignored metrical questions or had
failed to appreciate the potential utility of the subject for a student

of classical poetry. But Triclinius came across a copy of the ancient metrical treatise by Hephaestion and grasped the essentials of it with a view to correcting the many passages in classical texts which were suspect or undoubtedly corrupt. It seems likely that he or his elder contemporaries were the first to emend texts systematically, and in the case of Triclinius enough documents survive to allow us a view of him at work. Though his knowledge of metre was by no means perfect he could correct iambics; sometimes he achieved a result that has won the general approval of modern critics, but often he resorted to facile measures such as the insertion of stopgap words to heal a metrical fault, and it is evident that he was not sensitive to questions of linguistic style in classical poetry. In more complicated metres than iambics he was less sure of his ground, but had one vital weapon: he knew that the lyrics of the chorus in tragedy and comedy were intended to have exact metrical responsion, and the text of Euripides which contains his autograph corrections (Laur. 32.2) shows him willing to use Procrustean violence in order to achieve the desired result (see p. 211). Despite his many mistakes in the use of his knowledge it remains the most important step forward in the treatment of poetic texts at this date. Textual criticism was thus raised again to the level which it had reached in the ancient world, but the task awaiting the critic had increased, since the practice of copying by hand for a millennium and more had necessarily introduced many new errors into the texts.

Triclinius' other main work was a redrafting of the scholia on various authors. He sifted the material of the old scholia and selected what he believed to be most useful for school instruction. The resulting new commentary contained a certain number of additional glosses or other elementary notes added by himself, and it tended to omit or reduce parts of the scholia which are most valuable for modern scholars; ancient learning was not always directly relevant to the text and Triclinius did not have the modern scholar's reasons for wishing to preserve it. Being conscious of the importance of his metrical knowledge he composed a separate metrical commentary on many plays; in the case of Aristophanes he had some guidance from the ancient metrical commentary by Heliodorus which survived in the old scholia. In his autograph

copies he arranged in separate columns the metrical commentary
of his own composition and the old scholia which he had revised.

By his work on text and scholia, which was on the whole more
thorough and competent than that of his colleagues, Triclinius
deserves to be counted as the forerunner of modern editors. Like
other scholars he hunted for fresh manuscripts in the hope of improving the texts. In some of his notes he refers to the different
readings of the various copies that he had been able to consult.
On one occasion his searches appear to have been rewarded by
a dramatic discovery: he came across a text of nine plays of
Euripides that were otherwise almost unknown in Byzantium; the
copies of this book that he had prepared by his pupils or in a local
scriptorium, to which he added a good many alterations in his own
hand, are our only source for the text of these plays. We therefore
owe largely to Triclinius our knowledge of about half the surviving
work of Euripides.

Planudes and Triclinius may be selected as the most important
representatives of their age, and the latest Byzantines whose activities had any lasting effect on classical texts. Though they were
not followed by men of comparable ability, they were not without
colleagues and rivals in their own day, and the work of the latter
can be seen in much the same way from surviving manuscripts.
Some manuscripts of this comparatively late date are important
for the constitution of texts. They contain good readings which are
due to the acumen of contemporary scholars or represent branches
of tradition that cannot be traced earlier. Classical studies enjoyed great popularity; not only the literature was being read, but
technical and scientific works written in antiquity were still
sufficiently up to date to demand and reward attention. With some
justification the period is referred to as the Palaeologan Renaissance, the name being drawn from that of the ruling house of the
time. Secondary education seems to have increased substantially
although the general condition of the empire was anything but
satisfactory. Schoolmasters devoted themselves to the elucidation
or correction of texts that can scarcely have formed part of the
regular school curriculum; we have seen for instance how Planudes
worked on Nonnus and scientific texts, while Triclinius' study of
the newly found Euripidean plays apparently had no bearing on the

school programme, for there is no evidence that any of them was added to the normal syllabus. This consisted of Attic or Atticist prose writers, textbooks of the art of rhetoric, especially Hermogenes and Aphthonius, and the poets, primarily Homer (Plate IV) and the selected plays of tragedy and comedy. By the late thirteenth century it had become the custom to read three plays of each tragedian and Aristophanes, sometimes known as the 'triad'; the habit may go back to the twelfth century or earlier, for Tzetzes composed a full commentary on only the three Aristophanic comedies that later were standard reading. Most manuscripts of these four authors contain only the triad; some of the later manuscripts have only one or two plays, which may well be an indication that the curriculum had been still further reduced. The plays outside the triad might easily have been lost through neglect, but fortunately they were preserved just long enough to be rescued by the Italian visitors and collectors of the Renaissance; all the most important manuscripts of these texts reached Italy during the Renaissance and many are still to be found there. The dramatic texts are only one instance of a general process. The chief merit of the Byzantines was that they took an interest in a wide range of classical texts and thus preserved them until scholars of another nation were in a position to use and appreciate them. The tradition of scholarship was taken up by the Italian humanists, who resembled their Byzantine colleagues in many ways. A vast number of manuscripts were brought back from the Byzantine empire in the last century of its history, and the collectors were active long after, so that today the libraries of the Greek East are virtually denuded of classical texts. This process was undoubtedly necessary in order to ensure the survival of Greek literature.

3. THE LATIN WEST

The sixth century saw the final collapse of what remained of the Roman empire in the West. In Italy the relatively enlightened rule of Theodoric (493–526) was given distinction by the two most notable figures of the transition period from the ancient to the medieval world, Boethius and Cassiodorus; but it was followed by the destruction of the Ostrogothic kingdom by the Byzantines and a spectacular cultural decline. The provinces were to fare little better. North Africa, now in Vandal hands, was soon to pass beyond the pale of Western culture; some of its literary achievement, such as the *Latin Anthology*, was transmitted in time to Europe and so to posterity. Spain, prey to external attack and internal strife, was to see a revival of Visigothic culture in the later sixth and early seventh centuries, reaching a modest peak in Isidore of Seville, but it too was to succumb in the early eighth century to the Moslem invaders. Though traces of the older Roman culture lingered on among the upper classes in Gaul, the Frankish Merovingian dynasty founded by Clovis (481–511) was grotesquely ill-suited to foster any cultural continuity.

The ravages of conquest and barbarism made the prospects for cultural life extremely bleak, and within the narrowing world of culture the place allotted to classical Latin literature was insecure. Education and the care of books were rapidly passing into the hands of the Church, and the Christians of this period were predominantly hostile to pagan literature. Decimated by the continued destruction of war, faced by hostility or neglect at the hands of the new intellectuals, the Latin classics seemed to have a slim chance of survival.

But the fundamental condition for their survival obtained: there were still books. We do not know how much survived of the twenty-eight public libraries of which Rome could boast in the fourth century; but there were remnants at least of the great private libraries of the age of the Symmachi, there were important collections in such ecclesiastical centres as Rome and Ravenna and

Monastic and other centres of Western Europe

Verona, and books were beginning to find a refuge in the monasteries. The luxury copies of Vergil show that the book trade had flourished down to the end of the fifth century and the beautiful monastic productions which survive from sixth-century Italy demonstrate that nothing had been lost in the art of producing books when it passed into the hands of the Church. Many of the handsome capital and uncial manuscripts of the fourth and fifth centuries have survived, though in most cases only in fragments; their contents include remnants of Plautus and Terence, Ovid, Vergil, Lucan, a varied selection of Cicero's works, Sallust, Livy, the Elder Pliny, the tragedies and prose works of Seneca, Fronto, and Gellius. From this and other evidence it is clear that it was still possible in the year 500, at least in Italy, to obtain copies of most of the Latin authors. Some, like Catullus and Propertius, were probably scarce, and much of early Latin literature had been lost for ever, but even in the sixth century a Spanish bishop, Martin of Braga, was able to plagiarize a work of Seneca now lost and which could barely have survived him.

The bulk of Latin literature was still extant; moreover, the machinery for its transmission to later ages was already being set up in the shape of the monastic library and scriptorium. It was the monastic centres which were destined, often in spite of themselves, to play the major part in both preserving and transmitting what remained of pagan antiquity; a more slender, but at times vital, line of descent can be traced through the schools and libraries which became associated with the great cathedrals.

An early and conspicuous example of the monastic tradition was the monastery of Vivarium which Cassiodorus founded some time after 540 on his estates at Squillace in the extreme south of Italy. It owed much of its conception and character to the urgencies of the times, when the devastation of war and conquest was threatening to destroy cultural centres and even the books on which learning and literacy depended. Cassiodorus endowed his foundation with a good working library and put a strong emphasis on education and the copying of manuscripts. His educational program is set out in the two books of his *Institutiones divinarum et saecularium litterarum*, composed c. 562. Although endowed with no exceptional intellectual gifts, Cassiodorus appears in retrospect as a man of vision who foresaw the role which monasteries were to play in succeeding centuries, who grasped the crucial fact that with the disintegration of political life these retreats provided the main hope for intellectual continuity. But he also had a practical bent and an eye for detail in keeping with a long and successful career in the Ostrogothic civil service. He realized the need for Latin translations of the Greek authorities on exegesis, philosophy, and science, and he was influential in both augmenting and disseminating the increasing body of Greek learning available in Latin dress. He had a particular appreciation for the convenience of the omnibus volume and had related texts bound together whenever possible; one of his composite volumes contained Cicero's *De inventione*, Quintilian, and the *Ars rhetorica* of Fortunatianus, a book for which Lupus of Ferrières understandably searched far and wide in the ninth century. He insisted on the importance of the meticulous copying of books, paid great attention to orthography and presentation, and with moving eloquence conferred a new dignity upon the scribe: 'felix intentio, laudanda sedulitas, manu hominibus praedicare, digitis linguas aperire, salutem mortalibus tacitum dare, et contra diaboli subreptiones illicitas calamo atramentoque pugnare' (*Inst.* 1.30.1).

Cassiodorus' services to the classical tradition could easily be exaggerated; indeed, one of his main preoccupations had been to erode the secular monopoly of higher education. The pagan authors found a place in both his library and his educational program, but they were reduced to the rank of teaching books and manuals. The only classical works which to our certain knowledge he put on his shelves were Cicero's *De inventione*, Seneca's *De forma mundi* (now lost), Columella, Quintilian, Apuleius' *De interpretatione*, some Aristotle, and a number of technical works; of the poets, whom he quotes and on whom he had been brought up, apparently nothing. The library of his contemporary Symmachus, for example, who had a much more positive attitude to pagan culture, would probably have had a very different flavour. Nor does Vivarium appear to have played any direct part in the transmission of classical texts. His monastery seems to have died with him, and the theory once held, that its books passed in time to the great monastery of Bobbio, founded in northern Italy in

614, and so provided a direct link between antiquity and the Middle Ages, now lies in ruins: such of its books as can be traced appear to have found their way in the main to Rome, possibly to the Lateran Library, and from there to have been dispersed by the generosity of successive popes. A few manuscripts have been identified which were either written at Vivarium or had ancestors which originated in Cassiodorus' library, among them the famous codex Amiatinus of the Vulgate (see p. 228), but these do not include any classical texts. Cassiodorus is important for many reasons and not least because he provides us with our only example of a sixth-century library; but there must have been other—and from the classical point of view better—collections of which we know nothing.

More limited in aim, but immeasurably greater in effect, was the founding of Monte Cassino c. 529 by Benedict of Nursia, who, by the promulgation of his Rule, laid the foundation on which monastic life in the West was based for centuries to come. Apart from setting aside a period each day for reading—a spiritual rather than intellectual operation—the Benedictine Rule had nothing to say about intellectual pursuits, and the copying of books had no explicit part in the monastic ideal; but, in saying nothing, it left the way open for liberal influences when the time was ripe, and reading could in any case not be carried on without books.

While Italy had enjoyed its late Renaissance in the first half of the sixth century, the blossoming of Visigothic culture in Spain did not come until the late sixth and early seventh centuries. This revival largely owes its place in the history of classical culture to the achievement of its greatest writer, Isidore of Seville (c. 570–636). Owing to the phenomenally rapid spread of his works throughout Europe, an amazing accomplishment for the pre-Carolingian period, Isidore was quickly established as one of the most influential agents in the transmission and elucidation of ancient learning. His *Etymologies* was at the same time the last product of the Roman encyclopedic tradition and the starting-point for most medieval compilations; its most frequently copied section, the first three books covering the subjects of the *trivium* and *quadrivium*, must have contributed enormously to the consolidation of the medieval educational system. This systematically arranged encyclopedia, packed with information and misinformation on every topic from angels to the parts of the saddle, descends so often into false etymologizing and the uncritical parade of absurd bric-à-brac that it cannot be read without a smile. But Isidore wins one's respect, and even affection, by his obvious appreciation of knowledge for its own sake. Hostility to pagan literature is explicit in some of his public pronouncements, and he was more at home in the neutral pages of the scholiast and compiler than the classical authors themselves, whom with a few exceptions he quotes at second-hand; but his curiosity knew no barriers and he took for granted the independent value of profane culture. When he culls from the fathers of the Church the scraps of classical poetry and pagan learning which they contain and re-allocates them to their proper place in the traditional system of knowledge, this bishop is paradoxically recreating in a resecularized form the basic structure of ancient learning.

However, the process which has preserved Latin literature for us could not begin until there was a more sympathetic and more positive attitude to classical authors than generally obtained on the continent in the Dark Ages. Christians still lived in the shadow of pagan literature; its achievement dwarfed their own, and its threat to morals and doctrine was a real one. This was to change when Latin culture was transplanted to a distant soil, where those eager to learn the language of the Church could turn to antiquity without any sense of inferiority or fear, since rivalry was out of the question and men at large were protected from the dangers of ancient paganism by simple ignorance of the Latin language. But this spirit did not percolate on any scale to the continent of Europe until the Carolingian Revival in the late eighth century, and in the meantime much of classical literature perished.

Although few ages are so dark that they are not penetrated by a few shafts of light, the period from roughly 550 to 750 was one of almost unrelieved gloom for the Latin classics on the continent; they virtually ceased being copied. Among the mass of patristic, biblical, and liturgical manuscripts which survive from this period there are precious few classical texts: from the sixth century we have scraps of two Juvenal manuscripts, remnants of one of the Elder and one of the Younger Pliny, but at least two of these belong to the early part of the century; from the seventh century we have a fragment of Lucan; from the early eighth century nothing.

The fate which often overtook the handsome books of antiquity is dismally illustrated by the surviving palimpsests—manuscripts in which the original texts have been washed off to make way for works which at the time were in greater demand. Many texts which had escaped destruction in the crumbling empire of the West perished within the walls of the monastery; some of them may have been too tattered when they arrived to be of practical use, and there was no respect for rags, however venerable. The peak period for this operation was the seventh and early eighth century, and although palimpsests survive from many centres, the bulk of them have come from the Irish foundations of Luxeuil and Bobbio. Texts perished, not because pagan authors were under attack, but because no one was interested in reading them, and parchment was too precious to carry an obsolete text; Christian works, heretical or superfluous, also went to the wall, while the ancient grammarians, of particular interest to the Irish, often have the upper hand. But the toll of classical authors was very heavy: amongst those palimpsested we find Plautus and Terence, Cicero and Livy, the Elder and Younger Pliny, Sallust and Seneca, Vergil and Ovid, Lucan, Juvenal and Persius, Gellius and Fronto. Fronto survives in three palimpsests, fated always to be the underdog. Among the texts which have survived solely in this mutilated form are some of outstanding interest, such as the *De republica* of Cicero (Vat. lat. 5757, Plate X) written in uncials of the fourth or fifth century and covered at Bobbio in the seventh with Augustine on the Psalms, a fifth-century copy of the *De amicitia* and *De vita patris* of Seneca (Vat. Pal. lat. 24) which succumbed in the late sixth or early seventh century to the Old Testament, and a fifth-century codex of Sallust's *Histories* (Orléans 192 + Vat. Reg. lat. 1283B + Berlin lat. qu. 364) which, in France and probably at Fleury, was supplanted at the turn of the seventh century by Jerome. Other important palimpsests are the Ambrosian Plautus (Ambros. S.P. 9/13-20, *olim* G. 82 sup.) and the Verona Livy (Verona XL (38)), both of the fifth century.

II. IRELAND AND ENGLAND

A new intellectual movement which was to put a higher value on classical texts than the price of their parchment had already begun in a remote outpost of Christianity. This was Ireland, possessed of a Latin culture as early as the late fifth century and destined to play a vital part in the civilization of Europe. The amount of actual classical literature known in Ireland in pre-Carolingian times is much debated and appears to have been small indeed; the close acquaintance with Latin poetry revealed by their major literary figure, Columban (c. 543–615), relates to the continental phase of his life and may belong more to the context of late antique culture than that of the monasteries of Ireland. The important feature of their culture was therefore not its classical content but the intensive and uninhibited way in which they read what books they possessed, their enthusiasm and aptitude for learning, however peculiar and bogus that learning sometimes was, and the industry which produced in the course of the seventh and eight centuries a remarkable amount of grammatical and exegetical work. The Irish also had remarkable artistic talents: from the half-uncial manuscripts which they had acquired from Gaul in the fifth and sixth centuries they developed a beautiful half-uncial of their own, seen in its finest form in the Book of Kells, and a more practical and equally individual minuscule script. Their importance for the transmission of classical texts begins when they leave Ireland, impelled by a missionary zeal of far-reaching consequence. The establishment of Iona as the centre of Celtic Christianity outside Ireland by Columba c. 563 marked the effective beginning of the conversion of Scotland and led on in time to the foundation of such important monasteries as Lindisfarne in Northumbria and Malmesbury in the south-west. Even more spectacular was the continental mission of Columban, who blazed a trail across Europe marked out by such important monastic foundations as those of Luxeuil in Burgundy (590), from which Corbie was founded a century later, Bobbio in northern Italy (614), and Saint Gall, which developed from a hermitage which his pupil Gallus established in Switzerland c. 613. The *Scotti peregrini* became a colourful feature of the continental scene in the eighth and ninth centuries and had a large contribution to make, as such men as Virgil of Salzburg, Dungal, Sedulius Scottus, John Scottus Eriugena serve to demonstrate. However much these scholars became part of the Carolingian revival, their learning tended to retain its strong Irish accent.

While the Latin culture of Ireland was percolating through northern England, a more direct link with Rome and its past was re-established in the south when, in 597, Gregory the Great sent Augustine to England with a mission to convert the Anglo-Saxons to Christianity. Canterbury became the centre of Roman Christianity and Augustine its first archbishop. More significant, because more effective, was the second mission of 668, headed by Theodore of Tarsus and Hadrian of Niridanum, which succeeded in establishing the Roman Church throughout the country. Theodore was a Greek, Hadrian an African by birth; both were men of wide learning. An important feature of the renewed contact with Rome was the inflow of books. To Augustine Gregory had sent the necessary vestments and vessels for carrying on divine service *nec non et codices plurimos* (Bede, *Hist. eccl.* 1.29). These would be bibles, service-books, and the like, but most of them were doubtless written in uncials, and it was these books which led to to the development in England of a fine uncial script which enjoyed a couple of centuries of glory before giving way in the eight century to the minuscule introduced into Northumbria by the Irish. Theodore and Hadrian came with an educational and literary program; they must have brought a large number of books, Latin and Greek, probably pagan and Christian, but we have no details. The Anglo-Latin culture which grew out of the converging influences of Ireland and Rome created a need for books of all kinds; some came from France and Spain, but the main source was Italy, Rome, and the South. Wilfrid (c. 634–709), bishop of York and abbot of Ripon, made several journeys to Rome and will not have come back empty-handed, and the same applies to Aldhelm; but the great traveller of the age was Benedict Biscop, the founder of the twin monasteries of Wearmouth and Jarrow (674 and 682), who made no less than six trips to Italy. The fifth is the most famed: *innumerabilem librorum omnis generis copiam adportavit* (Bede, *Hist. abbatum* 6). A distinguished place in English history is owed to Benedict Biscop and his protégé abbot Ceolfrid, who made it possible for a local boy who had apparently never set foot outside Northumbria, Bede, to acquire a breadth of scholarship unrivalled in the Europe of his day and to leap the seemingly unbridgeable gulf which separated his world from that of the later Roman empire. We know of further importations of books in the eighth century, and the result can be seen in the rich libraries which grew up at Canterbury and York.

We know something of the width of reading of the English scholars of the seventh and eighth centuries from the writings of Aldhelm (c. 639–709) and Bede (673–735), the one a product of Wessex and Kent, the other of Northumbria. Their range of reference was doubtless exceptional, but it is evidence of the books available to scholars in England. The impressive roll of classical authors named or quoted shows a healthy respect for the classical tradition rather than first-hand knowledge, for much of it is derived from Macrobius and Isidore and the grammarians. Further reductions of the list may be necessary, but Aldhelm appears to have known Vergil and Lucan, Persius and Juvenal, the Elder Pliny, some Cicero, possibly Ovid, while Bede had first-hand knowledge of a large number of grammarians, Vergil, some books of the Elder Pliny, Macrobius and Eutropius, more dubiously Ovid and Lucan. This is impressive and is corroborated by evidence of a slightly later date which we owe to the fortunate chance that Alcuin (c. 735–804), in a poem in praise of York, gives us a glimpse of the contents of that great library. When it comes to cataloguing, a poem is a far cry from a card-index: some authors and titles are excluded by metrical exigencies, so that the list is vague and incomplete. However, among a rich collection of theological names, we have a number of *auctores*: Vergil, Statius, Lucan, Cicero, Pliny, and Pompeius. Cicero, given the epithet *rhetor*, will mean the *De inventione*, and Pompeius will be Justinus' epitome of Pompeius Trogus. Such hints as we have reveal in England a broader and more systematic knowledge of both Christian and pagan literature than could be paralleled elsewhere at this period.

III. THE ANGLO-SAXON MISSIONARIES

The rich and vigorous culture which blossomed in Anglo-Saxon England soon spread to the continent. The Irish had passed on their missionary impulse, and the most famous of the successors of Columban were Willibrord (658–739), a native of Northumbria, and Boniface (c. 675–754), a product of Wessex. Willibrord set out on his mission to the Frisian people in 690 and so inaugurated a period of Anglo-Saxon influence on the continent which was to last into the ninth century; his consecration as archbishop of the Frisians by the Pope and at the suggestion of Pippin II marked the first step in cooperation between the Carolingian house and the Papacy. Boniface eventually settled on central Germany as his sphere of activity; but his missionary venture, forwarded by the active help of successive Carolingian patrons, particularly Charles Martel, by papal encouragement, and not least by his own tremendous capacity for ecclesiastical organization, so snowballed that it led to the reform of the whole Frankish Church and the establishment of Germany as a province of the Church of Rome. Among his theological opponents was a colourful Irishman, Virgil of Salzburg, who administered the see from 746–84, a man of wide learning with a talent for satire; he claims our interest because his cosmological take-off, the so-called *Cosmographia* of Aethicus Ister, reveals him as the first person north of the Alps to know the geographical work of Pomponius Mela and establishes a link in a chain of transmission which leads from ancient Ravenna to the Renaissance (see pp. 94, 115). One of his countrymen, if not Virgil himself, may well be responsible for the pro-Irish gloss which crept into Mela's text: the unflattering description of the ancient Irish as *omnium virtutum ignari magis quam aliae gentes* (3.6.53) received the comment *aliquatenus tamen gnari*.

One result of this alliance of missionary enthusiasm and temporal interest was the rise of important episcopal centres, like Mainz and Würzburg, and a new wave of monastic foundations, both needing libraries and scriptoria. Among the monasteries were Fulda, founded in 744 by Boniface's pupil Sturmi, and the closely allied Hersfeld, established c. 770 by his helper, the Anglo-Saxon Lullus. But two other important monasteries, Reichenau on Lake Constance (724) and its daughter-house of Murbach (727), were founded by Pirmin, a man of obscure origin, thought to have fled from Visigothic Spain with the coming of the Arabs in 711.

With them the Anglo-Saxons brought a script, books, a liberal intellectual outlook, and the recognition that a well-stocked and well-balanced library was the basis of ecclesiastical education. Books must have been imported on some scale, and not only from England; the letters of Boniface and Lullus are full of requests for books. The Anglo-Saxon script became established in centres under insular influence and was often practised alongside continental hands in the same scriptorium. Pockets of insular writing flourished until the middle of the ninth century, and some of its features, particularly abbreviation signs, were incorporated into the tradition of continental script.

IV. INSULAR INFLUENCE ON CLASSICAL TEXTS

The impact of Anglo-Latin culture on the intellectual rebirth of the continent, which finally culminated in the person of Alcuin, together with the practical provision of books, scriptoria, and scribes, must have had an immeasurable effect on the revival—and hence the survival—of Latin literature. But it is not easy to demonstrate this in detail, as the evidence is fragmentary and disparate. A couple of classical manuscripts have survived which were actually written in the eighth century in Northumbria; these show that part of the textual tradition of these authors actually passed at one stage through northern England. One of these two manuscripts contains the first six books of Pliny's *Natural History* (Voss. lat. F. 4, Plate XII), the other is just a single leaf of Justinus (Weinheim, MS. Fischer). Both manuscripts were written in Northumbria and both the works which they contain were, as we have seen, in the library at York. The Justinus manuscript actually made the journey which one suspects in the case of some other classical texts: it crossed the Channel and found its way to the Carolingian court, where it fathered the transalpine—and best—family of Justinus manuscripts. A recently published fragment containing excerpts of Servius' commentary on the *Aeneid* appears to have been written in south-west England in the latter part of the eighth century (Spangenburg, Pfarrbibliothek S.N.); it is later associated with Fulda and it has been conjectured that it may have been taken to Germany by Boniface or one of his circle.

For some other authors we have manuscripts which were written in insular script on the continent (paradoxically known as 'continental insular'), and the text of these authors clearly owes much to the missionary activity of the English and the Irish. Texts which survive in manuscripts known to have been written or housed in insular monastic and episcopal centres on the continent are equally beneficiaries of the movement, though their script may show no trace of it. The same applies to those texts which show 'insular symptoms', i.e. errors which are best explained as originating in the faulty transcription of letters or abbreviations peculiar to English or Irish hands. These indicate that the text went through an insular tradition at an earlier stage in its history than that represented by the extant manuscripts. But such hypotheses have to be treated with caution: symptoms, especially when few in number, can be wrongly diagnosed, and insular ancestry, like the Scottish grandmother, is more often claimed than substantiated. The authors which go back with at least a high degree of probability to an insular parent include Ammianus Marcellinus, the *Tusculan disputations* of Cicero, the epic poetry of Statius and Valerius Flaccus, the *De architectura* of Vitruvius, and claims can be made for others. The great centres of insular activity were Hersfeld and Fulda, which played a dominant part in the preservation of some texts. But their contribution belongs more to the story of the Carolingian revival, and will be more appropriately described in that context.

V. THE CAROLINGIAN REVIVAL

The classical revival of the late eighth and early ninth centuries, without doubt the most momentous and critical stage in the transmission of the legacy of Rome, was played out against the background of a reconstituted empire which stretched from the Elbe to the Ebro, from Calais to Rome, welded together for a time into a political and spiritual whole by the commanding personality of an emperor who added to his military and material resources the blessing of Rome. Although the political achievement of Charlemagne (768–814) crumbled in the hands of his successors, the cultural movement which it fostered retained its impetus in the ninth century and survived into the tenth.

The secular and ecclesiastical administration of a vast empire called for a large number of trained priests and functionaries. As the only common denominator in a heterogeneous realm and as the repository of both the classical and the Christian heritage of an earlier age, the Church was the obvious means of implementing the educational program necessary to produce a trained executive. But under the Merovingians the Church had fallen on evil days; some of the priests were so ignorant of Latin that Boniface heard one carrying out a baptism of dubious efficacy *in nomine patria et filia et spiritus sancti* (*Epist.* 68), and knowledge of antiquity had worn so thin that the author of one sermon was under the unfortunate impression that Venus was a man. Reform had begun under Pippin the Short; but now the need was greater, and Charlemagne felt a strong personal responsibility to raise the intellectual and cultural level of the clergy, and through them of his subjects:

igitur quia curae nobis est ut nostrarum ecclesiarum ad meliora proficiat status, oblitteratam paene maiorum nostrorum desidia reparare vigilanti studio litterarum satagimus officinam, et ad pernoscenda studia liberalium artium nostro etiam quos possumus invitamus exemplo (*Epist. gen.*, *MGH*, *Legum sectio II*, *Capit. Regum Francorum I* (1883), p. 80).

When it came to creating an educated class out of next to nothing, the Anglo-Saxons were past masters, and it was a shrewd move on the part of Charles to turn to York, at this time the educational centre of England and indeed of Europe, and in 782 to invite Alcuin, the head of its school, to take charge of his palace school and be his adviser on educational matters.

Alcuin was above all an efficient teacher. There was nothing ambitious about the educational system which he transplanted to the continent and there refined: elementary and utilitarian, it aimed at literacy rather than literature, and the classical content, cut and dried, was entirely subsidiary to the Christian purpose. The Carolingian educational program waned before it could become widely established, but the setting up by imperial edict of schools attached to both the monasteries and the cathedrals guaranteed that a basic standard of literacy would be maintained at least here and there in the Europe of the future, to blossom into something greater when circumstances were favourable. But Carolingian culture was not chained to the schoolroom. Alcuin could rise to greater heights when he wished, and the court became the point of fruitful interaction between poets and scholars attracted to it from the whole of Europe, including men of imagination and elegance and learning, such as Peter of Pisa and Paul the Deacon from Italy, the Irish scholar Dungal, the poet Theodulfus from Spain. From this circle there emanated a higher and more secular cultural stream; men were found who rose above the rather constipated limits of much Carolingian thought and literature and approached the ancient classics with genuine intellectual curiosity and honest aesthetic appreciation. An important result of a rapidly developing and highly organized educational program, spreading from the court to the monasteries and cathedrals, was the need for books; these were produced on an unprecedented scale, in a flurry of activity which salvaged for us the greater part of Latin literature.

VI. THE DEVELOPMENT OF CAROLINE MINUSCULE

In keeping with the thoroughness and uniformity of the new order was the universal adoption of a new script, the Caroline minuscule (Plate XIII), which, though it developed too early for Charlemagne or Alcuin to have had a hand in it, doubtless owed its acceptance and refinement to their encouragement. The late seventh and eight centuries had been a period of universal experimentation in the art of writing, inspired by the need for a more economical and up-to-date script. While the Irish and the English had been developing a minuscule script out of half-uncial, other minuscule hands had come into being on the continent. These had a more humble origin, developing not from the uncial book-hands, though in places these influenced their evolution, but from the old Roman cursive which had remained as the script of business and officialdom. Out of this unpromising script was forged a calligraphic book-hand which evolved along its own lines in different regions and produced the 'national hands' of Spain, southern Italy, and Gaul—Visigothic, Beneventan, and Merovingian.

The Visigothic script, which flourished in Spain from the early eighth to the twelfth century, concerns us least, for there are very few extant classical manuscripts written in this hand and very little evidence that it was instrumental in the transmission of classical texts. Beneventan, so called because it was conterminous with the old duchy of Benevento—its designation as Lombardic is now obsolete—has a marked similarity to Visigothic and became the normal script of Italy south of Rome and parts of the Dalmatian coast (Plate XIV). This fine hand, built up entirely from cursive elements, came into being in the eighth century, reached its peak in the eleventh, and lingered on into the fifteenth, though in the thirteenth it gave way to Caroline minuscule as the vehicle for literary texts. The great centre was Monte Cassino (see p. 96), but a modified script emerged under Byzantine influence along the Adriatic coast and particularly at Bari, and a number of classical texts, including works of Terence, Cicero, Sallust, Vergil, and Ovid, are written in this local Apulian variety.

The early minuscule scripts of Merovingian Gaul are important, not as vehicles for the transmission of classical texts—in which they played little part—but as forerunners of the Carolingian hands. From these scripts, more fluid than those of Italy and Spain, the calligraphic urge of the craftsman evolved, after trial and error, a minuscule which was destined to become the normal script of Western Europe. The first calligraphic minuscule of France was produced at Luxeuil and bears the name of that great Irish foundation; it reached its peak about 700. In the eighth century the palm passed to Corbie, where in the second half of the century no less than three scripts can be distinguished, all in use at the same time —known technically as the en script, the ab script, and the Maurdramn type. In the biblical books produced at Corbie under abbot Maurdramn (772–80) we see emerging from these pre-Caroline scripts the first example of a developed Caroline minuscule. The cursive elements are eliminated, the letters are rounded, separate, and regular, and the result is an unsurpassed grace and lucidity, which must have had a tremendous effect on the survival of classical literature by casting it in a form which all could read with both ease and pleasure. It became universal throughout the Carolingian empire in the course of a few decades, crossed to England in the tenth century, and by the end of the twelfth had swept its rivals from the field.

VII. CAROLINGIAN LIBRARIES AND THE LATIN CLASSICS

Recent research has enabled us to see to the heart of the Carolingian classical revival by demonstrating that a list of authors preserved in a manuscript at Berlin (Diez B. 66), and remarkable for the richness and rarity of its content, can be nothing less than a partial catalogue of books in the court library of Charlemagne about the year 790. The list includes Lucan, Statius' *Thebaid,* Terence, Juvenal, Tibullus, Horace's *Ars poetica,* Claudian, Martial, some of Cicero's speeches (the *Verrines, Catilinarians, Pro rege Deiotaro*), and a collection of orations excerpted from the *Bella* and *Historiae* of Sallust. Other classical works quoted in the court poetry of the time suggest the presence in the library of such additional rarities as Grattius' *Cynegetica* and Statius' *Silvae.* It is reasonable to assume from passages in Alcuin's correspondence that it also possessed a copy of the Elder Pliny. Some of the books in this impressive list will have been ancient codices written in capitals and uncials.

It is clear from the evidence that abbots and bishops who had the right connections could enrich their libraries with copies taken from the books in the palace library; and after Charlemagne's death, although the details of the way in which his library was dispersed are unknown, many of the books found their way to monastic libraries. There is a remarkable correlation between the items in the palace list and the works known to have been copied at Corbie about the middle of the century: the unique Corbie manuscript which contains the well-known collection of speeches and letters taken from Sallust (Vat. lat. 3864) is the most striking example. Another tell-tale item is the group of three Ciceronian speeches which reappear in the important codex Holkhamicus, now in the British Museum (Add. 47678): this was written at Tours in the early years of the ninth century—Alcuin was abbot of Saint Martin's at Tours from 796–804—and it is easy to guess where its parent came from. Again, one of the most famous manuscripts of Livy is the codex Puteanus of the third decade (Paris lat. 5730, Plate XI), written in the fifth century in Italy and the source of all the later manuscripts: this was copied at Tours about the year 800 (its copy is Vat. Reg. lat. 762, Plate XIII) and again at Corbie about the middle of the ninth century (Laur. 63.20), a pattern which strongly suggests that the home of the Puteanus was to be found in the palace. Other classical manuscripts copied in France at the turn of the century may well owe their contents to the same fruitful source, and the science of palaeography, progressing in this field at a breathless pace, will in time doubtless throw much more light on the movement of books.

Gathering impetus with each decade, the copying of books went on apace through the length and breadth of Charlemagne's empire. Such ancient classical manuscripts as could be found, with their imposing majuscule scripts, were transformed, often at speed, into minuscule copies, and these in time begot further copies, branching out into those complex patterns to which the theory of stemmatics has reduced this fascinating process. Some idea of the scale, perhaps exceptional, on which classical books were copied can be had from those Latin manuscripts which were written at Corbie during a short period after the middle of the century. The exemplars from which they were copied came in part from the palace, and the credit for the burst of activity which produced them probably belongs to the Corbie librarian, Hadoard: they include a large collection of Cicero's philosophical works, the first and third decades of Livy, Sallust, Columella, the Elder Seneca, the Younger Pliny, Caesar's *Gallic War*, the *Ad Herennium*, Macrobius' commentary on the *Somnium Scipionis*, Statius' *Thebaid*, Martial, Ovid's *Heroides* and *Amores*, Terence, Vitruvius, and Vegetius. It is clear from extant catalogues of Carolingian libraries and from other evidence that comparable collections existed, or were being built up, at such centres as Tours, Fleury, Ferrières, Auxerre, Lorsch, Reichenau, and Saint Gall. The multiplication of popular texts meant that the contents of these libraries were inevitably somewhat repetitive: rather than examine them in detail, it will be more interesting to single out the more remarkable items and then attempt a survey of what the Carolingian revival had succeeded in rescuing from the wreck of antiquity.

Though a recent foundation (764), the monastery of Lorsch, in Hesse, enjoyed the special patronage of Charlemagne and rapidly built up one of the richest Carolingian libraries. The famous codex Pithoeanus of Juvenal and Persius (Montpellier 125) was written at Lorsch, and it possessed copies of Cicero's *Letters*, which were a rarity at the time. Among the manuscripts which came into its possession were some very remarkable books. These include the fifth-century codex which is our only source for the fifth decade of Livy (Vienna lat. 15) and which had earlier been circulating in the Low Countries; the main manuscript of Seneca's *De bene-ficiis* and *De clementia* (Vat. Pal. lat. 1547), written in northern Italy about the year 800 and one of the earliest classical manu-scripts of the Carolingian period; the codex Palatinus of Vergil (Vat. Pal. lat. 1631), written in rustic capitals of the late fifth or early sixth century; a famous palimpsest from Italy (Vat. Pal. lat. 24), which had been made up from scraps of some of the oldest surviving books of antiquity, including codices of Seneca, Lucan, Fronto, and Gellius.

The importance of the insular foundations of Fulda and Hers-feld has already been mentioned. From these come the two manu-scripts of Ammianus Marcellinus from which the rest derive, and we owe the survival of the *Opera minora* of Tacitus and the *De grammaticis* of Suetonius to a manuscript written at either Hersfeld or Fulda and preserved at the former. Besides contributing im-portant manuscripts to the textual tradition of some authors, such as the Younger Pliny and Aulus Gellius, Fulda played a dominant role in the history of other texts: there is good reason to believe that it housed the archetypes of the *Tusculans* and Vitruvius; of the two Carolingian manuscripts of Columella, one was written at Corbie, the other at Fulda; the prime source for the *Historia Augusta* (Vat. Pal. lat. 899) must have been associated with Fulda, for one of its copies is written in the characteristic script; books 1–6 of the *Annals* of Tacitus have come down to us in a manuscript written at Fulda and preserved at Corvey, a daughter-house of Corbie; finally, to end on a lighter note, while one of the early manuscripts of the cookery book of Apicius is a show-piece of the script of Tours, the other (written in a mixture of Anglo-Saxon minuscule and continental script) points almost certainly to Fulda.

Other monasteries and their treasures must be mentioned more briefly. The group of Caesar manuscripts which contain only the *Gallic War* seem to go back to Fleury, which is almost certainly the source of the text of Petronius. Bobbio possessed both a Lucretius

and a Valerius Flaccus, two rare poets. Two of the great Vergil
codices, the Augusteus and the Romanus (Vat. lat. 3256 and 3867),
have the *ex-libris* of the abbey of Saint Denis at Paris and may
have been preserved there from this early period. Reichenau possessed a number of scarce items, Ovid's *Metamorphoses* and *Ars
amatoria*, Silius Italicus, and the *Natural Questions* of Seneca.

If one were to take stock at the end of the ninth century of the
classical books available, it would be clear that some authors were
so well entrenched in the literary and educational tradition and so
thick on the shelves of the libraries that their survival was no
longer in question: to this group we can assign Vergil and Horace
(the *Satires* and *Epistles* rather than the lyrics, which were less
popular in the Middle Ages), Lucan, Juvenal and Persius, Terence,
the epics of Statius, some of the rhetorical and philosophical works
of Cicero (the *Letters* and *Speeches* were still rare or unknown),
the *Catilina* and *Jugurtha* of Sallust, the Elder Pliny, Justinus, and
Vitruvius. The Elder Seneca and Valerius Maximus were available, as were Aulus Gellius and the *Letters* of Seneca, but Gellius
and Seneca both circulated in two separate parts, of which one
was much less common than the other, and at this period complete copies were rare or non-existent. Quintilian was less common
than one would expect (his place had been usurped by the *Ad
Herennium* and the *De inventione*), and he too was incomplete; most
of the manuscripts were *mutili*, though a complete text was put together in Germany in the tenth century. Martial and Suetonius
were not common, though Einhard's *Life of Charlemagne*, thanks to
a happy connection with Fulda, is a brilliant adaptation of Suetonius' literary method and a milestone in the development of secular
biography. Plautus, Lucretius, Livy, and the Younger Pliny were
even scarcer, and the great age of Ovid was still to come. Some
authors existed in so few copies—sometimes only one—that their
future was still precarious: Cicero's *Letters*, Tacitus, Columella,
Petronius, Apicius, Valerius Flaccus, and Ammianus were all
copied at this time, but not on a scale which would ensure their
survival through wars and acts of God and the less dramatic but
ever-present evils of mice and mould; it was going to need another
renovatio to make their position secure. The few or unique copies
of Tibullus and Catullus, Seneca's *Tragedies* and Statius' *Silvae*,

were virtually in hibernation, while Propertius, Seneca's *Dialogues*, Apuleius' *Golden Ass*, much of Tacitus, Manilius, Nepos, and Velleius Paterculus were still quite unknown.

One cannot consider these facts without marvelling at the slenderness of the thread on which the fate of the Latin classics hung. In the case of many texts a single copy survived into the Carolingian period, and often a battered one at that. When the great period of the revival was over, some of the great works of Latin literature were still but a single manuscript on a single shelf. The slightest accident could still have robbed us of some of our most precious texts, of Catullus and Propertius, Petronius or Tacitus. There are some extraordinary examples of survival: the fifth-century manuscript of Livy's fifth decade which found a home at Lorsch (Vienna lat. 15) survived until the sixteenth century without ever being copied. A mere mishap, and five more books of Livy would have disappeared without trace.

VIII. CAROLINGIAN SCHOLARSHIP

One of the more obvious aspects of the Carolingian age is the staggering amount of parchment it consumed: there was a tremendous spate of publication, ranging from creative poetry, through history, biography, hagiography, theology, philosophy, and biblical exegesis, to the handbooks on rhetoric, dialectic, metrics, and grammar. All of this has its relevance, for anything that involved a more sophisticated study and exploitation of the Latin language and literature furthered the classical tradition. But if, for our present purpose, we confine our attention to the study of classical literature and put some weight on the word scholarship, there are only a few men who need engage our attention.

One of the earliest glimpses of scholarly activity expended on a classical text in the Carolingian period is provided by the most celebrated manuscript of Lucretius, the codex Oblongus (Voss. lat. F. 30), written in north-eastern France during the first few years of the ninth century. This has been corrected and at times supplemented in an insular hand by the intriguing 'corrector Saxonicus', whose characteristic script has allowed the palaeographer to clothe him with flesh and blood: no Saxon at all, he has proved to be no less a person than the Irish scholar Dungal, the astronomical authority of his day, whom we see taking a not unexpected interest in our oldest extant text of Lucretius. A much larger place in the history of scholarship has been won by another Irishman, Sedulius Scottus, who was active at Liège in the middle of the century. Versatile and gifted, theologian and versifier as well as the author of grammatical commentaries on Priscian and others, Sedulius interests us most as the compiler of a *Collectaneum*, a collection of excerpts from various authors. This is largely a moral rag-bag of the type one meets frequently in the Middle Ages, but he shows some interest in the style of the authors excerpted and is truly remarkable for the range of his reading: he excerpts a large number of Ciceronian works (including the *Philippics, Pro Fonteio, Pro Flacco, In Pisonem*), Valerius Maximus, Macrobius, the military manuals of Frontinus and Vegetius, and the *Historia Augusta*. For Cicero's *Speeches* he seems to have used one of the important extant manuscripts (Vat. Arch. S. Petri H. 25), copied in Italy and probably from an uncial original. A similar collection has been left to us by Hadoard, the *custos librorum* at Corbie (see p. 87), written almost certainly in his own hand (Vat. Reg. lat. 1762 of the mid-ninth century). Hadoard shows much less respect for his authors: his moral maxims are torn from their context, denuded of the names and historical references which tie them to place and period, and Christianized where necessary. But his range is again noteworthy, particularly of Ciceronian works—*Academica priora, De natura deorum, De divinatione, De fato, Paradoxa, De legibus, Timaeus, Tusculanae disputationes, De officiis, De amicitia, De senectute De oratore.* He is of less textual importance than one might imagine, for some of the manuscripts he used are still extant. A more fascinating document, since it reflects the whole career and personal interests of the compiler, is the scrap-book (Saint Gall 878) of Walafrid Strabo (808–49), poet, tutor to the future Charles the Bald, and abbot of Reichenau. The extracts themselves fail to reveal his literary interests: the only pagan works of the classical period which he chose to excerpt were Columella and the *Letters* of Seneca, the first a not surprising choice for the author of a charming poem on his monastery garden. But the scrap-book has helped to demonstrate a more active intervention in the transmission of classical authors than is normal with an excerptor by revealing that the handsome hand which has supplemented and in places written or rewritten our oldest manuscript of Horace (Vat. Reg. lat. 1703 = R) belongs to Walafrid himself.

But the scholar who towers over his contemporaries is Lupus of Ferrières (c. 805–62). Author of the famous dictum *propter se ipsam appetenda sapientia* (Epist. 1), he alone of the men of his age gives a foretaste of the Renaissance. He was educated at Ferrières and completed his studies at Fulda under the greatest teacher of the post-Alcuinian period, Hrabanus Maurus (780–856); he returned to Ferrières in 836 and was abbot from 842 until his death. His letters are of great interest; despite his involvement in the affairs of the world, his correspondence is dominated by his scholarly interests. Anxious to increase the resources of the library at Ferrières, which had been modest enough in his student days, he writes far and wide in his search for books, to Einhard (who had now left the court and retired to Seligenstadt), to Tours, to York, to the Pope himself. However, he was not the only manuscript-hunter in the ninth century: his distinction rests on the fact that he is avid to obtain manuscripts of works which he already possesses, so that by collation he can correct and supplement his own text. He succeeded in filling up some of the gaps in the incomplete Valerius Maximus which had survived from antiquity by drawing on the rare epitome made by Julius Paris in the fourth century. The following extract from a letter written in 847 to a monk at Prüm will illustrate his practice (Epist. 69):

> Tullianas epistolas quas misisti cum nostris conferri faciam, ut ex utrisque, si possit fieri, veritas exculpatur. Tu autem huic nostro cursori Tullium in Arato [the *Aratea*] trade, ut ex eo quem me impetraturum credo, quae deesse illi Egil noster aperuit, suppleantur.

Glad to give as well as to receive, Lupus willingly replies to queries on points of grammar, prosody, or exegesis, and gives us a vivid glimpse of the intellectual life of a circle of Carolingian scholars. He wrote little, and the main monument of his humanism, apart from his letters, are the manuscripts of classical authors—more than a dozen in number—which reveal his handiwork. The most important of these in one respect is a manuscript of Cicero's *De oratore* in the British Museum (Harley 2736), written by Lupus himself; those which he has annotated include texts of Cicero, among them the oldest manuscript of the Leiden corpus of the philosophical works (Vienna lat. 189), Livy (VI–X), Valerius Maximus, Aulus Gellius, Macrobius (on the *Somnium Scipionis*), and Donatus (on *Aeneid* I–VI). We know that Einhard sent a Gellius to Fulda at Lupus' request and that Hrabanus was busy having it copied in 836 (Epist. 5). A manuscript of Gellius written at Fulda recently came to light (Leeuwarden, Prov. Bibl. van Friesland 55), but the hope that it might prove to have been the manuscript used by Lupus to correct his own copy of Gellius (Vat. Reg. lat. 597) has been disappointed. His practice of leaving spaces where lacunae are established or suspected, marking corruptions, and recording variants, reveals a sound scholarly approach to classical texts which outweighs the modest quality of his own critical contribution. In the field of biblical studies Lupus' practice of collating manuscripts had been strikingly anticipated by Theodulfus, bishop of Orléans and abbot of Fleury. Before his death in 821 he had made an edition of the Vulgate in which he foreshadowed modern editorial methods by using *sigla* in the margin to distinguish the sources of his variants, such as ā for the Alcuinian reading, s̄ for the Spanish recension.

Lupus was important as a teacher, and among his pupils was Heiric of Auxerre (c. 841–76), himself the teacher of such important figures in the next generation as Hucbald of Reims and Remigius of Auxerre. When one reflects that Lupus was taught by Hrabanus and Hrabanus in turn by Alcuin, one can clearly see one of the threads in the continuity of Carolingian education. Heiric occupies an important place in the history of classical texts. He published collections of excerpts from Valerius Maximus and Suetonius which he had taken down at Lupus' dictation. Lupus' manuscript of Valerius has come down to us (Berne 366). There were texts of Suetonius in the early ninth century at both Tours (Paris lat. 6115) and Fulda, and it was from Fulda that Lupus had tried, and probably succeeded, in obtaining his copy. Heiric is also the first person known to have used the excerpts of Petronius which were circulating in a manuscript now at Berne (357, written c. 870), and he is responsible for a collection of rare texts which have survived in a manuscript written at Auxerre in the years

860–2 and annotated by Heiric himself (Vat. lat. 4929). This odd little collection of texts is extremely interesting because we know something of both its earlier and its later history. Among its varied contents are two texts, Julius Paris' epitome of Valerius Maximus and the geography of Pomponius Mela, which both have a subscription recording that they were edited at Ravenna in the sixth century by Rusticius Helpidius Domnulus, a Christian poet who flourished in the second quarter of the century. Ravenna was the chief residence of many of the emperors in the fifth and sixth centuries and a thriving centre of intellectual life in late antiquity; after it was recovered from Byzantine dominion in the mid-eighth century it may have been, with Rome, one of the main sources of books for the early Carolingians. At all events, Mela had reached northern Europe by the second half of the eighth century since his work was known to Virgil of Salzburg (see p. 80), and both these texts eventually reached the circle of Lupus and Heiric. The continental Irish may have taken a hand in their transmission: in addition to being known to one famous Irishman, Virgil of Salzburg, Mela's text absorbed a pro-Irish gloss somewhere on its travels. It was Heiric who in turn passed on Helpidius' little encyclopedia to posterity: via a twelfth-century copy the contents of the Vaticanus reached Petrarch, who then ensured their wide distribution in the Renaissance.

IX. THE CAROLINGIAN TWILIGHT

The intellectual life of the Carolingian revival had been closely connected with the cohesion and security of Charlemagne's political achievement. During the course of the ninth and tenth century his empire suffered repeated attacks on all sides from the Vikings, Saracens, and Hungarians; whole regions were devastated and monasteries sacked, while internal disagreement led to its being split up in 843 into the separate political units which already foreshadow the fragmented face of modern Europe. However, the educational machine which Charlemagne and Alcuin had set in motion, working through the monastic and cathedral schools, had sufficient momentum to keep going until a new age could take over the classical tradition and exploit it more fully.

The tenth century was very much a period of transition from the

Carolingian age to the economic and intellectual expansion of the eleventh and twelfth centuries. There was a general sagging in the cultural level and a falling off in the production of classical manuscripts, but the Latin authors went on being studied and copied. Indeed, among the scholars of the age there were two whose breadth of learning could not have been paralleled in the previous century: these were Ratherius (c. 887–974), bishop of Liège and thrice bishop of Verona, and Gerbert of Reims (c. 950–1003).

Ratherius was one of the most turbulent figures in a turbulent century. Indeed, he doubtless owes much of the breadth of his classical knowledge to his varied changes of location, and these in turn to an impetuous temper and a vitriolic tongue, more heavily indebted to the Latin satirists than was comfortable for his fellow clergy, which forced him to scuttle in almost picaresque fashion to and fro across Europe. He claims our special attention for his knowledge of two rare texts, Plautus and Catullus. It is probable that he met the plays of Plautus in France, which was the original home of the Palatine family of manuscripts, and the same may be true of Catullus. For although the great discovery of Catullus' poems took place in Verona, the first sign that they had survived was the inclusion of poem 62 in the *florilegium Thuaneum* (Paris lat. 8071), written in France in the late ninth century. A monument to Ratherius' devotion to the classics still remains in the shape of the most important single manuscript of Livy's first decade (Laur. 63.19 = M), which was copied at Verona on his instructions. Some of the more explosive marginalia readily betray their author. A twin manuscript, possibly copied at the same time and presented to Otto I, found its way to the cathedral of Worms.

The Carolingian traditions were best maintained in Germany, especially under the Ottonian dynasty (936–1002), and as tutor to Otto III Gerbert was at the centre of this intellectual revival. A great teacher, a pioneer in mathematics, and an active collector of manuscripts, Gerbert was an outstanding figure; he was at different times abbot of Bobbio, archbishop of Reims and Ravenna, and finally Pope Silvester II. The emergence of the Holy Roman Empire meant fruitful contact between Germany and Italy, and the German schools of the late tenth and eleventh centuries made a significant contribution to the cause of classical learning. Another famous manuscript of Livy, this time a fifth-century uncial manuscript of the fourth decade, was found at Piacenza and taken to Germany by Otto III. It was given to Bamberg cathedral library by Henry II and now survives as a few scraps of binding; but at least two copies were taken from it, the one our main source for the text (Bamberg Class. 35, written in the eleventh century), the other the parent of two celebrated lost manuscripts, the first at one time at Speyer, the second at Chartres, whence it fathered the whole Renaissance tradition (see p. 115). Further evidence of the scholarly achievement of the German schools of this period is provided by an important omnibus volume of Cicero's works. This manuscript, which is now in the British Museum (Harley 2682), was written in Germany in the eleventh century and formerly belonged to Cologne cathedral. It contains a number of the speeches, letters, and philosophical works, and is a valuable textual witness for some of them.

While the cathedrals continued to increase in importance as intellectual centres, the monasteries had been through a period of decline, but this was arrested by the Cluniac reforms on the continent and the efforts of Dunstan and Ethelwold in England. In the tenth century England begins to import books from the continent and with them the continental script. The most important manuscript of Cicero's *Aratea* (Harley 647), written in France in the Carolingian period, had arrived in England by the end of the century and soon produced a couple of offspring on English soil. Manuscripts of Juvenal and Persius survive from tenth-century England, including an attractive one in insular minuscule (Cambridge, Trinity College O.4.10), which must be among the last of the classical manuscripts written in this script; and a book containing part of Ovid's *Ars amatoria* and written in Wales in the ninth century (Bodleian Library, Auct. F. 4.32) actually belonged to Dunstan.

X. THE RESURGENCE OF MONTE CASSINO

The most dramatic single event in the history of Latin scholarship in the eleventh century was the phenomenal revival of Monte Cassino; the mother monastery of the Benedictine order had her most brilliant hour at a time when Benedictinism was rapidly declining as the cultural force of Europe. The great efflorescence of artistic and intellectual activity which reached its peak under abbot Desiderius (1058–87) was accompanied by a renewed interest in the classics, and in the late eleventh and early twelfth century there was written at Monte Cassino and allied centres a wonderful series of important Beneventan manuscripts of classical and other authors. At one swoop a number of texts were recovered which might otherwise have been lost for ever; to this one monastery in this one period we owe the preservation of the later *Annals* and *Histories* of Tacitus (Plate XIV), the *Golden Ass* of Apuleius, the *Dialogues* of Seneca, Varro's *De lingua latina*, Frontinus' *De aquis*, and thirty-odd lines of Juvenal's sixth satire which are not to be found in any other manuscript. Monte Cassino had strong connections in the eleventh century with Germany, and the Tacitus in particular points back to Hersfeld and Fulda.

XI. THE TWELFTH-CENTURY RENAISSANCE

As we have already noted incidentally, education was gradually passing from the monks and the monasteries to the secular clergy in the cathedral and urban schools. The monasteries remained important for their libraries and scriptoria and indeed as cultural centres, but more creative intellectual life passed to the cathedral schools, which rapidly increased from the middle of the eleventh century and in a few cases later developed into the first universities. By then the intellectual map of Europe had changed dramatically. The great centre for the revival of Roman law was Bologna; the first medical school came into being at Salerno; the Norman kingdom of southern Italy and Sicily fostered the translation of Greek technical works into Latin, and with the reconquest of Spain from the Muslims Toledo emerged as the chief centre for the translating activity which brought Arabic science and scholarship within the reach of the West. To the north the main scene of intellectual activity had shifted to Norman France and Norman England, with Bec and Canterbury to the fore, though it took the English schools a long time to catch up with those of France. The literary side of the classical revival was mainly carried on in the schools of Orléans and Chartres, while philosophy and dialectic chose Paris for their home and made it the intellectual capital of Europe. The literary output of ancient Rome continued to be the basic stuff of education and remained the chief source of literary inspiration, but now it had a new role—to cater for the specialized needs of a complex society with a professional interest in law and medicine, rhetoric and logic. The exciting books for this age were Euclid and Ptolemy, the Digest, and such works of the Aristotelian and medical corpus as were rapidly becoming available. At the same time the study of ancient literature was both broadened and intensified. Increased wealth and elegance, together with the secularizing trends in art and literature, enabled people to take a more robust interest in a literature which had not been designed for the cloister. An age which had a rapidly developing literature of its own, both Latin and vernacular, was able to explore with understanding the techniques of ancient epic and history. Love poetry and the moral writings of the satirist were in the greatest demand: ancient literature catered for both the senses and the conscience. In the process it became transformed: Vergil was allegorized, Ovid moralized, the satirists encrusted with glosses and comment rarely in keeping with the original intention. The results were various. In his *De amicitia* Aelred of Rievaulx was able to rethink the problem of human relationships in Christian terms and rework Cicero's dialogue in a way which does no real violence to the model nor detracts from the charm and originality of his own treatment. Seneca, subtly blended with material from Christian writers, could inspire some noble passages, as in William of Saint Thierry, though he loses his identity in the process; in Gautier of Saint Victor, suitably twisted, he could be made to denounce the study of pagan authors. Borrowings from Ovid sparkle through some of the most erotic scenes in the elegiac comedy of the period, but he is commonly exploited as a manual on morals and much else, his tone and intention so grotesquely distorted that the *Remedia amoris* could become a school text and even the poet's nose, reputedly large for obvious reasons, be transformed into an organ supremely capable of discriminating between virtue and vice.

Vergil, Horace, Ovid, Lucan, Juvenal, Persius, Cicero, Seneca, Sallust were the staple literary diet of the twelfth century; Statius (excluding the *Silvae*) and Terence were popular, Quintilian was known but not much used, Martial increased in favour, while some

Plautus (the first eight plays) and Livy began to circulate. No age would have taken greater delight in the poetry of Catullus, Tibullus, and Propertius, but the rare or unique copies of these authors which were in existence lay unused, as did those of Tacitus, and Lucretius is a striking example of how a text can circulate in the ninth century and then virtually disappear from sight for the rest of the Middle Ages. The classical emphasis of the revival can be gauged from the fact that in the extant palimpsests the ancient authors begin to appear more frequently in the upper texts: the tables have turned, but attacks on the educational use of the classics continued.

Some notion of the acquaintance with Latin literature enjoyed by the foremost intellects of the period can be derived from the works of two Englishmen, William of Malmesbury (died c. 1143) and John of Salisbury (c. 1110–80), the first the greatest historian of the period, the second the finest representative of the literary revival of the twelfth century. As librarian of Malmesbury, William had at his disposal an excellent library, which he did much himself to improve, and an easy access to the world of books; in addition to the usual run of school texts, he had read parts of Caesar and Livy, Suetonius, Plautus (apparently the *Pseudolus*, one of the rare plays), Petronius, and the *Apocolocyntosis* of Seneca; he was also the first person in the Middle Ages to quote from the whole corpus of Seneca's *Letters*. A real researcher, with strong historical and antiquarian interests, William has earned an honoured place in the history of classical scholarship. His particular concern was to seek out related texts and put them together, and some of his collections, often autograph, still survive. One of his historical collections, containing Vegetius, Frontinus, and Eutropius (Oxford, Lincoln College, lat. 100), is a good example. His massive attempt at an omnibus Cicero still exists in a later copy (Cambridge, University Library, Dd. 13.2); it contains an explicit defence of his classical interests and what is perhaps the first attempt at an edition of the fragments of the *Hortensius* and *De republica*, carefully culled from the works of Augustine. John of Salisbury, educated at Chartres and Paris and unrivalled in the Middle Ages as a stylist, not only absorbed a great deal of patristic, medieval, and classical literature, but was also able to bring it to bear on the practical problems of his day. His favourite reading was Cicero, Seneca, and the *exempla* of Valerius Maximus, but his strong classical interest led him to authors not commonly found, to the *Strategemata* of Frontinus and the *Historia Augusta*, while he was remarkable in knowing the whole extant text of Petronius. He used Heiric's excerpts for Suetonius and may at times be dependent on other *florilegia*. His caustic attacks on the encroachment of dialectic show that the purely literary revival is on the wane.

William of Malmesbury and John of Salisbury were of course exceptional, and among their contemporaries were many who were content to give their writings a spurious air of learning by pillaging the encyclopedists, the grammarians, and the *florilegia*: second-hand learning had come to stay. Robert of Cricklade dedicated to Henry II a nine-book *defloratio* of the Elder Pliny, William of Malmesbury compiled a *Polyhistor*, Étienne of Rouen prepared an abridgement of Quintilian. Some of the miscellaneous *florilegia*, when they were put together by someone who had access to a wide selection of books, are of considerable textual importance in that they tap a tradition at an earlier stage than that represented by the extant manuscripts and draw on a different source. The *florilegium Gallicum*, put together in northern France in the twelfth century, is a good example; it contains extracts from a large number of authors and has some contribution to make to the text of Tibullus, Petronius, Valerius Flaccus, and others. An early thirteenth-century *florilegium* of mainly classical authors (Paris lat. 15155, with portions elsewhere) contains the only pre-fourteenth century extracts from Propertius and also excerpts from the *Laus Pisonis*. Wibald, abbot of Corvey from 1146 to 1158, like William of Malmesbury before him, had the ambitious notion of putting the whole of Cicero into one volume, and he almost succeeded, for there can be little doubt that the most comprehensive manuscript of Cicero's works, written at Corvey in the twelfth century (Berlin lat. fol. 252), is the very volume. Containing oratorical and philosophical works, an imposing range of speeches, and part of the *Epistulae ad familiares*, it is an important textual source and an impressive witness to the humanism of the twelfth century.

If one were to ask how the Renaissance of the late eleventh and twelfth century affected the textual transmission of our classical texts, the answer seems to be that it consolidated the gains of the Carolingian revival. Authors central to medieval education or agreeable to the taste of the time simply poured from the scriptoria; in the case of popular writers like Ovid and Seneca, we have four or five times as many manuscripts from the twelfth century as from all previous centuries put together. Many of these manuscripts are textually worthless, containing nothing of value which is not found in a purer form in earlier witnesses, but often the twelfth-century broadening of the tradition has resulted in gains to the text. The best manuscript of Cicero's *Ad familiares* belongs to the ninth century (Laur. 49.9); but the errors and gaps in its text have to be remedied by calling in the other branch of the tradition, Carolingian in origin but largely represented by manuscripts of the twelfth century. Other texts survive entirely in manuscripts of this period: such texts of Seneca's *Natural Questions* as existed in the Carolingian era have perished and it is the descendants of this tradition, copied in the twelfth and thirteenth centuries, which have preserved the text for us.

XII. THE SCHOLASTIC AGE

In the late twelfth and throughout the thirteenth century the schools and universities were more concerned with assimilating and organizing the material and ideas brought to the surface by the recent intellectual ferment than with making fresh discoveries. The skills employed in the systematization of acquired knowledge and the unification of dogma were those of dialectic and logic, and these subtle sciences dominated not only philosophy, theology, and the fields of specialized knowledge, but grammar and literary exegesis as well. When the classical heritage was absorbed into the systems of contemporary thought, with its strong tendency to allegorize and elaborate, it was bound to become distorted. It also suffered in other ways. With so much else to occupy the mind, the wide reading of ancient authors gave way to the more practical manuals, the *auctores* to the *artes*, and the new grammars and rhetorics which came into use were often scholastic in character. The classics still remained a valuable quarry for moral anecdote and could provide a curious age with information of all sorts; but form and style were no longer part of the attraction, and matter could be more easily assimilated when reduced to excerpts and *exempla*. At the same time the writers of the twelfth and thirteenth centuries took their place alongside the ancient authors; although they did not displace them, the monopoly of the past had been broken.

For these reasons the century which witnessed the final triumph of the Middle Ages in many fields is not a particularly enticing one for the classical scholar. Manuscripts pour on to the market, but the text of those authors who have been copied for generations is getting more and more corrupt; the proportion of grain to chaff is getting smaller, and the manuscripts themselves, with their heavy Gothic appearance, are less alluring than those of previous centuries. Despite all this, the classics survived the tide of scholasticism and made significant advances where least expected. The heroes of the period were the builders of the mighty philosophical and theological systems, but amongst those intent on the organization of knowledge were some who gave an important place to pagan literature. Vincent of Beauvais, who died about 1264, is the most monumental encyclopedist of the Middle Ages; his *Speculum maius* was an attempt to put the whole sum of knowledge into one corpus. Like so many others, he was anti-pagan in principle, but he saw the value of profane texts and defends his use of them with a good conscience. He draws heavily on classical authors; Ovid and Seneca far outdistance the others, Vergil is eclipsed. A large part of his classical quotations are taken from secondary sources, and the appearance of rare authors like Tibullus is explained by his dependence on earlier compilations, in particular the *florilegium Gallicum*.

About 1250 and within a few years of the publication of the *Speculum maius* Richard of Fournival, a native of Amiens and later chancellor of its cathedral, was compiling his *Biblionomia*. In it he lays out the literature and wisdom of the world for the guidance of his fellow citizens in the form of an elaborate garden in which the various branches of knowledge each have their plot. This charming analogy quickly crystallizes into a picture of a library in which the books are laid out on desks according to their subject. This systematic bibliography is not, as has sometimes been thought, the imaginary projection of a bibliophile, but the actual catalogue of Fournival's own carefully collected library. It must have contained about 300 volumes and in size and range could challenge the monastic and cathedral libraries of his day. It contained some rare classical texts and among the most noteworthy are three items in the *opera poetarum*: Tibullus, Propertius, and Seneca's *Tragedies*. His copy of Tibullus may have descended ultimately from the manuscript at one time in the palace library of Charlemagne, for one of the earliest of the *florilegia* in which Tibullus occasionally surfaces also contains a collection of the poetry of the Carolingian court circle. His manuscript passed in 1272, with the bulk of his collection, to the library of the Sorbonne, but it is now lost; had it survived, it would have been our oldest manuscript of Tibullus, if not the source of much of the Renaissance tradition. But Fournival's manuscripts of Propertius and the *Tragedies* do survive and have now been identified. Seneca's *Tragedies* had shown signs of life; some excerpts had appeared in the *florilegium Thuaneum* (Paris lat. 8071), written in France in the ninth century, and our oldest complete manuscript, the codex Etruscus (Laur. 37.13 = E), goes back to the eleventh, but the plays had remained almost unknown. It is not until the thirteenth century that manuscripts of the other and main stream of the tradition (known as A) begin to appear; this re-emerged in northern France, though the oldest of its representatives (Cambridge, Corpus Christi College 406) appears to have been written in England. The manuscript known to editors as P (Paris lat. 8260) was written for Richard of Fournival. Propertius is a new name to the Middle Ages; one of the greatest of the Roman poets, he had to wait until the scholastic age to see the light again, and for his text we are heavily indebted, as with so many discoveries to come, to a new phenomenon, the wealthy private book collector. The book which Fournival had made for him is our manuscript A (Voss. lat. Q. 38), written by the same scribe as copied his Seneca; it is one of the two most important witnesses to the text and the parent of the humanist tradition.

The *Tragedies* were not the only text of Seneca to achieve circulation in northern Europe at this time. The *Dialogues* reached the schools of Paris in the first half of the thirteenth century, having worked their way north from Monte Cassino. They were known to John of Garland as early as 1220 and fifty years later, somewhat tardily but with tremendous excitement, their 'discovery' was announced by Roger Bacon. Though this text too begins to circulate again in northern France, among the first to make use of it were Roger Bacon and John of Wales, both Franciscans and both as much at home in Oxford as in Paris. They serve to draw attention to the less spectacular but not inconsiderable contribution to the promotion of classical studies already being made by the English friars. Some of the English Franciscans actually compiled in the thirteenth century a *Registrum librorum Angliae*, a union catalogue of books available in English libraries, a remarkable bibliographical project in which some classical authors were included. John of Wales's treatises, such as the *Communiloquium* and *Compendiloquium*, were full of references to the ancients and opened a wide and flattering window on classical antiquity; they were intended not only as aids for the teacher and preacher, but also as manuals for polite conversation. Somewhat later Nicholas Trevet, a Dominican but again mainly associated with Oxford and Paris, achieved such a wide reputation for erudition and the exegesis of antique texts that he received commissions from Italy to write commentaries on Livy and Seneca's *Tragedies* (see p. 114). These prepared the way for the classicizing group of friars who have been shown to have been active in England in the early fourteenth century. This loosely knit group, of which the most important are perhaps Thomas Waleys and Robert Holcot, did much to popularize a knowledge of the ancient world by introducing classical allusions to illustrate their biblical commentaries and sermons and helping to create an audience with a taste for ancient history and myth. With his classical scholarship, seen at its best in his commentary on the first ten books of the *De civitate dei*, completed in 1332, his admiration for the ancients, and his knowledge of rare texts, Thomas Waleys comes very close to being a humanist and doubtless owes much of his special quality to periods spent at Bologna and Avignon. He claims to have seen a copy of Apuleius' *Metamorphoses* and can quote from Livy's rare fourth decade, thanks to a book lent to him by the bishop of Modena. The fondness for classical learning common to the group might have developed into humanism had circumstances been different; as it was, their lack of stylistic sophistication, their medieval ways of thinking, their profession, and their lack of contact with a leisured highbrow milieu prevented this from happening; the movement took a different direction and faded out.

Thus more and more was added to the vast body of classical books and learning which had been accumulating over the centuries. Classical studies survived and advanced and were successfully adapted to new tastes and conditions, but in a context in which they were never really emancipated, could never really catch fire. It was left to the humanists of the Renaissance, who drew on this great medieval heritage with curiously little sense of debt, to exploit what had been achieved in a new and vital way.

XIII. GREEK IN THE WEST IN THE MIDDLE AGES

Under the Roman empire Italy had been to all intents and purposes a bilingual country, but with the decline of the empire Greek fell out of use except in the south of Italy and Sicily, where many towns were by origin Greek colonies. Cassiodorus' monastery Vivarium near Squillace is known to have had a collection of Greek books, but there is no sign that they contributed in any tangible way to the preservation of Greek. And in all the other parts of Western Europe, where the language had never been so firmly established, if indeed it was spoken at all, a knowledge of Greek became an attainment of exceptional rarity throughout the Middle Ages. Even diplomatic correspondence was sometimes delayed for lack of suitably qualified translators and interpreters.

For a brief period in the ninth century some interest in Greek can be traced. A few bilingual biblical manuscripts survive, proved by their handwriting to be products of the Latin world; they are thought to come from the scriptorium at Saint Gall. In 827 the Byzantine emperor sent a copy of Pseudo-Dionysius the Areopagite to the French king (still preserved as Paris gr. 437), which served as the basis for a translation of this highly popular forgery into Latin. A few years later the Irishman John Scottus Eriugena used the manuscript for his own translation of these works, and he also made some translations from Gregory of Nyssa, Gregory of Nazianzus, and Maximus the Confessor. But though some of his versions were widely read he did not create a tradition of Greek learning, and no other Greek texts were accessible for the time being except Boethius' versions of some of Aristotle's writings on

logic and a version of Plato's *Timaeus* made in the fourth century
by Chalcidius.

In the twelfth century the range of translations was increased
substantially. Some of the credit belongs to two figures who are
still very obscure, Burgundio of Pisa (1110–93), who had spent the
years 1135–8 in Constantinople as an interpreter, and James of
Venice, a canon lawyer whose version of Aristotle's *Analytica
posteriora* was known to John of Salisbury in 1159. Slightly better
known are the inelegant and literal versions of Plato, Euclid, and
Ptolemy made in Sicily c. 1160 under the aegis of Henricus
Aristippus, archdeacon of Catania (d. 1162), who is said to have
acquired some manuscripts sent as a gift by the Byzantine emperor
to the Norman king of Sicily. Aristippus himself translated Plato's
Phaedo and *Meno*, some works of Aristotle, and perhaps Hero's
Pneumatica, which discusses steam-engines, 'penny-in-the-slot'
machines, and other gadgets which have a surprisingly modern
ring about them. He is praised also for his assistance in making the
versions of Euclid, Proclus, and Ptolemy. Another important
figure in this circle was the admiral Eugenius, who translated
Ptolemy's *Optics* from the Arabic into Latin (the Greek is now lost).
The main interests of these men were clearly scientific.

Yet the influence of these translators was perhaps slightly less
than would have been expected, for Gerard of Cremona seems to
have translated Ptolemy's *Almagest* from the Arabic in Toledo c.
1175, apparently in ignorance of the existing version. For the
diffusion of Aristotelianism the work of Arabic scholars in Spain
who did not know the original Greek text was also important.
Arabic versions and commentaries by Avicenna and other scholars,
especially Averroes (d. 1198), were turned into Latin in Toledo in
the middle and late twelfth century. A large proportion of the
Aristotelian corpus became known and circulated rapidly to other
part of Europe.

In the thirteenth century a few eminent men show more than a
passing acquaintance with Greek. Robert Grosseteste (c. 1168–
1253), though he learnt it late in life and always needed help from
native speakers, studied Aristotle and translated the *Ethics*; he also
translated Pseudo-Dionysius the Areopagite (his copy of the Greek
text is in the Bodleian Library, Canonici gr. 97). His pupil Roger

Bacon (c. 1214–94) wrote a Greek grammar (Oxford, Corpus Christi College 148), but despite his insistence that texts should be studied in the original rather than the often unintelligible translations he had few if any followers. A Flemish contemporary, William of Moerbeke, translated parts of Archimedes and Aristotle, the latter perhaps at the request of Thomas Aquinas. He lived for a time in Greece and can be traced at Nicaea in 1260; later he became the Latin archbishop of Corinth. Another figure of importance was a Greek from Reggio called Nicholas (fl. c. 1308–45), who settled at the court of the Angevin kings at Naples and made versions of many works ascribed to Galen. Some of these survive in his Latin text only.

4. THE RENAISSANCE

I. HUMANISM

It will be convenient for the purpose of this brief survey to regard the Renaissance as the period extending from about 1300 to the middle of the sixteenth century. A cultural movement which is recognizable as humanism, the stimulating force of the Renaissance, was at work in certain parts of Italy by the end of the thirteenth century; by the middle of the sixteenth it had spread to most of Western Europe and had transformed, among so many other things, the transmission and study of classical antiquity. The scholar of the late Renaissance had at his disposal almost as much of the literature of Greece and Rome as we possess ourselves; most of it he could read, at ease and at no great cost, in print; and the translation of Greek into Latin, and of both into the vernacular languages, had made a large part of ancient literature available to the public at large. On the scholarly side, the foundations of historical and textual criticism had been securely laid.

Although humanism eventually acted upon all areas of intellectual and artistic life, it was primarily a literary activity and was closely connected with the study and imitation of classical literature. The origin of the nineteenth-century term 'humanism' has been traced to the word *umanista*, coined in the student slang of the Italian universities of the late fifteenth century, on the analogy of such words as *legista* and *iurista*, to denote the professional teacher of the humanities, the *studia humanitatis*, which by this time had crystallized as the study of grammar, rhetoric, history, poetry, and moral philosophy, a canon as important for what it excluded as for what it contained. The philosophical overtones which humanism later developed are only in part the result of its originally classical emphasis, the teaching, study, and promotion of classical literature.

Many humanists, particularly in the fifteenth century, were professional teachers of the humanities; in this capacity they stepped into the place of the medieval *dictatores*, the men who had taught the art of composing letters, speeches, and other documents essential to diplomacy and public life. But the *dictamen* was an essentially medieval phenomenon, elaborate, stereotyped, smelling of the handbook and fair copy. The cultivation of style depended very little on the use of classical models, poetry was neglected, and classical studies generally in Italy seem to have been in some respects considerably less 'humane' than elsewhere. It is therefore not easy to see why humanism should have emerged from precisely this stable. There appears to be no simple answer, but it has been pointed out that most of the early humanists were notaries or lawyers or in some way associated with the legal profession. The law schools of Italy held a dominant position and the revival of Roman Law at Bologna had reforged a link with antiquity. The *dictatores* had been particularly active in the twelfth and thirteenth centuries, and the strongly grammatical and rhetorical emphasis of the education which lawyers would have received as a preliminary to their legal training, however much it may have lost its classical flavour, would impart a good command of Latin and a strong sense of style. Other important factors were the secular nature of Italian education, the existence of a sophisticated urban culture and of a professional class who had the training and the means and the leisure to pursue their classical interests and yet were sufficiently involved in civic life to make practical use, when the opportunity offered, of the new rhetoric. Some allowance must be made too for the personality of some of the individuals concerned, a Lovato or a Petrarch, who were gifted with the ability to communicate to others their enthusiasm and sense of excitement, and to the simple fact that there were libraries within reach which could provide the right sort of text to give humanism a new direction and emphasize the break with the past. Nor, as humanism broadened and extended its influence to other fields, was the practical aim of the *dictator* superseded, but the way to speaking and writing well was seen to lie in the use of classical models; the Latin classics were revived, not only as an academic study, but as the stuff of which eloquence was made, and it was this command of the Latin tongue which enabled the Renaissance man to impress his peers, denounce his enemies, thunder in defence of creed or city. In turn this led to a more sympathetic and comprehensive study of all aspects of ancient life and to that feeling of identification, however illusory, with the men and ideals of the ancient world which is the mark of neoclassicism.

This attempt to get closer to the classical spirit and to relive and rethink the past in terms of the present completely transcends the medieval approach to ancient letters. At last Latin literature was emancipated from the role for which it had been so badly cast, that of playing second-fiddle to religion; humanism was fundamentally secular, and the thin but unbroken tradition of lay education in Italy had doubtless contributed to this. The humanists were men of the world, sometimes teachers of grammar or literature, more commonly notaries, papal secretaries, chancellors of cities. They were usually book collectors, often on a large scale, and the growth of private libraries and a commercial book trade helped to break the long ecclesiastical monopoly of learning. At the same time the movement quickly gained a foothold within the Church and soon humanists were to be found in the highest positions of its hierarchy.

II. THE FIRST HUMANISTS

The beginnings of humanism are clearly detectable in a small literary coterie which grew up in Padua in the second half of the thirteenth century. The leader of these prehumanists was a Paduan judge, Lovato Lovati (1241–1309), who had a keen interest in classical poetry, a remarkable flair for unearthing texts unknown for centuries, and the ability to communicate his enthusiasm to a circle of friends. His surviving works are some collections of poems, in particular his *Metrical Epistles*. It is evident from these that Lovato was at best a mediocre poet, despite a freshness in his attempt to capture the spirit of his classical models; what is staggering about these poems is the knowledge of Roman poetry which they reveal. Since the clues to his classical models are echoes rather than direct quotations, the evidence is not always as clear-cut as one could wish, but there is enough of it to command respect. An age ahead of his contemporaries, Lovato appears to have been acquainted with Lucretius, Catullus, the *Odes* of Horace, the whole of Tibullus, Propertius, Martial, the *Silvae* of Statius, Valerius Flaccus, and such little-known works as Ovid's *Ibis*. The chronology of humanism has had to be drastically revised: Petrarch was not the first humanist to know Propertius, or Salutati to possess a complete Tibullus; Lovato knew Lucretius and Valerius Flaccus a century and a half before they were discovered by Poggio, and was making use of Catullus almost fifty years before the traditional date of his resurrection in Verona. Other members of the same circle were acquainted with a similar range of Latin poets, unprecedented since antiquity and not equalled again until the fifteenth century.

A dramatic clue to the source of some of Lovato's texts has been found in a manuscript in the British Museum (Add. 19906), containing *inter alia* Justinus' *Epitome* and Lovato's poems, and written by Lovato himself about 1290. At the end of the Justinus he copied the subscription which he found in his exemplar, and this reveals that the manuscript which he was using had been written in the monastery of Pomposa, in the Po delta, just before 1100. Among the classical texts known to have been at Pomposa as early as the eleventh century was a great rarity, the *Tragedies* of Seneca. The collateral discovery that Lovato made use of the famous eleventh-century codex Etruscus of the *Tragedies* (Laur. 37.13) at one swoop provides a home for the misnamed Etruscus and confirms that Lovato had succeeded in tapping the resources of one of the great medieval libraries of northern Italy. It is an easy guess that another source was the Chapter Library at Verona. However, not all the questions raised by the richness of his finds have yet been answered; when these texts were rediscovered later, they came to light in France and Switzerland and Germany, beyond the ken of this parochial group. Padua is an isolated and as yet obscure chapter in the story of the rediscovery of antiquity.

Lovato has also left us a short note on the metre and prosody of Senecan tragedy, remarkable in that it is derived, not from the medieval manuals, but from an intelligent study of Seneca's own practice. It was elaborated by his successors and is an indication of the intense interest which the prehumanists took in Roman tragedy. He also tried his hand at archaeology, and identified a skeleton which some workmen had turned up as the remains of the legendary founder of Padua, the Trojan Antenor, a gorgeous error. From all this it is clear that something new had begun.

Something of a contrast is provided by another Paduan judge of the same circle, Geremia da Montagnone (c. 1255–1321), who had no literary ambitions and trod the well-beaten path of the didactic florilegist: his *Compendium moralium notabilium*, probably put together in the first decade of the fourteenth century, enjoyed a wide circulation and was eventually printed in Venice in 1505. Geremia is more typical of his period; but in some respects his compendium plants him firmly in the humanist group. His reading is vast, his excerpts are systematically arranged, with chapter and verse added, and he seems to be quoting at first hand from the authors themselves; his notions of chronological sequence are not bad for his time, and he makes a nice distinction (e.g. *poeta* and *versilogus*) between classical and medieval writers. His quotations from Catullus and Martial, from Horace's *Odes* and Ovid's *Ibis*, together with his lavish use of Seneca's tragedies, show clearly the influence of the local humanism.

Lovato's spiritual successor was his friend and fellow townsman Albertino Mussato (1262–1329). A notary by profession, Mussato achieved distinction in the worlds of politics, diplomacy, and literature. Strongly influenced by Lovato, he read the same Latin poets and delved more deeply into Senecan tragedy; he also wrote *Historiae* modelled on Livy, Sallust, and Caesar. His greatest literary success came in 1315: in order to open the eyes of the Paduans to the danger of falling into the clutches of the lord of Verona, Cangrande della Scala, he wrote a Senecan tragedy, the *Ecerinis*, which dealt in lurid colour with the rise and fall of Padua's own former tyrant, Ezzelino III. The first tragedy to be written in classical metres since antiquity was a tremendous literary and political success; the Paduans crowned its author with laurels and so revived a Roman custom which caught the imagination of the Renaissance and was a fitting compliment for the pioneer of modern classical drama.

Although limited in its influence by the weakness in communications and the fragmentation of political life in Italy, Paduan humanism soon percolated to the neighbouring town of Vicenza, where the notary Benvenuto Campesani (1255–1323) composed in the early years of the fourteenth century his famous and enigmatic epigram celebrating the return to Verona of her long-lost poet Catullus. Verona fostered a more scholarly tradition of humanism.

which was nourished by the Chapter Library. Among its treasures were two important prose texts, the lost *Veronensis* of Pliny's *Letters* which had been known to Ratherius, and the ninth-century manuscript of the *Historia Augusta*, which had travelled down to Verona in time to have an enormous influence on Renaissance historiography. Both were used by Giovanni de Matociis (fl. 1306–20), custodian of the cathedral, who, in addition to his major work, the *Historia Imperialis*, produced the first critical work on literary history to be written in the Renaissance, his *Brevis adnotatio de duobus Pliniis*. Basing himself on the Verona Pliny and a text of Suetonius, he was able to split the composite Pliny of the Middle Ages into the Elder and the Younger. The Chapter Library also had its own florilegist: in 1329 someone who had access to the books put together a *Flores moralium auctoritatum* (Verona CLXVIII (155)) which, while being partly derived from other florilegia, contained excerpts from rare texts known to have been at Verona, from Catullus, the Younger Pliny, the *Historia Augusta*, Varro's *Res rusticae*, and Cicero's *Letters to Atticus and Quintus*.

III. THE CONSOLIDATION OF HUMANISM: PETRARCH AND HIS GENERATION

Although recent research has shown that the prehumanists had advanced much further along the road to humanism than had been supposed, especially in their acquisition of a new body of Latin poetry, the éclat with which Petrarch (1304–74) makes his dramatic entry has hardly been dimmed. He dwarfs his precursors in every respect: he was an immeasurably greater poet and greater man than any of them; his horizons were wider and his influence, never cramped within the limits of town or province, extended over most of Western Europe; he had the vision and the ability to unite the two existing strands of humanism, the literary and the scholarly, and to combine aims which reached for the moon with the capacity for painstaking research; he went further than anyone else in trying to revive within the framework of a Christian society the ideals of ancient Rome, and his attempts to get close to the great figures of the past, and indeed to rival their achievement, though flirting with the vainglorious, unleashed passions and ambitions which were to reanimate the whole cultural legacy of the ancient world and bring it to bear upon contemporary modes of thought and literature.

It was fortunate for Petrarch, and indeed for the continuity of the classical tradition in the West, that for a critical period in the fourteenth century (1309–77) the papal curia transferred its seat from Rome to Avignon. Avignon was well placed to be a point of cultural contact between the north and the south, and the attraction to the papal court of men of different nationalities and intellectual outlook had important consequences. In particular, educated churchmen and lawyers, whose growing interest in classical texts demanded more knowledge of the ancient world than their schooling had provided, began to draw on the medieval legacy of the north. The monastic and cathedral libraries of France lay within reach, and for help in reading the more difficult classical texts they turned to Oxford, to the polymath Nicholas Trevet, who wrote at the express request of a pope and a cardinal his commentaries on Livy (c. 1318) and the *Tragedies* of Seneca (c. 1315). Thus when Petrarch arrived at Avignon he found an older generation with an active interest in texts which had been little read for centuries. Petrarch owed much to this stimulating society; at the same time he had the imagination and the historical sense to see the inadequacy of looking at antiquity through the eyes of the Middle Ages and broke away to recreate it for himself.

In the British Museum is preserved a manuscript of Livy (Harley 2493, Plate XV) which has been shown to illustrate as well as any single document can the importance of Avignon as a bridge between the Middle Ages and the Renaissance and the part played in this story by Petrarch. This volume, which originally contained books 1–10 and 21–40, was put together by Petrarch when he was still in his early twenties; parts of it he copied in his own hand. The nucleus of the book is a manuscript of Livy's third decade, written about 1200 and ultimately derived, as are all the complete manuscripts which have survived, from the extant Puteanus; to this central portion Petrarch added about the year 1325 a copy of the first decade, then, a few years later, of the fourth. By 1329 he was the proud owner of a Livy which was more complete and had a better text than any other in existence. The various decades of Livy's *History* had followed their separate fates through the Middle Ages and it was a considerable achievement to have put three of them under one cover, expecially as the fourth decade was a great rarity in Petrarch's day; the remaining extant books of Livy (41–5) were not discovered until the sixteenth century. The whole text was supplemented, corrected, annotated—and so in a sense edited—by Petrarch himself; of special value are the variants recorded in his notes to books 26–30, because these were taken from a manuscript independent of the Puteanus. It is evident that for these books, as well as for the fourth decade, he had access to a manuscript of the same tradition as the lost codex of Speyer cathedral used by two scholars, Beatus Rhenanus and Gelenius, for the Froben edition of 1535, from which editors have painfully tried to recover its readings. The story of Petrarch's great find has now been unravelled. In 1328 Landolfo Colonna, a member of the Colonna family whose patronage Petrarch enjoyed and who had for a long time been a canon of Chartres, brought to Avignon a copy of an ancient manuscript of Livy which he had found in Chartres cathedral. The *vetus Carnotensis*, as this manuscript has been christened, was a close relative of the lost Spirensis, and both derive, for the fourth decade, from the fifth-century uncial manuscript which Otto III found at Piacenza and carried off to Germany (see p. 96). Petrarch's great book of Livy later passed into the possession of Lorenzo Valla, whose famous emendations can be found in its margins (see p. 126).

A similar tale has been told of the text of Pomponius Mela. We have already seen (p. 94) how a collection of rare texts, including Mela and Julius Paris, were edited at Ravenna in the sixth century by Rusticius Helpidius and survive in a copy made in the ninth century at Auxerre and annotated by Heiric (Vat. lat. 4929). These texts had a long and important career in the Renaissance, and all the humanist copies derive from the Auxerre archetype via a twelfth-century manuscript, now lost, which Petrarch had acquired at Avignon. We know this because Petrarch's notes were often copied along with the text, and in the earliest of the humanist copies (Ambros. H. 14 inf.) we find, for instance, the revealing remark: *Avinio. Ubi nunc sumus 1335.* The textual history of Propertius too illustrates the same pattern. The earliest manuscript of this author (Gud. lat. 224 = N), which was at one time in the region of Metz, reached Italy in time to influence most of the humanist tradition; but this tradition descends in direct line from the other early Propertius manuscript (Voss. lat. Q. 38 = A), which never left northern Europe. The link between the Vossianus and the humanist manuscripts is a copy of A which had belonged to Petrarch. Via Petrarch's copy we get back to A; and A takes us back, via the Sorbonne library—where it was at the time of Petrarch's trip to Paris in 1333—to the booky garden of Richard of Fournival, and through him to the medieval libraries of northern France. As with Livy, so with Mela and Propertius; amid the gay distractions of papal Avignon the young Petrarch became the converging point of threads of transmission which stretched back through the Middle Ages to antiquity itself, and forward again, with complex ramifications, into the High Renaissance.

This happy conjunction of book collector and scholar meant that in time Petrarch acquired a classical library which for breadth and quality had no equal in his day. We can to a certain extent reconstruct his collection of Cicero texts, an author whom he regarded as his *alter ego* and for whom he scoured the whole of Europe. It is an impressive list: almost all the philosophical works, most of the *rhetorica*, the *Letters to Atticus and Quintus*, and a remarkable range of speeches which he had built up over a lifetime, extending from the *Pro Archia* which he discovered at Liège in 1333 and copied himself, to the *Pro Cluentio* which Boccaccio transcribed for him in 1355 from an eleventh-century manuscript in Monte Cassino (Laur. 51.10). The *Letters to Atticus* were a discovery of supreme importance to him, worthy of an immediate letter to Cicero himself. He found them, as had others before him, in the Chapter Library at Verona, in 1345. It is on these letters, and in practice still more on those of Seneca (whose works he possessed *in toto*) that his own letters, the most charming and valuable of his prose writings, are modelled.

More significant than the mere range of his books was the intensity with which he read and re-read those which he thought important; for it was easy in the Renaissance to degenerate into a mere book collector. The patience with which he corrected and annotated his texts can be seen in the embryonic editions of the Harleian Livy and the Ambrosian Vergil (S.P. 10/27, *olim* A. 79

inf.), his own copy of his favourite poet. By a stroke of good fortune, in addition to reconstructing much of Petrarch's library and seeing him hard at work on his books, we have an intimate record of his literary tastes, for on the flyleaf of a manuscript in Paris (lat. 2201) we have what a brilliant piece of decipherment has proved to be Petrarch's own list of his favourite books. The list is instructive, both for the works which it contains and their order of priority, and for those it does not contain; but it must be remembered that the list belongs to the earlier period of his life and that some of the books which he prized were among his later discoveries. Cicero not unexpectedly heads the list, his 'moral' works taking precedence. Next comes Seneca: the *Letters* have pride of place; the *Tragedies* come later, and in a second and more select list on the same page they are explicitly excluded from the inner circle. The next main section is devoted to history, headed by Valerius Maximus and Livy; there is a special category of *exempla*, in which Macrobius and Gellius find their home. Poetry follows, with Vergil, Lucan, Statius, Horace, Ovid, and Juvenal; Horace is qualified *praesertim in odis*, a complete reversal of medieval taste. At the end come the technical works, grammar, dialectic, and astrology. Augustine is favoured with a list to himself, and with Boethius' *De consolatione* he makes up the sum of the Christian content. The only Greek work is Aristotle's *Ethics* (in Latin, of course), and this disappears from the select list. Of the law, in which Petrarch received his formal education at Bologna, nothing; the writers of the Middle Ages are likewise rejected, made redundant by direct contact with antiquity.

One of the first to fall under the influence of Petrarch's humanism was his younger contemporary Boccaccio (1313–75). Under the patronage of its ruler, Robert of Anjou (1309–43), Naples had emerged as an important intellectual centre quite early in the century and it was here that Boccaccio spent his youth. His early works, written in Italian, belong to the medieval tradition of rhetoric and romance; it was largely his admiration for Petrarch, whom in 1350 he got to know personally, which made him turn from the vernacular to Latin, from literature to scholarship. As a scholar he fell far behind Petrarch; he lacked the patience even to be good at copying manuscripts. He was in the main a gatherer of facts about ancient life and literature, and his encyclopedic treatises on ancient biography, geography, and mythology, enjoyed a considerable vogue in the Renaissance and did much to promote the understanding of classical literature. He had a passionate interest in poetry, and this led him along the lesser-known paths of Latin literature to poetry unknown to Petrarch, to Ovid's *Ibis*, and the *Appendix Vergiliana*; our oldest manuscript of the *Priapea* (Laur. 33.31) is in his hand.

Among the prose works which he possessed was a group which clearly indicate that a new stream of the medieval tradition had broken through to the surface: his acquaintance with the *Annals* and *Histories* of Tacitus, Apuleius' *Golden Ass*, and Varro's *De lingua latina*, can only mean that someone had unlocked the riches of Monte Cassino. It has now been shown that much of the credit for these discoveries lies with a humanist known to both Boccaccio and Petrarch, Zanobi da Strada. As secretary to the bishop in whose jurisdiction Monte Cassino lay, he had access to the monastery and lived there from 1355 to 1357; marginalia in all three of the early manuscripts of Apuleius (including the mysterious *spurcum additamentum* at *Met.* 10.21.1) are in his hand and bear witness to his keen interest in the contents of the library. The texts which Monte Cassino alone had preserved through the Middle Ages were soon in the hands of the Florentine humanists, and the key person in this operation was obviously their man in Monte Cassino, Zanobi da Strada. But Boccaccio played his part in this: we know that in 1355 he returned to Florence from a brief visit to Naples with a Beneventan manuscript (Laur. 51.10) containing *inter alia* two unknown works, Varro's *De lingua latina* and Cicero's *Pro Cluentio*, and that he copied out these texts for Petrarch. His library could boast copies of both Tacitus and Apuleius (his autograph Apuleius is still extant—Laur. 54.32); the Monte Cassino Tacitus eventually turned up in Florence, and Boccaccio has been suspected of playing a sinister part in its removal.

Although he was not in the front rank as a scholar, Boccaccio did put his genius and enthusiasm behind the humanist movement and helped to mark out the lines along which it was to develop. He naturalized humanism in Florence and made the first attempt, even if for the time being an abortive one, to establish Greeks studies in the city which was to become the centre of the teaching of Greek in the West.

IV. COLUCCIO SALUTATI (1331–1406)

The combination of creative genius and humanist inquiry gives Petrarch and Boccaccio an aura which would elude a man who followed mere scholarly pursuits. Coluccio Salutati had little literary talent and his scholarship was not of a very high order; but he was a powerful and critical link in the development of humanism, second in importance only to Petrarch. He had corresponded with Petrarch in his later years, knew Boccaccio well, and was strongly influenced by both. Inspired by the previous generation, he passed on the torch to the next great wave of humanists, many of whom he could claim as his disciples, among them Poggio Bracciolini and Leonardo Bruni. From the death of Petrarch in 1374 until his own death in 1406 Coluccio presided over the humanist movement.

Although a disconcerting taste for allegorical exegesis makes it clear that Coluccio had one foot still in the Middle Ages, he possessed in full measure the characteristic qualities of the humanist. As chancellor of Florence for over thirty years, he was able to consummate the powerful alliance which had grown up between humanism and politics, to use his Latin and his learning to lash his antagonists, whether enemies of Florence or detractors of classical literature. He read the ancient authors passionately and at first hand and achieved that easy intimacy with them which we have seen in Petrarch. To the humanist spirit he added the elements of classical scholarship: he was an active collator of manuscripts, showed remarkable grasp of the ways in which texts are corrupted, made some creditable contributions to textual criticism (his emendation of Scipio Nasica to Scipio Asina in Valerius Maximus (6.9.1) is well known), and has been recognized as a pioneer in this field. Above all, it was he who invited Chrysoloras to Florence (see p. 131) and so made possible, in 1397, the real beginning of Greek studies in Western Europe.

Not the least thing about Coluccio was his library; more than a hundred of his books have been identified. One of them is a classical text copied throughout in his own hand, the *Tragedies* of Seneca

E

(Brit. Mus. Add. 11987), to which he had added Mussato's *Ecerinis*. Although his books have less intrinsic interest than those of Petrarch, this fine collection was an important cultural instrument both during his lifetime and after it was dispersed. Among his more remarkable volumes were the oldest complete manuscript of Tibullus (Ambros. R. 26 sup. = A), one of the three primary witnesses to the text of Catullus (Ottob. lat. 1829 = R), and—his greatest find—a copy of Cicero's *Ad familiares*. Cicero's *Letters* had a special significance for the early humanists; they felt that they now knew Cicero intimately, that they could travel back in time to the classical period and relive moments with the person who was for them the greatest of the Romans. The *Ad familiares* were found in the cathedral library at Vercelli by Pasquino Cappelli, chancellor of Milan, who had instituted a search at Coluccio's instigation. Coluccio was really looking for a manuscript of the *Letters to Atticus*, which Petrarch had known, and he was beside himself with joy to receive (in 1392) the unexpected bonus of a completely unknown collection. In the following year he obtained a copy of the *Letters to Atticus*, and so became the first person for centuries to possess both collections; his copies still survive (Laur. 49.7 and 49.18; the second is the important manuscript M of the *Ad Atticum*). The Vercelli codex was eventually taken to Florence and there it remains (Laur. 49.9), the only surviving Carolingian manuscript of Cicero's *Letters*. It is interesting to observe that the rounded picture of Cicero which emerged from his letters provoked very different reactions from Petrarch and Coluccio. While Petrarch was upset to discover that Cicero had left philosophy for a life of action and intrigue, it was his blending of intellectual pursuits with a political career that roused the admiration of Coluccio and the later Renaissance.

V. THE GREAT AGE OF DISCOVERY: POGGIO BRACCIOLINI (1380–1459)

The gradual rediscovery of ancient literature runs like a powerful current through the Renaissance from the days of Paduan prehumanism into the second half of the fifteenth century and beyond. Lovato, Petrarch, Zanobi, and Coluccio had been pre-eminent among those who had added to the list of classical works made accessible to the writers and thinkers of their time; but for sheer ability in turning up lost texts they were all outdone by Poggio Bracciolini, an arresting person, who found time as papal secretary to indulge in a variety of literary pursuits, ranging from history and moral essays to polemic and pornography of such accomplished scurrility that it becomes clear that the more robust writings of antiquity had not been rediscovered for nothing.

The great opportunity for another break-through in the discovery of classical texts came when the Council of Constance (1414–17) was summoned to heal the Great Schism and settle other ecclesiastical problems. The whole papal court moved to Constance, and the humanists who were assisting at the conference soon perceived, as men do, that there were interesting activities not included in the agenda; they devoted their spare time to the search for classical texts. Poggio made a number of expeditions, the first in 1415 to the monastery of Cluny in Burgundy, where he found an ancient manuscript of Cicero's speeches, containing the *Pro Cluentio*, *Pro Roscio Amerino*, *Pro Murena*, *Pro Milone*, and *Pro Caelio*. The *Pro Roscio* and *Pro Murena* were previously unknown. This manuscript, which was at least as early as the eighth century, is known as the *vetus Cluniacensis*, and its partial reconstruction from copies and extracts in 1905 is perhaps the greatest achievement of the English Ciceronian scholar A. C. Clark. The text of the lost Cluniacensis is most accurately mirrored in a manuscript which was in part copied from it before it was carried off to Italy by Poggio (Paris lat. 14749). This manuscript has now yielded up its secret and revealed the hand of the French humanist Nicholas of Clémanges.

His next foray was in the summer of 1416, this time to Saint Gall in company with three humanist friends, Bartolomeo da Montepulciano, Cencio Rustici, and Zomino da Pistoia. The result was three major discoveries: a complete Quintilian (previous humanists had had to make do with *mutili*), Asconius' *Commentary* on five of Cicero's speeches, and a manuscript containing four books (i-iv.377) of the *Argonautica* of Valerius Flaccus. Poggio's manuscript of Quintilian is of little value, but for Asconius we depend on three copies which resulted from this trip, one made by Poggio, one (and the best) by Zomino, and one derived from Bartolomeo's

autograph. The lost Sangallensis of the *Argonautica* has to be reconstructed from a similar trio, one certainly in Poggio's hand
(Madrid, Bibl. Nac. 8514, *olim* X. 81, which also contains his
Asconius); but for Valerius we have a complete and more important ninth-century manuscript from Fulda (Vat. lat. 3277), which
was itself eventually taken to Italy.

Early in 1417, armed with official sanction, Poggio and Bartolomeo made a highly organized expedition to Saint Gall and other
monasteries of the area: their finds included Lucretius, Silius
Italicus, and Manilius. The manuscripts which they found have
perished, but their legacy remains. The copy of Manilius which
Poggio had made is an important witness to the text (Madrid,
Bibl. Nac. 3678, *olim* M. 31); his Lucretius fathered the whole
race of *Itali*, and all our manuscripts of Silius go back to the
copies made as a result of this expedition. At the same time Poggio
acquired from Fulda their famous manuscript of Ammianus (Vat.
lat. 1873), which he took off to Italy; he also set eyes on their
Apicius, and this too was eventually taken to Rome, by Enoch of
Ascoli in 1455. Now or at some later date he also obtained a manuscript of Columella (an author already known in Italy), and his
manuscript was probably the insular codex at Fulda, which reached
Italy in the fifteenth century.

In the summer of 1417 Poggio went on more extended travels in
France and Germany. He made two important discoveries. The
first was eight unknown speeches of Cicero: the *Pro Caecina*, *Pro
Roscio comoedo*, *De lege agraria* i–iii, *Pro Rabirio perduellionis reo*,
In Pisonem, *Pro Rabirio Postumo*. He found the *Pro Caecina* at
Langres, the others probably in Cologne cathedral. His autograph
copy of these speeches has now been discovered (Vat. lat. 11458)
and so done away with a tedious process of reconstruction. The
second find was one of the rarest of texts, the *Silvae* of Statius;
our manuscripts of these poems all descend from the copy which
was made for him (Madrid, Bibl. Nac. 3678, *olim* M. 31).

When the Council was over, Poggio spent some years in England,
where his only find was what he described as a *particula Petronii*,
i.e. the *excerpta vulgaria*; it is from this manuscript that all the
fifteenth-century copies descend. On his way home in 1423 he
found at Cologne a second manuscript of Petronius containing the

Cena Trimalchionis, and from the copy which was made for him descends our unique source for the complete *Cena* (Paris lat. 7989). It disappeared from view while on loan to Niccolò Niccoli, fortunately to reappear at Trau in Dalmatia about 1650.

Poggio's achievements in the field of discovery were prodigious; his personal intervention in the history of many important texts was decisive and influential. But recent studies have added another feather to his cap: he appears to have been the inventor of the humanistic script (Plate XVI). As time went by, and particularly from the beginning of the thirteenth century, Caroline minuscule had become more angular and thick and considerably less attractive, developing into what is known as the Gothic hand. The humanistic script was a deliberate return to an earlier form of Caroline minuscule; the earliest book written in this hand by Poggio can be dated to 1402–3. The influence of Coluccio may have been at work, and it was another of his protégés, Niccolò Niccoli, who seems to have developed the cursive form of the new script. With the advent of printing the formal hand developed into the roman fount, the cursive into italic.

The bulk of Latin literature known to us had now been recovered. The more important of the remaining discoveries may be mentioned more briefly. In 1421, in the cathedral of Lodi, to the south-east of Milan, Gerardo Landriani found a collection of *rhetorica*, including the *De oratore* and *Orator* (previously only known through *mutili*) and an unknown work, the *Brutus*. In 1429 Nicolaus of Cues brought to Rome an eleventh-century German manuscript of Plautus (Vat. lat. 3870), which contained, among others, the twelve plays which were still unknown. The unique manuscript of Tacitus' *Opera minora* (Iesi lat. 8) had been known to Poggio as early as 1425, but attempts to entice it from Hersfeld had failed: in 1455 it was finally brought to Rome, probably by Enoch of Ascoli. The remaining unknown part of Tacitus, *Annals* 1–6, was filched from Corvey and arrived in Rome in 1508. Other fifteenth-century discoveries included Cornelius Nepos, Celsus, Frontinus' *De aquis*, and the *Panegyrici Latini*.

With the finding of a large number of grammatical works at Bobbio in 1493 ended what Sabbadini called the heroic age of discovery. But important texts continued to see the light. In 1501–4

Sannazaro found in France the archetype of the pseudo-Ovidian *Halieutica* and the *Cynegetica* of Grattius (Vienna lat. 277) and its no less interesting and important copy (for the Vienna manuscript is now incomplete) containing the *florilegium Thuaneum*. But most of the discoveries of the early sixteenth century were associated with the scholarly activity now centred at Basle, the home at this time of Erasmus and Beatus Rhenanus and such printers as Froben and Cratander. Beatus Rhenanus discovered Velleius Paterculus at Murbach in 1515 and produced the *editio princeps* in 1520. By using an important new manuscript Cratander was able to print in 1528 an edition of Cicero which contained five letters to Brutus never seen before and for which his book remains the unique source. In 1527 Grynaeus found the surviving books of Livy's fifth decade at Lorsch. Such finds were rarely to be the lot of later scholars, but the excitement of discovery continued, buoyed up by two new sources, palimpsests and papyri.

It should be remembered in this context that the humanists also had a capacity for losing manuscripts. Once they had carefully copied a text, they were liable to have little interest in the manuscript which had preserved it. The Cluny and Lodi manuscripts of Cicero, the Veronenses of Catullus and Pliny have perished; only a few leaves survive of the Hersfeld Tacitus; the *Cena Trimalchionis* was nearly lost again for ever. Other manuscripts unnamed and unsung survived into the Renaissance (their existence can be inferred from their humanist progeny), but not beyond it. In the sixteenth century the situation was worse; many fine codices went along the one-way road to the printing press. Among them were the Murbach codex of the *Historia Augusta* lent to Erasmus, the fifth-century manuscript of Pliny's *Letters* (the unique source for book X, now reduced to a fragment) which Aldus managed to borrow from the abbey of Saint Victor at Paris, the manuscripts of Livy from Worms and Speyer which were used by Beatus Rhenanus and Gelenius. The Murbach codex of Velleius Paterculus which they used for their edition survived but later disappeared, being last heard of in the sale-room in 1786.

VI. LATIN SCHOLARSHIP IN THE FIFTEENTH CENTURY: VALLA AND POLITIAN

The quickened interest in all aspects of ancient life and literature, fostered by the continual excitement of new discoveries, led to a vigorous growth in all the main disciplines and techniques which are necessary to a full understanding of classical antiquity. While archaeology, numismatics, epigraphy, and the study of Roman institutions were launched along sound lines by such men as Flavio Biondo (1392–1463), historical and textual criticism, which are fundamental to the study of classical texts, were developed with singular brilliance by two humanists who may be regarded as representing what was best in the scholarship of the fifteenth century, Lorenzo Valla (1407–57) and Angelo Poliziano (1454–94). As attention will be focused on these two figures, it should be emphasized that they are in a class apart. The average scholar of the time did not reach these heights, though there is evidence that a great deal of sound and scrupulous work was done on Latin texts during this period. A valuable body of corrections and conjectures was rapidly amassed, often depreciated because anonymous. But there were also the dabblers, men whose confidence in emending and elucidating classical texts had outstripped their scholarly equipment and whose facile jottings, even when they were not intended to infect the traditional text, might easily do so. There was a temptation to embellish, to produce the readable and elegant text which the customer expected. Hence the caution with which editors use the manuscripts of this period.

It was now possible to study the works of Latin literature with greater ease and in greater depth. A contributory factor of supreme importance was the increasing number of splendid libraries, founded or enriched by generous and influential patrons, among them the Visconti in Pavia, Duke Federigo of Urbino, Alfonso V in Naples, the Medici in Florence, Pope Nicholas V in Rome. In the train of the library-builders came the highly organized entrepreneur like the bookseller Vespasiano da Bisticci (1421–98), who was prepared to lay on forty-five scribes when a library was on order; and, as the manuscript gave way to the printed book, classical texts and the scholarly work that began to gather around them could be disseminated without restriction or limit.

The critical standards of this surging humanism were carefully probed by Lorenzo Valla. Trained in Latin and Greek by the best teachers of his day, among them Aurispa and Leonardo Bruni, and gifted with exceptional ability, Valla was clearly destined to make his mark. But his vain and aggressive nature, which prompted him to tilt at every sacred cow and was to involve him in a series of venomous polemics, particularly with Panormita and Poggio, might have seriously hampered his career, had it not been for the protection and patronage, first of Alfonso V, then of Nicholas V. Nicholas opened the doors of the Curia to this *enfant terrible*, and under his successor he became papal secretary. From 1450 he held a chair of rhetoric at Rome.

An early victim of his critical powers was the Donation of Constantine, a notorious document, fabricated as early as the eighth or ninth century, which strengthened papal claims to temporal power by recording the legendary gift of Rome and the provinces of Italy by Constantine to the Pope: in 1440 Valla proved, on historical and linguistic grounds, that the Donation was a forgery. It is not surprising that he likewise attacked the authenticity of the spurious correspondence between Seneca and Saint Paul, which had had an undeserved run since the days of Jerome. His most famous work is his *Elegantiae*, dealing with points of Latin style, usage, and grammar. Composed while he was at Naples, it was first printed in 1471; by 1536 it had appeared in no less than 59 editions, a standard authority on the Latin language for both the fifteenth and sixteenth centuries. Its critical and independent scholarship marks the highest point which the study of Latin had so far attained. It was followed, in 1446–7, by his *Emendationes sex librorum Titi Livi* (books 21–26). Written with a scathing brilliance recurrent in later works of this sort, this philological masterpiece was designed to discredit two other scholars at the court of Alfonso, Panormita and Facio, and made it painfully plain that only the best could play at the fashionable game of emending Livy. One of the weapons in his arsenal was the great Livy volume which had been put together by Petrarch, and his autograph notes can still be seen in its margins (Plate XV). He dared to emend the Vulgate itself, and his notes and corrections (1449), based on a study of the Greek original and early patristic texts, were fully appreciated by Erasmus, who had them printed in 1505. He also found time to be a prolific translator from the Greek.

Politian was born at Montepulciano and educated at Florence. 1454-1494 He showed a precocious talent and was taken at an early age into the household of Lorenzo de' Medici, who made him tutor to his children and remained his lifelong friend and patron; by the age of thirty he was a professor of such repute that he attracted scholars from all over Europe to his lectures on Greek and Latin literature. As well as being an influential teacher, he was the finest poet of his time, both in Italian and in Latin; and as a scholar he at times transcends his age and moves out of reach of any of his contemporaries.

Politian won his prominent position in the history of the classical tradition both by his exact scholarship and by the way in which he opened the eyes of his contemporaries to the full perspective of ancient literature. Valla had recommended the study of Quintilian, but his insistence on a classical norm in the writing of Latin had tended to foster the predominant cult of Ciceronian Latin. Politian firmly rejected Ciceronianism and chose to create an eclectic style of his own which exploited the whole range of Latin: '*non exprimis*' *inquit aliquis* '*Ciceronem*'. *Quid tum? Non enim sum Cicero, me tamen* (*ut opinor*) *exprimo* (*Epist.* 8.16). In the same way he was the first to give serious attention to the prose and poetry of the Silver Age.

Politian's great work of scholarship was his *Miscellanea*, a collection of a hundred chapters of varying length on different points of scholarship which well displays the many sides of his learning. The first part (*Centuria prima*) was published in Florence in 1489; an autograph draft of a second series of chapters recently came to light and has only just been printed. The work is similar in style to the *Attic Nights* of Aulus Gellius; again the influence of late authors is evident. A few examples of the topics discussed will show the character of the book: the origin of the names of the days of the week, the original meaning of the word 'panic', the significance of a coin struck by Brutus showing his portrait with a cap and two daggers are typical problems. To settle the question of how to spell the name Vergil Politian invokes the evidence of some inscriptions and the spelling of very old manuscripts. He uses the text of Callimachus to emend a corrupt passage in Catullus (66.48). In an important chapter for the development of textual criticism (*Misc.* xviii) he points out that the manuscript of the *Epistulae ad familiares* which was made for Coluccio in 1392 (Laur. 49.7 = P) is a copy of the Vercelli manuscript (Laur. 49.9 = M), and demonstrates that P itself, in which a number of leaves have been displaced through an error in binding, must be the parent of a whole family of later manuscripts in which the sequence of a group of letters has similarly been disturbed. This methodical application of the principle of *eliminatio codicum descriptorum* (see p. 188) is not found again until the nineteenth century. In the *Letters to Atticus* (15.4.4) he emends the vulgate reading *cera* to *cerula* on the strength of the reading *ceruia* in M, the best of the Italian manuscripts (Laur. 49.18). The principle that conjectural emendation must start from the earliest recoverable stage of the tradition, employed more than once by Politian, was not fully exploited until the age of Lachmann.

Although his conviction that later manuscripts are derivative was too sweeping, Politian's constant recourse to the oldest manuscripts available and his distrust of humanist copies was bound to produce solid results. In this he was helped enormously by the improved library facilities of his day and the advent of the printed book; between 1465 and 1475 the bulk of the Latin classics were put into print. He made full use of libraries, both public and private, in Florence and elsewhere, particularly that of the Medici; no less than thirty-five Medicean manuscripts were out on loan to him at the time of his death. Among the many great classical manuscripts which he is known to have examined or collated were such important witnesses as the Bembinus of Terence (Vat. lat. 3226 of the fourth to fifth century), the Romanus of Vergil (Vat. lat. 3867 of the fifth to sixth century), the Etruscus of Seneca's *Tragedies*, the Neapolitanus of Propertius, and (though this is less certain) the Vaticanus of Valerius Flaccus. Some manuscripts which he used have been lost and his careful collations, usually entered (by him or for him) into his copy of an early printed edition, have the status of important witnesses to the text. Examples are the Parma edition of Ovid in the Bodleian Library, with his autograph readings from the lost Marcianus of the *Tristia*, his copy of the first edition of the *Silvae* with his collations of a manuscript which is thought by some to have been the one which Poggio found in 1417, and his *editio princeps* of the *Scriptores rei rusticae*; this contains collations of an early manuscript of Columella (doubtless Ambros. L. 85 sup. from Fulda), and, more important, of the lost archetype of the agricultural works of Cato and Varro.

His keen interest in the more technical writings of antiquity is further illustrated by a massive edition of the Elder Pliny (Rome, 1473) now at Oxford; this contains a transcript of Politian's notes and collations, the latter taken from five different manuscripts (carefully distinguished with the sigla *a b c d e*) and the important critical work of a contemporary scholar, the *Castigationes Plinianae* of Ermolao Barbaro. For Apicius he was able to collate the two ninth-century manuscripts on which the text is based (E and V), from Fulda and Tours respectively. The Fulda manuscript is now in New York, while a fragment of Politian's own manuscript of Apicius, complete with his collations of E and V, eventually came to light in Russia (Leningrad 627/1, *olim* V. 644), a remarkable and colourful history for a cookery book. He studied and copied important medical texts, including the manuscript of Celsus discovered by Giovanni Lamola in Milan in 1427 (Laur. 73.1); and the copy which he caused to be made of an old manuscript of the *Ars veterinaria* of Pelagonius is now the unique source for the text (Riccardianus 1179). Its *subscriptio*, which is typical, demonstrates the sound and scholarly way in which Politian dealt with manuscript evidence:

Hunc librum de codice sanequam vetusto Angelus Politianus, Medicae domus alumnus et Laurenti cliens, curavit exscribendum; dein ipse cum exemplari contulit et certa fide emendavit, ita tamen ut ab illo mutaret nihil, set et quae depravata inveniret relinqueret intacta, neque suum ausus est unquam iudicium interponere. Quod si priores institutum servassent, minus multo mendosos codices haberemus. Qui legis boni consule et vale. Florentiae, anno MCCCCLXXXV, Decembri mense.

VII. GREEK STUDIES: DIPLOMATS, REFUGEES AND BOOK COLLECTORS

The introduction of Greek studies to the city states of central and northern Italy might have been expected to come about at an early date and without difficulty through contact with the Greek-speaking communities of the extreme south and Sicily. But the south was quite isolated from the rest of the peninsula and had not shared the growth in wealth and other progress of the bigger northern cities, a state of affairs which was not altered until well into the present century. Occasionally men of ability from these regions travelled to the north on diplomatic missions, and in the fourteenth century two of them received an enthusiastic welcome from the leading scholars and writers of the day. It is well known how Petrarch took lessons from the monk Barlaam, whom he met at the papal court at Avignon. But though the monk was admitted by his most bitter theological opponents to be a master of theology and logic, his ability as a teacher left something to be desired, and Petrarch never succeeded in learning enough Greek to read the copy of Homer that a Byzantine ambassador gave him (Ambros. I. 98 inf.). Another opportunity to learn Greek arose in 1360, when Barlaam's pupil Leonzio Pilato was intercepted by Boccaccio at Florence on his way north to Avignon; he was induced to stay and lecture on Greek, in return for an annual stipend from the Florentine government, but being a man of restless and impatient character he did not stay many years. The first translations that he was persuaded to make were some Homer together with about four hundred lines of Euripides' *Hecuba* for Boccaccio and some of Plutarch's *Lives* for Coluccio Salutati. The style of these versions was very rough, and Coluccio set to work to improve the latinity of the Homer translation, which was done in word-for-word style. The opening lines of the *Iliad* ran as follows in Leonzio's version:

> iram cane dea Pelidae Achillis
> pestiferam quae innumerabiles dolores Achivis posuit,
> multas autem robustas animas ad infernum antemisit . . .

More fruitful than the contacts with the south of Italy were those with Constantinople itself. The declining fortunes of the

Greek empire made it necessary to send frequent diplomatic missions abroad to beg help against the Turkish invader; monarchs as far distant as the king of England received these appeals. We have already seen how a knowledge of Latin literature was made available to the Byzantines through Maximus Planudes, who had served on an embassy sent to Venice. It was almost exactly a century later that another Byzantine diplomat, Manuel Chrysoloras, became the first man to give regular lectures on Greek in Italy. He began in Florence in 1397, which is therefore a date of fundamental importance in the cultural history of Europe, and continued his courses for a number of years, combining this activity with diplomatic business. He had several notable pupils including Guarino and Leonardo Bruni. One important result of his teaching was that Latin translations of Greek texts were prepared, and he insisted that the old word-for-word style of translation should be abandoned, and that attention should be given to ensuring some literary merit in the version. An indication of his influence as an instructor is that his textbook of Greek grammar entitled *Erotemata* gained a considerable circulation, and eventually became the first Greek grammar to be printed (in 1471); it was later used by such famous men as Erasmus and Reuchlin.

During the fifteenth century the opportunities for an Italian to learn Greek improved. A number of Byzantines came to live in Italy, and after the defeat of their country in 1453 there was a stream of refugees, who generally reached Italy by way of Crete and Venice, and who were all anxious to earn a living by teaching their native language or copying texts. Fortunately for them the revival in knowledge of classical Latin caused a widespread desire to read the Greek authors so frequently quoted or mentioned in it. But it is difficult to estimate how many Italians in fact learnt Greek to a standard which permitted them to read a text with ease. Enthusiasm for the new language might soon be lost through the lack of a gifted teacher or the irritating drawbacks of unsystematic grammatical textbooks; even Erasmus complained of the effort required to master the language. Some Italians, including Politian, are known to have taught themselves by taking a Latin translation, for example the traditional version of the Bible or Theodore Gaza's rendering of Aristotle, and using it as a key to elucidate the Greek text. In the absence of a teacher or a satisfactory grammar this was an exceptionally difficult undertaking. Many would-be scholars must have been obliged to content themselves with reading Latin translations: a great number of these were produced, especially under the patronage of Pope Nicholas V (1447–55), who commissioned versions of Thucydides, Herodotus, Xenophon, Plato, Aristotle, Theophrastus, Ptolemy, and Strabo. A small minority of students had the energy or the means to seek instruction in Constantinople itself; two of the more famous fifteenth-century figures who did this were Filelfo (1398–1481) and Guarino (1374–1460).

Another reason for travel to the East was the chance of bringing back manuscripts which might well include new texts. Some collectors had remarkable success, and Giovanni Aurispa came back to Italy in 1423 with 238 Greek books (Plate IV); an equally large modern collection of Greek printed texts would be considered substantial, but one must not exaggerate the merits of the Aurispa library, since it doubtless contained a large number of duplicated titles. Probably Filelfo's collection of forty Greek books was more typical of the private libraries formed at the time. Rulers of Italian states collected also. From Florence Lorenzo de' Medici dispatched Janus Lascaris, one of the scholar refugees, on a journey to various Byzantine provinces in 1492 in search of manuscripts. The papal collections also grew rapidly. Venice acquired the basis of its large collection rather differently in 1468 through the gift of Cardinal Bessarion; he had collected for some time with the object of forming a complete library of Greek literature, giving his agents instructions to search in many territories of the former empire, and it is known that a part of his collection, including the newly discovered text of Quintus of Smyrna and perhaps the famous codex Venetus of Aristophanes (Marc. gr. 474), was acquired from the monastery of Saint Nicholas at Otranto.

VIII. GREEK SCHOLARSHIP IN THE FIFTEENTH CENTURY: BESSARION AND POLITIAN

A comprehensive account of Greek studies in the fifteenth century would need to deal with a large number of the more eminent humanists, but for this short introduction it must suffice to select two of the most notable scholars as typical of the aims and achievements of the period. One of these two represents the learning of the Greeks, the other shows what the Italians were able to learn from their masters.

The earlier of the two figures is cardinal Bessarion (c. 1400–1472). He was born in Trebizond and educated in Constantinople at the school run by George Chrysococces, where he first met the Italian Filelfo with whom he was to correspond frequently in later life. He became a monk in 1423, and spent the years 1431–6 at Mistra in the Peloponnese in the circle of the freethinker George Gemistus Plethon, from whom he probably acquired his admiration for Plato. Through Plethon he was introduced to the emperor and came to be employed on government business; the emperor made him abbot of a monastery in the capital in 1436 and in the following year promoted him to the see of Nicaea. In 1438 he came to Italy as a member of the delegation sent to the Council of Florence and Ferrara to negotiate a union between the Greek and Roman churches. More than one attempt had been made to restore church unity, and now the need to end the schism was made acute by the rapid disintegration of the Byzantine empire, which governed no more than a tiny proportion of its former territories; hopes of Western military aid might be realized after a reunion of the church. The proceedings of the council were protracted, but in the end an agreement was reached between the two parties, very largely owing to the forceful arguments of Bessarion, who had to overcome determined opposition from members of his own delegation. The union was abortive, since the mass of the population in the Greek empire, encouraged by many of the clergy, refused to accept the act of union as a just compromise; the minority who accepted the union became a separate sect, known as the Greek Uniate Church, which thus owes its existence to Bessarion. Despite the failure of the council to have any lasting political effect Bessarion's services to the Church did not pass unnoticed by the pope; he became a cardinal and resided permanently in Italy, taking a considerable part in church affairs, and on more than one occasion he was nearly elected pope.

The cardinal's house in Rome was a centre of literary activity, where Greeks and Italians mixed freely; of the former the two most famous were Theodore Gaza and George Trapezuntios, who translated various works into Latin, while among the Italians were Poggio and Valla. Bessarion's wide knowledge and expert command of Latin caused him to be dubbed by Valla '*Latinorum Graecissimus, Graecorum Latinissimus*'. His library was exceptionally large; the Greek books alone amounted to some five hundred volumes towards the end of his life and included many important copies of classical texts, for his tastes were not confined to theology and philosophy. He took great care over them, as may be seen from the possession-notes, shelf-marks, and other notes he inserted on the flyleaves. He had not always been a keen collector, since he had relied on the book trade in Constantinople as an adequate source of supply; but one of his letters states that the fall of the Greek empire in 1453 made him form the plan of building as complete a collection as possible of Greek books, in the intention of placing it eventually at the disposal of those Greeks who survived the fall of the empire and reached Italy. This statement of his plans shows one of his main reasons for presenting his collection during his own lifetime (1468) to the city of Venice to form the basis of a public library, for it was in Venice that a high proportion of Greek refugees tended to congregate.

Bessarion's own literary work included a Latin translation of Aristotle's *Metaphysics*, and a long book against the critics of Plato. A good many pamphlets and letters also survive. Two of the former are of interest for our present purpose. The first arose out of the negotiations for church unity. The crucial point in the argument between the Greeks and the Latins concerned the procession of the Holy Spirit: is it of the same or merely similar nature to God the Father? Bessarion's great success was that he found a passage in Saint Basil's tract *Against Eunomius* which clearly enunciated the view of the Latin Church, and should therefore have formed the basis of a reconciliation, since the authority of Saint Basil in the Greek Church was beyond criticism. Bessarion's opponents at the council, members of the Greek delegation who wanted a successful conclusion to the discussions only if everything went their own way, claimed that the passage was not a genuine statement by Saint Basil, that an earlier Greek church reformer or the Italians had forged it, and that they had manuscripts which omitted the words in question. Though sure of his ground Bessarion was temporarily at a loss to prove his point and had to rely on other less decisive evidence to convince the opposition. But when he returned briefly to Constantinople he determined to settle the matter to his satisfaction and began to examine all the copies of the text that he could lay his hands on. At the time of the council only one of the six copies of the work that could be found appeared to favour Bessarion's opponents, and that gave every sign of having been tampered with, for the vital passage had been deleted and other words substituted for it. Research in the monastic libraries of the capital soon yielded two old copies of the text, one on paper dated to the middle of the twelfth century, and the other on parchment of still greater age; the text of both these copies supported Bessarion, while only very recent copies of the text, which appeared to have been written at the time of the council or just after, supported the other view. Bessarion used the age of the two old copies as his decisive argument; they were both older than the date of certain earlier Greek churchmen who had favoured union with the West, and so could not have been forged by them; and as to the notion that they had been forged by the Italians, the high quality of the Greek was sufficient reply to the suggestion.

After this example of scholarly method used to refute the unscrupulous manipulation of texts we come to Bessarion's other short work which shows his scholarship to advantage, and here too the context is theological. After a reading from Saint John's Gospel as part of the liturgy conducted in his house in Rome, lively conversation began as to the correct text of John 21:22. The reading had been performed from the Latin Vulgate, which erroneously gave the word *sic* instead of *si* (the Greek has ἐάν). Bessarion pointed out in discussion that this was a simple case of a copyist's error, involving only one letter. His audience was not completely persuaded, and so he wrote a pamphlet to prove his point. Here several important principles are enunciated, and the whole matter is discussed with a common sense that seems natural to us but was not welcome to the narrow-minded conservatism of men who regarded every word of Saint Jerome's translation as sacred. Bessarion states that the Greek text is the original and must have precedence over the Latin translation, and is able to claim Augustine's authority for this proposition. He also shows that early quotations of the Greek text in Origen, Cyril, and Chrysostom all have the same wording. Then he shows that the whole context of the passage is not suited to the reading of the Vulgate. The work is of great importance and anticipates the attitude of Erasmus in regarding the Greek text of the New Testament as the only proper basis for interpretation. It may owe something to Valla, who frequently met Bessarion and had previously written but not published a tract entitled *Adnotationes in Novum Testamentum*, in which he called into question the Vulgate's accuracy.

To the Greek bishop who settled in Italy and whose scholarly activity was devoted mainly to theology and philosophy Politian (1454–94) offers a striking contrast. He is famous as a poet in his vernacular language and in Latin, but was equally distinguished as a scholar. Though primarily interested in ancient literature he had a proper understanding of the subsidiary branches of knowledge, such as epigraphy and numismatics, and the contribution that they can make to a general understanding of the ancient world. The combination of poet and scholar in Politian has an interesting analogy in the Hellenistic world; the same description suits Callimachus and Eratosthenes, and it is perhaps not entirely a coincidence that Politian was the first scholar to give serious attention to Hellenistic poetry.

His ability as a Latinist and his appreciation of the importance of old manuscripts have been described above. It may merely be worth remarking in passing that he changed the direction of Greek and Latin studies in rather the same way, by encouraging an interest in post-classical authors; just as in Latin he had pointed out the merits of Quintilian, Suetonius, and the Silver Latin poets, so in Greek he lectured on Callimachus and Theocritus. As a Greek scholar he was the first Italian of whom it was generally agreed that he equalled native Greeks in knowledge of the language. Such a claim appears in his own works. In a latter to Matthias Corvinus, king of Hungary (*Epist.* 9.1), where he offers his literary services, either as a translator of classical texts or official panegyrist of the king's successes, he states that he knows as much Greek as the Greeks themselves, and is the first Italian to do so for a thousand years. The same boast is implied in the opening of his inaugural lecture on Homer. Whatever vanity there may be in this claim, it can easily be justified. Politian is the first Italian of the Renaissance who did work of permanent value on a Greek text, so that his name can still be found in the apparatus criticus of a modern edition. (Valla's contributions to the text of Thucydides are more probably due to the merits of the manuscripts he used than to his own ingenuity.) One other notable testimony to Politian's linguistic power is that from the age of seventeen he composed epigrams in Greek. About fifty of these survive in various metres, and though they are faulty in a number of matters of scansion and prosody they display considerable knowledge of the language, especially in the use of a wide vocabulary.

His works include several translations from the Greek. There is a fluent version of the late historian Herodian and some short essays by Epictetus and Plutarch. But most important prose authors had already been translated, and so Politian could turn his energy in other directions. The work which best displays the many sides of his learning is the *Miscellanea*. Most of the chapters deal with matters of Latin scholarship, but numerous Greek authors are quoted as evidence to justify or reinforce an argument. One example already mentioned is his use of the text of Callimachus to emend a corrupt passage is Catullus (66.48). Perhaps the most significant chapter is the one which gives a text of Callimachus' fifth hymn, *The bath of Pallas*, accompanied by a translation into elegant elegiacs. Here he prints the Greek text without accents in order to avoid anachronism, a point of scholarly precision in which he has not been followed by later generations, and makes a very good job of preparing the first edition of the hymn.

IX. THE FIRST PRINTED GREEK TEXTS: ALDUS MANUTIUS AND MARCUS MUSURUS

While the new art of printing soon led to a spate of editions of Latin classics from the seventies of the fifteenth century onwards, for Greek texts the situation was quite different. Part of the reason for this may have been the difficulty of designing a suitable fount of type, in which the number of sorts would not be unreasonably increased by the various combinations of letters with accents and breathings. Certainly some of the early printers, in a mistaken desire to reproduce in print the appearance of contemporary Greek script, devised founts of type that were expensive to operate with and unsatisfactory in appearance. Even the famous Aldine founts, which served for a very long time as the models for later typographers, are open to both these criticisms. But not all early printers failed in this way; the type-face designed by the famous Frenchman Nicholas Jenson, who worked in Venice, was an excellent piece of work, and still better in some ways was that used for printing passages of Greek in Politian's *Miscellanea*: here the accents and breathings were omitted and ligatures avoided, so that the text bore no close resemblance to written script but was far more easily legible. It is surprising that one of these simpler founts was not immediately accepted as the standard.

More serious than the typographical difficulty was the lack of demand for Greek texts in sufficient numbers to make an edition pay. Knowledge of Greek was quite restricted, and Latin translations could be printed instead in editions large enough to be profitable. A striking example of this is that Plato was not printed in Greek until 1513, but Marsilio Ficino's translation appeared in 1485 in an edition of 1,025 copies. Not only was this an uncommonly large edition, for the average number of copies of all publications at this date is thought to have been 250 or a little more, but it was sold out within six years, and another printing took place. But in contrast to this the Greek text of the *editio princeps* of Isocrates, which appeared in Milan in 1493, sold so slowly that in 1535 the remaining copies were reissued with a new title-page. Before the Aldine press was set up the total number of volumes printed in Greek was scarcely more than a dozen. Several of these were grammars by Chrysoloras and Constantine Lascaris, and the only major classical texts apart from Isocrates were Homer, Theocritus, and the Greek Anthology.

Aldus Manutius (1449–1515) had the idea of setting up a publishing house primarily for the printing of Greek texts. The notion came to him while he was living in Carpi, a town near Modena, acting as tutor to the sons of the ruler. Florence might seem to be the obvious place for the location of this enterprise, in view of its intellectual pre-eminence, but the death of Lorenzo de' Medici had removed the most influential patron of learning and letters. On the other hand Venice possessed a larger library of Greek books than had been assembled by the Medici family; this resulted from the gift of Bessarion. Probably more important to Aldus was the great reputation of Venice as a centre of the printing trade; more than half the books printed in Italy before 1500 were published there. Skilled and experienced workmen would be available for the new firm.

From 1494 to 1515 the Aldine press issued a great series of editions of classical texts: with the death of Aldus in the latter year the firm declined. The printing of Latin texts had advanced to the point that Aldus' books include only one first edition of a Latin text, and an unimportant one at that. But in Greek he was responsible for the first printing of nearly all the major authors, and during his twenty years in business he had almost a monopoly of preparing Greek texts. In Venice and its territories he had privileges from the government which amounted to a patent for the exclusive right to use type-faces designed or commissioned by himself.

His great project could not have been realized without the help of numerous scholarly friends, both Greek and Italian. The man who undertook much the most significant single share of the scholarly work was the Cretan Marcus Musurus (1470–1517). Aldus himself must probably be counted a considerable scholar in his own right. But it is not always easy to tell how much of the work was done by him or Musurus or some other members of the circle. The title-pages of Aldine books and the dedicatory letters written by Aldus often do not name the editor of the text. In such cases the most likely solution to the problem is that the work was shared by several of the publisher's friends. By 1502 at the latest the title-pages refer to the Academy or Neakademia, a club formed by Aldus for the promotion of Greek studies. It had a set of rules drawn up in Greek, one of which was that at meetings Greek should be the only language permitted. About thirty or forty members can be identified. Permanent residence in Venice was not necessary for membership, since Musurus, who taught at Padua and at Carpi for a time, appears to have been a member. Visiting foreign scholars were welcomed; the most famous example was Erasmus.

The quantity of first editions brought out by the press during its most active periods testifies to the enthusiasm of the collaborators

and the efficient organization of the printing. The first Greek
book to appear was a short text, Musaeus, doubtless chosen as an
easy experiment before proceeding to more difficult ventures. After
this came a text of Theocritus and Hesiod more complete than the
one already in print. Then the press settled to the enormous task of
editing Aristotle and Theophrastus, the result being a series of
five folio volumes brought out between 1495 and 1498. The only
interval in the activity of the firm was caused by the war of the
League of Cambrai against Venice, and no Greek books could be
produced during the years 1505–7 and 1510–12. The most remarkable years for the publication of major classical texts were 1502–4,
which saw the first editions of Sophocles, Euripides, Herodotus,
Thucydides, and Demosthenes. But Aldus did not confine himself
to major authors: he published Herodian's *History*, Pollux,
Stephanus of Byzantium, and Philostratus' *Life of Apollonius*, to
mention only a selection. In the preface to the last of these he
stated bluntly, with a candour not normal among publishers, what
a worthless text he believed this to be (*nihil unquam memini me
legere deterius*). Nearly all the Aldine books were classical texts;
Christian writers only occasionally appeared. At one time Aldus
seems to have projected an Old Testament in Hebrew, Greek, and
Latin, together with a New Testament in Greek and Latin, but
nothing came of this during his own lifetime.

The task of an editor at this date was full of difficulties. Manuscripts had to be obtained to serve as copy for the typesetters, and
if, as often happened, the text was corrupt, the editor might attempt
either to emend it or to find better manuscripts. The prefaces give
some indications of these hardships. Aldus tells us that in the whole
of Italy he had been able to find only one copy of Theophrastus. At
the end of his introduction to Thucydides he says that he would
willingly have added Xenophon and Gemistus Plethon to the same
volume, but had to postpone it for lack of manuscripts. Musurus
in his preface to the epistolographi says that some passages in
Alciphron were so corrupt that he could not put them right, and
asks readers to excuse the unintelligible state of the text as printed.
Musurus' procedure can be observed a little more closely in some
of his other books. The first large volume for which he was undoubtedly responsible is the Aristophanes of 1498 (Plate VIII),

and it can be established that he worked from at least four manuscripts in preparing it. One of these survives in Modena (Estensis *a*. U. 5.10). A text of the comedies had to be constructed from these four books and submitted to the typesetter. An equally substantial task was the redaction of the scholia, which were printed in the margins in just the same position as they had in a medieval manuscript. The scholia in the manuscripts at Musurus' disposal were of different types, and he had an enormous task in selecting and combining the notes into a form that could be printed. To this clerical labour was added the need to restore the correct text, which he did in a number of passages. Similar clerical labour awaited him a number of years later, when he came to edit the lexicon of Hesychius, a Greek dictionary compiled in the sixth century. This survives in only one manuscript (now Marc. gr. 622). Rather than write out the whole text afresh to provide the printer's copy Musurus himself wrote in the manuscript all the necessary corrections and instructions to the printer. As the script contained numerous abbreviations Musurus wrote out in full, either above the line or in the margin, each abbreviated word. He also corrected a large number of mistakes, and the most recent editor has remarked that every page has some emendation which shows Musurus' skill and linguistic knowledge. One rather amusing instance of his skill, which shows him going to greater lengths than modern critics would think necessary, arises in another text, the third pastoral poem of Moschus. Here there is a gap in the text between lines 92 and 93, which Musurus filled by six hexameter lines of his own. Though these lines consist largely of echoes from the similar poems of Theocritus, and were probably not intended to do more than indicate the general sense required by the context, they have sometimes been regarded as genuine lines of the poem, supposedly recovered by Musurus from a unique manuscript that is now lost.

Musurus' contribution to classical scholarship is not easy to estimate exactly, because in most cases the copy of an author which he submitted to the printer is lost, and the best potential source of evidence is thereby denied to us. But if he was personally responsible for all the good readings which appear for the first time in editions that he saw through the press, there can be no doubt that he was the most talented classical scholar ever produced by his nation.

x. ERASMUS (c. 1469–1536)

We must now turn to consider the level of scholarship that could be achieved by a native of northern Europe. The figure who commands attention is Erasmus. Though originally a monk at Steyn near Gouda, he contrived to obtain permanent leave from his monastery, and it was in Paris that he began to take up Greek. He found the language difficult, and did not benefit much from the tuition of a Greek refugee called George Hermonymus. In 1506 he went to Italy with the intention of improving his knowledge of the language, and in due course made contact with Aldus. Erasmus was by this time tolerably well known in literary circles through the publication of the first edition of the *Adagia*, a collection of proverbs with accompanying comments, and the *Enchiridion militis Christiani*, in which the blunt expression of his view of piety had caused some offence to ecclesiastical authorities. Erasmus had added fuel to the flames in 1505 by supervising the printing of another book that was not welcome to the clerical establishment, Lorenzo Valla's *Adnotationes in Novum Testamentum*, which treated the text of the Bible not as if it were sacred but like any other literary monument. It was therefore natural that Erasmus should soon be in touch with Aldus, and in due course he visited Venice, staying as a guest in the printer's house for several months. In one of his later *Colloquia*, called *Opulentia sordida*, he gives a vivid description of the miserable food and house-keeping, but there is reason to think that this is much exaggerated by Erasmus for the purpose of replying to a scurrilous polemic by Alberto Pio of Carpi. In Venice he naturally had the chance to acquire all the Greek he needed, and read the many texts that Aldus' private library could offer. One immediate result of his stay was the publication of a greatly enlarged version of the *Adagia*, incorporating material from the Greek sources that he had just begun to know well.

Much later in his career he wrote a pamphlet on the correct pronunciation of Greek, which led to the widespread adoption of what is called the Erasmian pronunciation. As a rule the Greek exiles taught classical Greek in the pronunciation of the modern language, which certainly is quite different from that used in the ancient world. Evidence to prove this had already been noted by the Spanish scholar Antonio Nebrija (1444–1522) and some members of the Aldine circle. The epithet Erasmian therefore fails to give credit for the discovery where it is due; but it is only fair to add that Erasmus himself did not claim to be the inventor of the new system, which he may be presumed to have met for the first time while staying with Aldus.

Fruitful and important though Erasmus' association with Aldus had been, he is better remembered for his long collaboration with one of the great printing houses of the north, that of Froben at Basle. Erasmus found the milieu congenial, took an active share in the editorial side of the business, and formed with Froben a friendship of considerable importance for the promotion of Christian humanism. One of the earliest and most spectacular fruits of this alliance was the first publication of the Greek text of the New Testament in 1516. By coincidence the Greek text was being set up in type at the same time in Spain at Alcalá (this edition also included the Old Testament with the Greek and Hebrew texts); but difficulties of various kinds prevented publication until 1520. It is worth noting that while Cardinal Ximénez, the chief editor of the Complutensian Polyglot, as it is sometimes known, recommended study of the Bible in the original languages, his views were perhaps not shared by all his collaborators; in one of the prefatory letters there is at least a hint that the Latin text is more to be trusted than the others. Erasmus, however, was quite clear in his own mind of the importance of establishing the original text of the New Testament. A good deal is known about his editorial procedure. He began working seriously at his projected edition during his stay in England in 1512–13, and had four manuscripts of the Greek text for consultation; one of these has been identified as the Leicester codex, a fifteenth-century copy. During the printing at Basle in 1515–16 he had five manuscripts by him, and one which has marks indicating that it was used as copy for the printer is still preserved (Basle A.N.IV.1). This is a twelfth-century manuscript of no particular value. It seems that Erasmus was aware of the likely value of really old manuscripts, but his palaeographical knowledge was inadequate for his need. In this respect he was clearly inferior to Politian and almost certainly to Bessarion; in general he relied on rather late books of no great merit, despite the evident possibility of discovering better and older texts by inquiry from his many correspondents. Though he rightly regarded codex B (Vat. gr. 1209) as of amazing age, and for a reprint of his edition obtained some collations of it through a friend, it does not seem that he ever used it systematically for the whole text. On the other hand he had a grossly exaggerated regard for a manuscript of the Apocalypse, which he thought might even date back to the apostolic age; modern scholarship has identified it as a twelfth-century codex (Schloss Harburg, I 1, 4⁰, 1).

Among many points arising out of the edition two may be mentioned here. In the book of Revelation his only manuscript lacked the last few verses and was unintelligible at other points; being determined to print a Greek text, Erasmus consulted the Vulgate in these passages and made his own Greek version of it. In so doing he exceeded the duty of an editor as it is now understood, and made some mistakes in his Greek. In the first epistle of John (5: 7) Erasmus had followed the Greek in omitting the so-called *comma Johanneum*, a statement of the doctrine of the Trinity which was found in the Vulgate. This caused some controversy, during which Erasmus unwisely offered to insert the words into any reprint of his edition if they could be found in a Greek manuscript. Not surprisingly a manuscript was written for the purpose without delay (Trinity College Dublin 30), and the promise had to be made good. But Erasmus took the chance of indicating his suspicions about the authenticity of the book. The episode shows how a lack of a set of logical principles for the evaluation of manuscripts handicapped scholars in their dealings with opponents who were willing to descend to forgery. Bessarion had had a similar experience at the Council of Florence, but it was easier for him to refute his opponents in controversy, since his aim was to prove a certain passage genuine by showing that it occurred in manuscripts earlier than the date of potential forgers; whereas Erasmus had no equally neat argument at his disposal, and could only appeal to the good authority of very old manuscripts.

Despite its shortcomings in these matters Erasmus' edition of the Greek New Testament represents a very great step forward in scholarship. Against stubborn opposition it established the principles that texts are to be studied in the original language rather than translations, and that texts of scripture are to be discussed and interpreted according to the same rules of logic and common sense as any others. The work of Valla and Bessarion had come to fruition.

Erasmus had been attracted to Basle in the first place because it had already become a centre for the publishing of patristic texts. His New Testament was immediately followed by his first edition of Jerome, and that by a long series of editions of the Fathers which he produced either alone or in collaboration with others, often returning again and again to revise the same author. These include Cyprian, Hilary, Ambrose, and Augustine, and are an impressive monument to his energy and learning, both on account of the massive labour involved and because the patristic writers had received comparatively little critical attention from early editors. While engaged on these mammoth operations, Erasmus still found time to work on classical texts, an essential part of his humanist program. His services to classical Greek are comparatively small, though he produced a number of translations and edited Aristotle and Demosthenes; the only author of whom he produced the *editio princeps* was Ptolemy (1533). His contribution to Latin literature is much greater; the authors he edited include Terence, Livy, Suetonius, the Elder Pliny, and Seneca. The last, which he edited twice (1515, 1529), has been recognized as representative of both his strength and his failings. The first edition was marred by characteristic haste. It went through the press in the absence of its editor, who in any case had enough on his plate with Jerome and the New Testament both in their last stages; the distinction between editor, copy-editor, and proof corrector being more than somewhat blurred, too much was left to others, whom Erasmus afterwards blamed for incompetence and worse. The text benefited from a refreshingly critical approach, but Erasmus knew how much better it should have been and returned to retrieve what he regarded as a disgrace in 1529. The second edition, prefaced by an admirably balanced and sensible essay on Seneca, produced two successful emendations for every one in the first edition and provides convincing proof of the judgement and scholarship of its editor. But again the printing was carried out in something of a fluster, with manuscripts continuing to arrive when parts of the book were already in print. He made judicious use of such manuscripts as he could muster, but they seem to have been an indifferent lot, with one signal exception. He had access to readings from the Lorsch manuscript of the *De beneficiis* and *De clementia* (cf. p. 88), the one manuscript in a large tradition of any real value. But he was inhibited by the critical methods of his day: instead of basing his text of these works upon this prime witness, he drew on it spasmodically to emend what he had before him, and a great opportunity was lost.

5. SOME ASPECTS OF SCHOLARSHIP SINCE THE RENAISSANCE

I. THE COUNTER-REFORMATION; THE HIGH RENAISSANCE IN ITALY

The progress of scholarship in the sixteenth century was hampered by continuing religious controversy. Although Bessarion had been stimulated by such controversy to write two short books of great importance for the development of critical method, it is not easy to discover equally fruitful controversies among the contemporaries of Erasmus or in the next generation. Erasmus himself, though he had exploited the work of Valla and Bessarion for his edition of the New Testament and was aware of Politian's eminence as a scholar, did not possess the palaeographical skill that might have led to further advances; and as he settled at Basle, while most of the best working libraries with manuscript collections were still at that date to be found south of the Alps, he could scarcely hope to add greatly to his experience in dealing with manuscripts. Religious disputes took up much of his time and energy in later years, and in 1524 we find him complaining (*Epist.* 1531) that the struggle between Luther and his opponents had become such a preoccupation in literary circles that the book trade was affected, and in the German-speaking parts of Europe it was hardly possible to sell books on any other topic. Elsewhere, and especially in Italy, the energies of literary men were consumed by another controversy in which Erasmus was once again a leading figure: the question was whether Cicero should be regarded as the one and only suitable model for Latin prose, and though the discussion had been going on intermittently since the days of Poggio and Valla, Erasmus succeeded in giving new life to the argument by publishing at Basle in 1528 a dialogue entitled *Ciceronianus*, in which he held up to ridicule many of the absurdities committed by unduly enthusiastic admirers of Cicero. The debate did not end with Erasmus, whose moderate view failed to win general acceptance. In the middle of the century the extreme pro-Ciceronians seem to have been in the majority, but later there was a change of taste, which affected reading habits and prose style. Literary men became more interested in the works of Seneca and Tacitus than in Cicero and allowed this interest to affect their manner of writing both in Latin and the vernaculars; one of the most important representatives of the new movement was the classical scholar Justus Lipsius.

The prospects for classical and biblical scholarship were not improved by the Counter-Reformation. The abolition of intellectual freedom implicit in the decisions of the Council of Trent (1545–63) could lead to nothing but stagnation. The authority of the Vulgate as the text of the Bible was reaffirmed. Erasmus' books were put on the index of prohibited literature, and although the Church did not make a systematic attempt to have them destroyed, the intellectual atmosphere of Catholic countries was not conducive to scholarship. The dispute between Catholics and Protestants was still being carried on bitterly at the beginning of the next century, and one indication of its power to deflect able minds from what might have been more profitable concerns is that Casaubon devoted two years or more to a refutation of the ecclesiastical history compiled by Cardinal Baronius.

However, the dark side of the picture must not be exaggerated. Although most Latin texts had by now appeared in printed editions, there were still some Greek authors of importance that had not been made generally available in the original language by the time of Erasmus' death, and these gradually appeared in the course of the century. In 1544 Josephus and Archimedes came out in Basle, while in Paris the king's printer Robert Estienne (1503–59) was very active during the same decade. His house produced the first editions of the church history of Eusebius and the Roman histories by Dionysius of Halicarnassus and Dio Cassius. He had already made a name by publishing his Latin dictionary in 1531, and he increased his reputation, and equally his unpopularity with the theological faculty at the Sorbonne, by a series of editions of the Bible. Between 1532 and 1540 he is known to have made some search for good manuscripts of the Vulgate, and in the preface to the 1551 edition, which is otherwise famous for the division of the text into verses universally adopted since that date, he makes an interesting comment on the value of the Vulgate. He asserts, not without justice, that it can be taken to represent the Greek text at a very early stage of its history. Despite an apparatus criticus reporting the variants of fifteen manuscripts his edition is critically disappointing in other respects.

The value of a relatively early translation had been correctly assessed in 1549 by the best Italian scholar of the day, Pier Vettori (1499–1585). In his edition of Aristotle's *Rhetoric* he used the medieval Latin version by William of Moerbeke, citing about 300 of its readings. In his preface he shows that its literal and inelegant form can be exploited to reveal precisely the Greek text of the exemplar used by the translator, and its use is chiefly that by being older than the Greek copies it has not suffered as much of the corruption that results inevitably from copying by hand. Vettori notes the frequent agreement of Moerbeke's version with the oldest and best Greek manuscript (Paris gr. 1741), whose readings he was able to use. Though he shows no knowledge of stemmatic theory as such and apparently did not realize that the Paris codex is even older than Moerbeke's version (though not therefore older than his exemplar), his procedure in dealing with this indirect or secondary tradition is of a scholarly competence that deserves mention in even the briefest survey.

Vettori was in touch with the Estienne family, and after Robert had been obliged to leave Paris and set up his printing house in Geneva, Vettori published with his son Henri (d. 1598) an edition of Aeschylus which was the first to include the full text of the *Agamemnon* (previously lines 323–1050 had been omitted). The younger Estienne was a figure at least as important as his father, but as far as classical scholarship is concerned his main achievement was the completion in 1572 of a work begun by his father, the *Thesaurus linguae graecae*. He was not responsible for the first Greek editions of the few remaining authors not yet printed, the most notable of these being Plotinus (1580), Photius' *Bibliotheca* (1601), and the mathematician Diophantus (1621).

Vettori's most able and active contemporary in Italy was Francesco Robortello of Udine (1516–67). He is generally best known for the *editio princeps* of Longinus *On the sublime* (1552) and an important edition of Aristotles' *Poetics* (1548), but he deserves notice here for another reason. In 1557 he wrote a short dissertation *De arte critica sive ratione corrigendi antiquorum libros disputatio,* which is apparently the first attempt to write a brief manual of textual criticism. Robortello claims to be the first to have devised a theory of emendation. After a short and rather slight section on the value of old manuscripts, in which he shows an awareness of the value of Latin texts written in 'Longobardic' script, by which he probably means pre-Caroline minuscule rather than Beneventan, he turns to the principles governing the art of conjecture. The critic is to test his ideas in the light of palaeography, style, and a general understanding of the subject-matter. Then follows a series of eight headings under which emendations can be classified, mostly illustrated with a few examples. The classification is not as clear as might be wished, but it deals with such essential notions as the intrusive gloss that has displaced the original reading and the possibility of error arising from incorrect division of words. The illustrations are mostly taken from Latin authors, but there are a few from Plutarch and Aristotle's *Rhetoric*, where he may have learnt from Vettori. There is no trace of stemmatic theory anywhere in the argument, and the palaeographical knowledge shown is rather disappointing in view of the many good manuscript collections accessible to him. Nevertheless it is very much to his credit that he attempted a systematic account of the way that the critic should go about his task of restoring classical texts to their original state.

The study of the broader aspects of classical antiquity in Italy during this period is well represented by Fulvio Orsini (1529–1600). Cold-shouldered as an illegitimate adjunct to the great family whose name he bore, Orsini owed the bent of his interests and his preferment in the first place to Gentile Delfini, a learned canon of the church of Saint John Lateran, where Orsini began as a chorister, and later to the patronage of the Farnese family, three of whose cardinals he served as librarian. A scholar and collector in the central Renaissance tradition, he had a number of important and original publications to his credit, such as his *Virgilius illustratus* (1567), which filled in the Greek literary background to Vergil, works on iconography (*Imagines et Elogia*, 1570) and numismatics (*Familiae Romanae*, 1577), and the *editio princeps* of the greater part of the fragmentary books of Polybius (1582). It was the breadth of his enthusiasms, ranging over the whole antiquarian world of art, sculpture, inscriptions, coins, and gems, which marked out his contribution to classical studies. He was well placed to make fruitful contacts with scholars of other countries, so that he knew Lipsius, helped Gruter, entertained Daniel and de Thou. His great archaeological collection ended up at Naples, but his books and manuscripts became one of the most important of the early acquisitions of the Vatican. These included a valuable collection of autograph manuscripts of the great humanists, from Petrarch to his own day, but also a number of books of great antiquity, the Augusteus of Virgil (Vat. lat. 3256), a present, not entirely unsolicited, from Claude Dupuy, and others obtained after protracted haggling from the legacy of Pietro Bembo, an important Pindar (Vat. gr. 1312), the Vaticanus of Virgil (Vat. lat. 3225), and the great Terence in rustic capitals which we still call the Bembinus (Vat. lat. 3226). But his activity at the centre of the antiquarian movement of his time was of no less significance than his achievements in the literary field.

Work on patristic authors also made some limited progress in the latter part of the sixteenth century. In 1550 appeared the first edition of Clement of Alexandria, edited by Vettori and printed in Florence but with a dedication to cardinal Cervini, the future Pope Marcellus II. The cardinal was interested in setting up a press at Rome, in order to produce theological texts in editions that would rival and if possible replace those of Erasmus, whose commentaries on the Scriptures and the Fathers were regarded as dangerous if not downright heretical. The creation of the Index in 1558 gave an impetus for several decades to the production of editions in full conformity with orthodoxy, but the results were variable both in quality and in quantity. The fight against heresy could not be entirely beneficial to scholarship, which received a setback in 1587 when Pope Sixtus V, at the foundation of the Typographia Vaticana, decreed that problems of textual criticism too difficult for the editorial staff to solve by their own efforts must be referred to himself. On the other hand it is known that the staff were capable of careful and intelligent work when left to their own devices, as can be deduced from surviving papers relating to a new edition of Saint Augustine.

The most notable literary event of Sixtus V's pontificate was the publication of the Latin Vulgate in 1590, accompanied by the threat of excommunication to anyone who should subsequently dare to change its readings or print the variants from the manuscripts. Notwithstanding the threat his successor Clement VIII in 1592 recalled the unsold copies and issued another edition differing in many passages, which became and remained the official text of the Roman Catholic Church until it began to be replaced by the Benedictine edition published in Rome from 1926 onwards.

The best achievements in patristic studies at this period fall a little later and come from an utterly different milieu. In Oxford, Thomas James (1573–1629), the first librarian of the Bodleian, who took a delight in showing the inadequacy of editions prepared by Catholic scholars on the continent, organized in 1610–12 a team of helpers to collate manuscripts of Gregory, Cyprian, and Ambrose. They found an extremely large number of erroneous or dubious readings in the printed texts and James compared his task to that of cleansing the Augean stables. He and his team are known to have worked on more than fifty manuscripts and he planned without success a series of patristic texts based on the best manuscripts. In this he foreshadowed the work of the Benedictines of Saint Maur, who were able to use some of his material. Still more significant is the edition of Saint John Chrysostom by Sir Henry Savile (1549–1622), Warden of Merton College Oxford and Provost of Eton, published at Eton in 1612 in eight folio volumes. To a considerable extent this edition of one of the most popular and influential of all the Fathers, both Greek and Latin, has not been superseded. Savile's papers for the edition amount to nearly 16,000 pages, and were by no means the only product of a busy life of scholarship in many fields. An indication of his industry is perhaps given by his wife's remark to him: 'Sir Henry, I would I were a book too, and then you would a little more respect me.'

II. THE BEGINNINGS OF HUMANISM AND SCHOLARSHIP IN FRANCE

The speed and vitality with which humanism had taken root and flourished in Italy was unparalleled elsewhere. In France classicism remained more traditionalist and made no such dramatic leap despite its being open to Italian influence, particularly through

Avignon, from the early fourteenth century onwards. But the strength and vitality of French medieval culture meant that French humanism could absorb what it needed from Italy without being too dependent on it and could strike out along its own path within the broad lines of its own tradition. The sensitivity of French scholars on this issue and the frequent signs of a reaction against Italian scholarship reflect both their debt to Italian humanism and the pride they took in the originality of their own achievement.

Pierre Bersuire (d. 1362) had been one of the first to benefit from the cultural interaction fostered at Avignon and from personal contact with Petrarch himself, who gave him his friendship and help with his classical studies. His translation of Livy into French was an important step in reinforcing the historian's new-found popularity and his *Ovidius moralisatus* shows some Petrarchan influence, but his medieval ways of thinking were too strong for even a Petrarch to change and he fell far short of being a humanist. But a powerful group who thoroughly deserved the name had emerged in France towards the end of the century, among them Jean de Montreuil (1334–1418) and his intimate friend Nicholas of Clémanges (c. 1360–1437). Though they owed their wide familiarity with classical authors, particularly Cicero, to contact with Italian humanists and imported texts, their humanism was firmly rooted in the north and they were well able to discover new texts on their own account. Cluny in particular had proved a rich source. Not even a Poggio can turn up a new text every time without being told where to look, and the presence of Jean de Montreuil at the Council of Constance may have had important side-effects. It can hardly have been a coincidence that Poggio found the *Pro Caecina* at Langres, where Nicholas of Clémanges, the great connoisseur of Cicero's speeches, had been canon and treasurer to the cathedral chapter. And although Poggio claims credit for the discovery of the vetus Cluniacensis of the speeches and indeed had it sent to Italy, it must be remembered that the best and most conscientious copy of the lost manuscript is the one made before it went to Italy, by Nicholas of Clémanges. Much of the achievement of this group remains to be told.

The apparently intermittent progress of French humanism was

strengthened by two events which took place in the second half of the fifteenth century, the appearance of the first teachers of Greek and the setting up of the first printing press in France. Earlier attempts to organize Greek studies at Paris had proved abortive and Gregorio Tifernate, who arrived in 1456, stayed only a few years. George Hermonymus of Sparta, who came to France in 1476, is best known for his failure to give much help as a teacher to either Budé or Erasmus. But with the arrival of Janus Lascaris in 1495 and Girolamo Aleandro in 1508, Greek studies began to flourish and became an important element in French humanism. The first printers were German, the first book was a collection of the model letters of the Italian humanist Gasparino Barzizza, but the promoter of the first press to operate in France was Guillaume Fichet, master in theology and librarian of the Sorbonne, who in 1470 obtained authorization to set up a printing press in the College itself. It made a decisively humanistic début; it used the Roman letter exclusively and its first publications were either straight Latin texts, Sallust, Cicero, Juvenal, Terence, and the like, or works bearing on the cultivation of Latin style, such as Valla's *Elegantiae* and Fichet's own *Rhetorica*. The first Greek book to be printed in France appeared in 1507.

The first great classical scholar of France is Guillaume Budé (1468–1540). Born into a wealthy family and not disinclined in his earlier years to the traditional pursuits of the upper class, Budé did not get down to serious study until he was well into his twenties and appears to have been largely self-taught. Years of hard work finally bore fruit. In 1505 he produced his translation of three of Plutarch's treatises into Latin and in 1508 a work of prime importance which established him as one of the founders of legal science. This was his commentary on part of the *Digest*, his *Annotationes in XXIV libros Pandectarum*, an attempt to cut through the medieval accretion of commentary and gloss and reconstitute the text and spirit of Roman law. Neither diplomatic and administrative duties nor a large family nor his fearful headaches stood in the way of Budé's dogged scholarship. In 1515 came his *De asse*, a study of ancient coinage and measures as much a pain to read as a milestone in the establishment of classical studies as a serious discipline. Thanks to a thorough knowledge of the ancient sources, and a practical bent which allowed him to use a balance and consult the local baker, he outstripped previous essays in the field and produced one of the scholarly masterpieces of the century. His *Commentarii linguae graecae* was more lexicographical in character and much of it was afterwards incorporated in the *Thesaurus* of Henri Estienne. His later works, such as his *De philologia* and *De transitu Hellenismi ad Christianismum*, were attempts to define the place of classical, and particularly Greek, studies in contemporary Christian society and justify the position, still somewhat uncomfortable, of the Christian humanist. A monument to one of his many services to scholarship still stands, the Collège de France; it was largely due to the firm pressure applied by Budé that Francis I was finally persuaded in 1530 to institute its precursor, the Collège des Lecteurs Royaux, which gave the study of the ancient languages a certain independence and emancipated them from the prejudices and traditionalist curricula of the university. By giving concrete expression to his view that there is more to humanism than elegance of form Budé initiated a strong trend in the French scholarship of the period, which accorded high respect to solid learning and a thorough understanding of all aspects of ancient life. Though interested primarily in illuminating the content of ancient texts, Budé knew that this depended on a close criticism of the sources themselves and his numismatic researches, for instance, have left an abiding mark on the text of the relevant parts of the Elder Pliny.

While Budé had been reluctantly drawn into the Ciceronian controversy, the Elder Scaliger (Julius Caesar, 1484–1558) had chosen, rather late in life, to make a quick reputation by writing two poisonous orations against the *Ciceronianus* of Erasmus. Though of Italian origin (whether high or low became a matter of lively international dispute), he had left Italy in 1525 to become physician to the bishop of Agen, settled there, and acquired a French wife and fifteen children, one of whom became even more famous than he. His work extends from commentaries on botanical and zoological works of Aristotle and Theophrastus, inspired by his professional interest in medicine, to philology and literary criticism. His *De causis linguae latinae* (1540) is remarkable for its time in aiming at a scientific analysis of the principles of the Latin language, but the work which earned him the fame for which he thirsted was his *Poetice*, published posthumously in 1561. In this he tries in a lucid and coherent manner to produce a theory of poetry relevant to Latin literature viewed as a continuum extending from the classical poets down to his contemporaries Erasmus and Dolet; nor is it less interesting as an essay in practical criticism.

Budé and Scaliger had not been primarily interested in textual criticism. But they were followed by a series of scholars who conspicuously advanced both the standard and the technique of editing classical texts. The first of these was Adrianus Turnebus (1512–65), who held chairs at Toulouse and Paris and was Royal Reader in Greek from 1547 until his death. As director of the Royal Press (1552–6), he published a series of Greek texts, including Aeschylus, Philo, and Sophocles. He also worked on Latin authors and produced an important edition of Cicero's *De legibus*. His most substantial work is his *Adversaria*, in thirty books, a miscellany of passages from ancient authors emended and explained, criticized by Joseph Scaliger as an *abortivus foetus*, not so much for its content, in which he found much to admire, but because it continued the Italian fashion of *Adversaria* promoted by Politian and Vettori. Turnebus is admired for his acumen, judgement, and conjectural gifts. Happy is the man who can leave such an abiding impression on the text of Aeschylus. His edition of Sophocles (1553) is also the *editio princeps* of the scholia of Triclinius. His text shows too much Triclinian influence; still, he posed the problem of the Triclinian recension, gave the text of Sophocles a new look, and added to the corpus of scholia available in his day. Though his editorial method was the standard *emendatio ope codicum* of his time, he saw the need to use older and better manuscripts than had generally been used for the early printed editions and knew a *codex vestustus* when he saw one. To him we owe our knowledge of an important manuscript of Plautus, the *Fragmenta Senonensia*, better known as the codex Turnebi. This was a fragmentary manuscript from the monastery of Sainte Colombe at Sens, which Turnebus had in his possession for a time and which may have perished when the monastery was burnt by the Calvinists in 1567. Apart from the readings quoted in his *Adversaria*, a transcript of part of Turnebus's collation made by the jurist François Duaren in the margins of a contemporary edition of Plautus came to light in 1897. Turnebus's manuscript or his collation of it was known to Lambinus and Scaliger and the book in which his collation is preserved is itself a commentary on the period, having passed from Duaren to the poets Tabourot and Belleau, to Scaliger and Daniel Heinsius.

Turnebus's counterpart in Latin scholarship was Denys Lambin, or Lambinus (1520–72). Before being appointed Royal Reader in 1561, Lambinus had been able to spend considerable periods in Italy, had met such scholars as Faernus and Muretus, and taken the opportunity to collate manuscripts in Italian libraries. This bore fruit when he came to publish his great series of Latin texts, of which the most celebrated are Horace (1561), Lucretius (1563), and the whole of Cicero (1565–6); not the least remarkable feature of these editions is the shortness of the interval between them. Lambinus had an unrivalled knowledge of the literature of the Golden Age, an acute intellect, and a fine feeling for language exemplified in the exquisite elegance of his own Latin style. He had a particular predilection for Lucretius and his masterly edition held the field until Lachmann. One of the five manuscripts he used was the ninth-century codex Quadratus (Leiden, Voss. lat. Q. 94 = Q), one of the two manuscripts on which the text is still based; it was then at the monastery of Saint Bertin, near Saint Omer, and he had access to a collation made for Turnebus. For Cicero's letters he used a manuscript of outstanding merit which belonged to the Lyons printer Jean de Tournes and was last heard of in 1580; for its readings we are dependent on three French scholars of this period, Lambinus, Turnebus, and Bosius.

The manuscript collectors of this age, often scholars and editors themselves, made a signal contribution to classical studies. Conspicuous among them is Pierre Daniel (c. 1530–1603), a jurist of Orléans, whose great coup was to succeed in buying manuscripts from Fleury after its sack by the Huguenots in 1562. His collection, now mainly at the Vatican or Berne, contained such important relics of the scholarly heritage of that region as Lupus's copy of Valerius Maximus (Berne 366). He also published *editiones principes* of the *Querolus* (1564) and the longer version of Servius (1600), still sometimes referred to as Servius Danielis. Another was

Pierre Pithou (1539–96), who published the first editions of the *Pervigilium Veneris* (1577) and the *Fables* of Phaedrus (1596), both based on ninth-century manuscripts which remain prime witnesses to the text. His use of good manuscripts enabled him to publish important editions of Petronius, and he was the first to use the Lorsch manuscript for the text of Juvenal and Persius (1585), the famous codex Pithoeanus, now to be found, with many other manuscripts of his, at Montpellier. Equally important was Jacques Bongars (c. 1554–1612), whose enormous library, partly derived from the collections of Daniel and Cujas and now at Berne, included such choice items as the famous Irish manuscript of Horace (Berne 363) and our best manuscript of Petronius (Berne 357). Indeed, the complicated history of the text of Petronius in the latter half of the sixteenth century epitomizes the activity of a group of French scholars of this period, Pierre Daniel, the Pithou brothers, Bongars, Scaliger, and the great professor of jurisprudence who had taught them all and may have inspired this particular interest, Jacques Cujas. Its complexity is also an indication of the difficulty of piecing together the elaborate web formed by the interrelationship of men and manuscripts in this period, even in the case of central texts, and of how much remains to be discovered about the ramifications of this type of scholarship.

At the end of the century the classical scholarship of Europe was dominated by two great Huguenots, Joseph Justus Scaliger (1540–1609) and Isaac Casaubon (1559–1614). Scaliger was as fortunate as Casaubon was ill-starred. Launched into Latin by his father, Scaliger enjoyed for thirty years the patronage of a French nobleman and when offered the chair at Leiden vacated by Lipsius his eminence as a scholar was such that he was allowed to accept the chair but decline the customary duties attached to it. His scholarship owes its strength to a massive learning in a number of fields and the capacity to treat an author or a subject as an organic whole. It is best seen in his great edition of Manilius (first edition, 1579), a worthy precursor to those of Bentley and Housman, and his *Thesaurus Temporum* (1606), a reconstruction of the chronological systems of the ancient world and a fundamental contribution to the study of history. His special interest in archaic Latin finds expression in his pioneering edition of Festus. His attempts at textual emendation were sometimes violent and spring paradoxically from a more scientific approach to the editing of texts. When editing Catullus, he sought to prove from the nature of corruptions in the manuscripts (the confusion of *a* and *u*) that they all descended from a common parent in pre-Caroline minuscule. Though he happened to be wrong, he did arrive at the notion of a medieval archetype. This concept, reinforced by his critical attitude to even good manuscripts, encouraged his taking considerable liberties with the transmitted text.

Scaliger was far from untouched by the religious troubles of his day, but the way they bedevilled the scholarship of the sixteenth century is more starkly illustrated in the case of his friend and younger contemporary Casaubon. Born in Geneva of refugee Protestant parents, obliged to learn his Greek hiding in a cave in the French mountains, unable to avoid being drawn into the wrangle because of his distinction as a scholar and forced to spend much of his time and talents on arid polemic, this great French scholar finally found rest as a naturalized Englishman in Westminster Abbey. With him the French scholarship of the period ended, as it had begun, on a chalcenteric note. He was a man of vast industry and erudition, but had the rarer gift of being able to use his learning as a commentator to illumine rather than impress. He appears to have chosen to work on those texts which offered the most scope to his wide knowledge, such as Diogenes Laertius, Strabo, and Athenaeus. His choice of difficult and often diffuse texts, with which most students of the classics have but a passing acquaintance, means that his services are not always recognized. For Casaubon is still with us. His *Animadversiones* on Athenaeus formed the core of Schweighäuser's commentary of 1801, Strabo is still usually cited by reference to Casaubon's pages, his notes on Persius loom large in Conington's commentary. Son-in-law to Henri Estienne and for a time sub-librarian to de Thou at the royal library, Casaubon was most at home in the world of books and manuscripts, able to find material for his own needs and to supply scholars all over Europe. His use of manuscript material has not been properly appraised, but he seems to have made no dramatic advances, except that his second edition of Theophrastus' *Characters* (1599) added five more characters (24–8) to those then known.

III. THE NETHERLANDS IN THE SIXTEENTH AND SEVENTEENTH CENTURIES

Although Erasmus could speak with disgust of the ignorance which obtained in the Netherlands in his youth, it is likely that there was a more widespread general level of literacy than elsewhere. A large measure of the credit for this must go to the Brothers of the Common Life, the members of a community founded at Deventer in the later fourteenth century who devoted a large part of their energy to educational projects and the copying of books. Among the many schools which owed their existence or excellence to them were those attended by Erasmus at Deventer and Hertogenbosch. The general level of literacy and the growth of prosperous mercantile towns helped to create conditions in which learning could flourish despite a late start.

It was the universities and the printing houses, often working closely together, which were largely responsible for the powerful classical tradition of the Netherlands. The university of Louvain was founded in 1425 and the establishment of the Collegium Trilingue for the study of Latin, Greek, and Hebrew in the same town about 1517 further strengthened its claim to be for a time one of the greatest intellectual centres of northern Europe. A similarly dominating position in the northern Netherlands was achieved by the university of Leiden, founded in 1575 to commemorate the heroic resistance of its inhabitants to siege by the forces of Spain. Just as the Protestant north and the Catholic south had their respective centres of higher learning, so they had equally famous traditions of printing. Although the early history of Dutch printing is obscure, it is interesting to observe that such a standard school-book as Donatus' *Ars minor* was printed in Holland about 1470, while in the south at Louvain John of Westphalia issued a number of standard classical authors as early as 1475. His successor in the business, Thierry Martens, was himself a scholar and a friend of Erasmus. From 1512 onwards he began to produce classical books to meet the needs of the university and printed the first Greek texts to be published in this part of Europe. In the great age of printing in the Netherlands, in the later sixteenth and seventeenth centuries, it was Plantin who held sway in the south and Elzevir in the north. Christopher Plantin settled in Antwerp in 1550; on his death in 1589 the business passed to his son-in-law Jan Moerentorf (Moretus) and continued on the same premises and in the same family for three centuries, when it was transformed into the Musée Plantin-Moretus. Though his most famous production was the eight-volume Polyglot Bible (1568–73), his vast and varied output contained an enormous number of classical editions, some of them magnificently produced. He was closely associated with such scholars as Canter and Lipsius, and published a number of *editiones principes* of Greek authors, including Nonnus (1569) and Stobaeus (1575). Louis Elzevir had established himself at Leiden, initially as a bookseller, in 1580. His first book, a text of Eutropius (1592), heralded a strong preoccupation with classical books which fortunately coincided with the great period of Dutch scholarship and so ensured a series of good scholarly texts. Particularly influential was the charming little duodecimo series of classical authors, inaugurated by his sons in 1629. At a guilder a volume they appealed to the student and carried both the name of Elzevir and a sound tradition of classical scholarship all over Europe, much as the great series of Greek and Latin texts begun in 1824 was to make the name of B. G. Teubner a household word and provide a sound basis for modern scholarship.

Although the greatest classical scholar to emerge in the Netherlands in the sixteenth century is undoubtedly Justus Lipsius, there were others whose special interests claim our attention. One of these is Wilhelm Canter (1542–75), whose speciality was Greek textual criticism. He is mainly known for his editions of the three tragedians, but he also edited the *editio princeps* of the *Eclogae* of Stobaeus for the Plantin Press. He makes a special claim for his treatment of the lyrics, and his edition of Euripides, printed by Plantin in 1571, is the first to pay particular attention to responsion and its role in emendation. He also wrote a short manual on textual criticism, *Syntagma de ratione emendandi scriptores Graecos*, appended to his Latin translation of the speeches of Aelius Aristides (1566). This is a systematic classification of the different types of error in Greek texts, brought under such headings as the confusion of certain letters, wrong word-division, omissions, additions and

transpositions, errors arising from assimilation or the misunderstanding of abbreviations, and illustrated with examples taken
almost exclusively from Aristides. He provides a brief but business-
like guide to the errors of scribes and, though little that he says
would come as news to the great critics of his day, it is a gain to
have certain valid principles of emendation explicitly set out, even
if the details need refinement. Franz Modius (1556–97) is less
noteworthy for his scholarship, though he edited a number of
Latin texts, than for his insistence that conjecture alone is useless
and even dangerous, that there must be a proper balance between
manuscript authority and emendation, that recension is an essential
preliminary to editing. In this conviction, and also obliged by the
political unrest of the Netherlands to be on the move, he systematically explored the manuscript collections of a wide area, extending
from northern France through the Low Countries to Fulda and
Bamberg. His activity is remarkable for its scale and his reports of
manuscript readings, found in his *Novantiquae lectiones* (1584),
acquire great value when the manuscripts themselves have been
destroyed, as in the case of the Cologne manuscript of Silius
Italicus. The only other first-hand report of the Cologne Silius is
provided by his friend and later enemy, Ludovicus Carrio (1547–
95), who was similarly active on a smaller scale. Jacob Cruquius
worked almost exclusively on Horace and owes his fame to his
invention of the ghostly 'commentator Cruquianus', now exorcized,
and to his timely examination of four Horace manuscripts at the
monastery of Saint Pierre au Mont-Blandin, near Ghent, just
before its destruction in 1566. One of these was the very important,
if controversial, Blandinius vetustissimus, which assures the Bruges
professor a fractional share of that immortality which Horace so
confidently forecast for himself.

It was a singular piece of good fortune for the new university of
Leiden that it should have attracted so soon after its inauguration
one of the most brilliant Latinists of the century. Justus Lipsius
(1547–1606) was a Catholic by upbringing and associated in his
early years with the university of Louvain, but his conversion to
the Protestant faith had opened the way for his being invited to the
chair of history at Leiden, which he held from 1579 to 1591, just
as his reconversion led to his return to Louvain in 1592, where he

was Professor of History at the university and of Latin at the Collegium Trilingue. His achievement was based on a thorough knowledge of the history and antiquities of Rome, reflected in his monographs and discussions on various topics from ancient warfare to dinner parties, and a close reading of the texts, which combined to produce a commentator and critic of the first order. Though he worked with good effect on Plautus and Propertius and Seneca's *Tragedies*, his main contribution was to the prose writers of the imperial period and he is best remembered for his editions of Tacitus (1574, frequently revised) and Seneca (1605). His interest in this period led him to modify his own prose style, initially Ciceronian in character, and to develop a pointed style which had considerable influence on both Latin and vernacular prose writing. His Tacitus is his greatest achievement and a random glance at the apparatus criticus of any modern edition, where his name appears with devastating regularity, will show how he was able to transform the text, despite a basically cautious approach to emendation. As a young man he had spent two years in Italy doing the fashionable things, studying the antiquities, exploring the libraries, and meeting Muretus, but he was luckier with his monuments than his manuscripts. He failed to examine the two Medicean manuscripts of Tacitus and had to rely on copies until his last edition, which appeared posthumously in 1607, where he was able to make use of the collations published in 1600 by an important and rather neglected scholar, Curzio Pichena, gratified to discover how often his conjectures were confirmed. His Seneca is a magnificent folio volume, published, as were so many of his works, by Plantin. He relied on poor manuscript material and his Seneca generally lacked the brilliance of his Tacitus, but it remains a fitting culmination to the labours of a man who had made such a thorough study of Stoicism in preparation for the work that he had been able to revive it as a living force in the troubled days of the Netherlands. His *Manuductio ad Stoicam philosophiam* and *Physiologia Stoicorum* (1604) give the first full account of Stoicism, while his own *De constantia* (1584), which owes much to Seneca in both thought and style, went through thirty-two editions and was translated into several languages.

In the seventeenth century the Netherlands were unaffected by the general decline in the level of classical scholarship which can be discerned in other countries. It maintained its flourishing tradition well into the eighteenth century, when the influence of Bentley, working through Hemsterhuys, contributed to a brilliant revival of Greek studies which more than compensated for the dogged industry of the Elder Burman and the incompetence of Havercamp. Leiden attracted powerful scholars from abroad and Dutch scholarship was enhanced by their influence. Joseph Scaliger had succeeded in 1593 to the chair at Leiden vacated by Lipsius, and occupied it until his death. The same chair, vacant from 1609 to 1631, was then again filled from abroad, to the chagrin of Vossius, by the appointment of the erudite but somewhat dilettante Salmasius (Claude de Saumaise, 1588–1653). He is known for his polemic with Milton, owned the famous codex Salmasianus of the Latin Anthology (Paris lat. 10318), and played a part, much smaller than has at times been supposed, in making known the contents of the famous manuscript of the Greek Anthology at Heidelberg (Heidelberg gr. 23 + Paris suppl. gr. 384); but he had done his best work before moving to Leiden.

G. J. Vossius (1577–1649) helped to give Dutch scholarship a broader basis by treating a wide range of subjects in a systematic and encyclopedic way. He was Professor of Rhetoric at Leiden for ten years until 1632, when he accepted the Chair of History at the newly founded Athenaeum at Amsterdam. He also became a non-resident prebendary of Canterbury. He wrote a comprehensive treatise on rhetoric and later a more influential *Poetic institutions* (1647), two notable contributions to Latin grammar and usage, his *Aristarchus* and *De vitiis sermonis et glossematis latino-barbaris*, while his *De historicis graecis* and *De historicis latinis* (1624, 1627), dictionaries of historians from antiquity to the sixteenth century, took him into the neglected field of literary history. His *De theologia gentili*, still almost medieval in its misconceptions, can claim to be one of the earliest books on classical mythology. His interest in the theory of poetry was shared by his contemporary Daniel Heinsius (1580–1655), the devoted protégé of Scaliger, who in 1611 published an edition of Aristotle's *Poetics* and a short treatise *De tragoediae constitutione*. The latter is a succinct and authoritative restatement of the Aristotelian view of tragedy, filled out with references to Horace's *Ars poetica* and illustrations from Greek tragedy and Seneca, and it had considerable influence on neoclassical drama and the French theatre in particular. He was an elegant versifier and a stimulating teacher, but he had a very mixed success as a textual critic and his greatest gift to this branch of classics was his son.

The editing of Latin authors continued to be the central activity of Dutch scholarship and it was carried on with distinction in the latter half of the seventeenth century by two great friends, J. F. Gronovius (1611–71) and Nicolaus Heinsius (1620–81), who dominated respectively the fields of prose and poetry. Gronovius had travelled in England, France, and Italy before settling at Leiden and had taken the opportunity to examine Latin manuscripts. It was in Florence in 1640 that he came across the codex Etruscus of Seneca's *Tragedies*, neglected since the Renaissance: he immediately recognized its worth and in his edition of 1661 firmly established its authority. He did other useful work on Latin poetry, but is best known for his numerous editions of the prose writers of the imperial period, including Livy, the Elder Pliny, both Senecas, Tacitus, and Gellius, an enormous output distinguished, as was his miscellaneous *Observationes*, by wide knowledge, good judgement, and balanced scholarship. Heinsius was more gifted. He held no academic post and could give to study only such time as remained from an active career in diplomacy and public life. His diplomatic missions had given him the chance to investigate many of the manuscript collections of Europe and his great store of accurate collations stood him in good stead. But his strength lay in his fine feeling for the elegance of Latin poetry, partly derived from his own skill in writing verse, a precise understanding of the niceties of diction and convention which made him a sensitive and almost uncanny critic. His main editions were of Ovid, Vergil, Valerius Flaccus, and the later poets Claudian and Prudentius, but he left notes on others which were published after his death and he did some work on Silver Latin prose. He lives on, and not merely as a model critic: work on the identification of the many manuscripts which he collated, particularly of Ovid, is still in progress, and those editors who follow in his footsteps admit with awe that what Heinsius thought still matters.

Isaac Vossius (1618–89) is best remembered as a bibliophile, or indeed as the free-thinking Anglican convert who dared to read Ovid during divine service in Saint George's Chapel. He had come to England in 1670, was given a doctorate at Oxford and a prebend at Windsor, and became a well-known if somewhat odd figure in the London society of Charles II. His versatile forays into the by-ways of erudition have left no permanent mark, but he had a decisive hand in shaping some of our greatest manuscript collections. Like Salmasius and Heinsius and Descartes, he had been invited to Stockholm by that extraordinary monarch, queen Christina of Sweden, and enjoyed her patronage from 1649 to 1652. Apart from tutoring her in Greek, he aided her in her ambition to build up a library comparable with that of the other courts of Europe. Among the manuscripts which he acquired for her were those of his father, Gerard Vossius, and the French jurist Paul Petau, who had himself bought part of Pierre Daniel's collection. The majority of the queen's manuscripts are now in the Vatican and constitute the Reginenses. But Vossius was not slow to exploit his expertise on his own behalf and he left behind a magnificent library. The Vossiani were offered to the Bodleian Library and Bentley was energetic in trying to promote their purchase, but they went instead to Leiden, and with them the two great manuscripts of Lucretius which, had they not been removed at a critical moment from Bentley's reach, might have changed the course of textual studies.

IV. RICHARD BENTLEY (1662–1742): CLASSICAL AND THEOLOGICAL STUDIES

The next figure of commanding importance in the history of textual criticism is Richard Bentley, who was Master of Trinity College Cambridge from 1699 onwards. Much of his time in that position was taken up by the academic intrigues that were endemic in Oxford and Cambridge colleges in the seventeenth and eighteenth centuries, but his amazing self-control enabled him to avoid being entirely distracted from scholarship, and the list of his works would be more than creditable to many men who enjoyed an undisturbed career. He began to make a name for himself in 1691 by the publication of the *Epistula ad Joannem Millium*. This was a series of observations on the text of John Malalas, an obscure and mediocre Byzantine chronicler of the sixth century, then being printed for the first time. Bentley's extraordinary learning allowed him to emend the text in many places and in passing he offered explanations and emendations of other and better-known authors. It was probably these, in conjunction with the attractive vivacity of his Latin style, which made the work well known in a short time, and his fame spread to a wider public than professional scholars, for in 1697 we find him a member of a small circle that included Newton, Wren, Locke, and John Evelyn.

A few years later Bentley distinguished himself again with his work on the epistles of Phalaris. Once again it was an obscure text of no literary merit that called forth his best efforts, but, as will be seen below, he cannot be accused of confining himself to a pedantic delight in the study of trivial authors. The letters, which purport to be by the early tyrant of Acragas, are in fact a composition of the Second Sophistic age, and there is no explicit testimony to their existence earlier than the anthology of John Stobaeus in the fifth century A.D. Bentley was by no means the first person to cast doubts on their authenticity; Politian had done so already. But there were still some scholars who believed them genuine, and when a new edition appeared the argument began again. It formed a small part of the controversy between the Ancients and the Moderns, and there were some who maintained that irrespective of their dubious authenticity the letters of Phalaris were one of the best literary products of antiquity. Bentley's *Dissertation*, although its conclusions did not win universal acceptance for a long time, was a masterly proof that the letters were a miserable and worthless forgery, marred by every kind of anachronism and composed in a dialect unknown to the supposed author, and the display of learning employed in order to demonstrate the conclusion made it clear that Bentley had no serious rival as a critic or commentator anywhere in Europe.

As a textual critic Bentley is perhaps best known for the work he did on Latin authors at a later stage in his career. His zest for emendation, which is relatively easy in authors whose texts are badly preserved and who have never received the attentions of a good critic, led him astray in dealing with such authors as Horace, and he earned notoriety by the amusing change he proposed to make in the fable of the fox caught in the granary (*Epistles* 1.7.29). Insisting that a fox will not eat grain Bentley proposed to read 'field-mouse' (*nitedula* instead of *vulpecula*), quite oblivious of the consideration that the author of the fable chose the animal as the representative of cunning greed at the expense of the facts of natural history. This insistence on logic, without consideration of poetic and other forms of literary licence, mars Bentley's contributions to the emendation of leading authors that he edited, namely Horace in 1711 and Terence in 1726, and the same is even more true of his attempt to restore the works of Milton to what he supposed to be their original state before a putative interpolator imposed on the blind poet with a series of alterations of the text. On the other hand, where hard facts were at a premium, as in the astronomical poem by Manilius, Bentley's gifts were given a great opportunity, and the opinion of experts is that he made contributions of the utmost brilliance to the interpretation of the hardest passages of this very hard poem, the edition of which appeared in 1739 although the work for it had been done long before.

Bentley made many emendations in the text of other authors, of which a high proportion have been accepted or seriously considered by subsequent editors. But two of his most valuable activities were projects that never came to fruition, editions of Homer and the New Testament. As far as Homer is concerned, his most notable discovery was that the metre of many lines could be explained by postulating the existence of the letter digamma, a notion which contributed as much as any other single discovery to the understanding of this text.

Though Bentley is commonly thought of as a classical scholar pure and simple because of his striking achievements in that field, he was also of sufficient competence in theology to be appointed Regius Professor of Divinity in 1717. Three years later he published a tiny pamphlet called *Proposals for an edition of the New Testament*, in which he announced explicitly that the text would be based on the oldest manuscripts of the Greek text and of the Vulgate. Bentley knew that in English libraries he could lay hands on more than one manuscript a thousand years old, and he arranged for some collations of equally old manuscripts in foreign libraries to be made. With the aid of this information he reckoned to be able to restore the text as it was in the best copies circulating at the time of the Council of Nicaea (A.D. 325). It is interesting to note that he did not hope to establish the authors' text exactly as it stood in the autographs, and in passing it should be said that one of his most distinguished followers, Lachmann, writing in 1830, announced his intention of restoring the text as it was c. A.D. 380. Bentley had already begun collations, and although the work never made much progress he was able to state in the *Proposals* with characteristic confidence 'I find that by taking 2,000 errors out of the Pope's Vulgate, and as many out of the Protestant Pope Stephens', I can set out an edition of each in columns, without using any book under 900 years old, that shall so exactly agree, word for word, and, what at first amazed me, order for order, that no two tallies, nor two indentures, can agree better' (the reference to order is an allusion to the many manuscript variants involving the order of words). He continued, however, with the much less characteristic promise 'I alter not a letter of my own head without the authority of these old witnesses', which is far from the principle he adopted in the textual criticism of secular authors.

Since his edition was never completed, the so-called *textus receptus*, in other words the text in the form which Erasmus and Estienne had given it, continued to be printed. Only very rarely did a bold critic show independence of mind and risk the annoyance of churchmen at large by printing other readings or his own conjectures, and it was not until 1881 that the principles of recension and textual criticism were rigorously applied to the new Testament in the edition of B. F. Westcott and F. J. A. Hort.

While Bentley would therefore appear to be a century and a half ahead of his time, it is only fair to record that his *Proposals* scarcely mark any advance on the work of the cantankerous French priest Richard Simon (1638–1712). For our purpose Simon's chief work is his *Histoire critique du texte du Nouveau Testament*, published in Rotterdam in 1689 (censorship and *odium theologicum* prevented publication in his own country) and translated into English in the same year. This seems to be the first attempt to write a monograph on the transmission of an ancient text, and despite its unattractive appearance and concern with polemic it contains important exemplifications of critical principles in the chapters on the manuscripts, and it is impossible to believe that Bentley did not know and approve of them. After observing that there is nothing in the Greek tradition like the Masoretic system for ensuring textual stability he states as his policy the investigation of the Greek manuscripts, the various versions and the scholia. There follows a survey of the history of the New Testament text from the time of Valla onwards, with comments on the printed editions, chiefly concerned with their success or otherwise in providing a satisfactory apparatus of variant readings. He knows that the great age of a manuscript does not automatically guarantee the truth of its readings, and he follows previous critics in the view that the Greek text should be tested by comparison with early patristic citations, since these are earlier than the schism of the Greek and Roman churches, as a result of which, according to some critics, the Greek text had been deliberately falsified. His use of the versions is admirably shown by his discussion of John 7: 39, where he exploits the Vulgate and Syriac versions in order to arrive at a view of the passage. It leads him to the surprisingly modern and sophisticated view that obscure or ambiguous texts were explained by scholia, and when these scholia were short they easily came to be incorporated into the text. As to the use of early Greek manuscripts, much of his time is spent on readings of the codex Bezae (Cambridge, University Library, Nn. II. 41, commonly known by the symbol D), which has a text very different from most other witnesses and presents some of the most awkward problems of criticism. But he was also aware of the importance of the Vatican codex B (Vat. gr. 1209) and the Alexandrinus (British Museum, MS. Royal I D VIII).

V. THE ORIGINS OF PALAEOGRAPHY

The first steps towards establishing the study of manuscripts on a firm basis were not taken until the end of the seventeenth century. Bessarion and Politian may be credited with some palaeographical knowledge, and the former at least found it useful in refuting his opponents at the Council of Florence. While the technique of editing and the art of textual criticism made steady progress in the late Renaissance and the following century, little or no interest was taken in the date and origin of the manuscripts being used for editions of classical and Christian texts. Once again it was religious controversy that led to progress. A quarrel broke out between the Jesuits and the Benedictines; a Jesuit called Daniel van Papenbroeck (1628–1714, otherwise known as Papebroch) proved in 1675 that a charter supposedly issued by the Merovingian king Dagobert in 646 and guaranteeing certain privileges to the Benedictines was a forgery. The French Benedictine order, which had recently been revived under the title of the Congregation of Saint Maur and was devoting itself to various scholarly enterprises, treated van Papenbroek's work as a challenge. One of its most able members, Dom Jean Mabillon (1632–1707), spent several years in studying charters and manuscripts, drawing up in a systematic way for the first time a series of criteria for testing the authenticity of medieval documents. The result was *De re diplomatica* (1681), to which we owe the word diplomatic, normally used as the technical term for the study of legal and official documents. Mabillon's work dealt also to a lesser extent with manuscripts, but was restricted to Latin. It was immediately recognized as a masterpiece, even by van Papenbroeck, who had a cordial exchange of letters with Mabillon, acknowledging that his attempt to prove the spuriousness of all Merovingian charters was an excess of scepticism. On the other hand his thesis about the charter of 646 was upheld.

Among the projects of the Congregation of Saint Maur were new editions of the Greek and Latin Fathers. A large group of monks was at work at the Parisian house of Saint-Germain-des-Prés. A knowledge of medieval charters had only limited application, but Mabillon's remarks on manuscripts stimulated one of his junior colleagues to look more closely at the writing of Greek manuscripts. Dom Bernard de Montfaucon (1655–1741) had been ordained in 1676 after illness had enforced his retirement from the army. Since 1687 he had been working on the edition of the Greek Fathers, and particularly on Athanasius. In the year after the death of Mabillon he produced *Palaeographia graeca*, and in this case too the title of his book invented a word that has been standard ever since. In its own field it was in some ways a greater achievement than Mabillon's book, since it remained the best book on the subject for about two centuries and it made the first attempt to understand the history of individual letter forms, which is fundamental to palaeography. The scope of the book is rather different, since very few medieval Greek charters or other documents were available to Montfaucon (they are still mostly to be found in the archives of the monasteries of Mount Athos, which Montfaucon never visited), and in any case the authenticity of these documents raised no issues for Montfaucon and his contemporaries. So he was able to devote himself to studying the manuscripts, and his examination of examples that can be dated with little or no doubt from the subscriptions of the scribes themselves was of permanent value. His other contribution to palaeography was *Bibliotheca Coisliniana* (1715), the first systematic description of a complete collection of manuscripts, in this case the fine collection of about 400 items that had been inherited by Coislin, the prince-bishop of Metz, from Séguier, Chancellor of France under Louis XIV. Although Thomas James, in his *Ecloga Oxonio-Cantabrigiensis* of 1600, had given a very useful list of the manuscripts in the libraries of the two English universities, he did not attempt to describe the manuscripts in any detail, and can scarcely be said to have anticipated Montfaucon. It may be worth adding in passing that Montfaucon was by no means a narrow specialist, concerned with nothing but manuscripts. His other works include a dictionary of classical antiquities in ten folio volumes, to which a further five were subsequently added as a supplement. It appeared in 1719 under the title of *Antiquité expliquée*; 1,800 were sold within ten months, and a second edition of 2,200 copies was called for.

Despite the enormous bulk of their writings, Mabillon and Montfaucon found time to travel, especially in Italy, to visit other manuscript collections that could offer material for their works. In Verona, where the wealth of the Chapter Library had been known to humanists of the Renaissance, the visitor of the late seventeenth century was told that the books could no longer be found. This tantalizing state of affairs roused the curiosity of a local aristocrat and antiquarian, the marquis Scipione Maffei (1675–1755). Besides making a name for himself by writing the tragedy *Merope*, which was a landmark in the revival of the Italian theatre, he found himself involved in historical controversy in 1712, when he wrote a pamphlet against the duke Francesco Farnese. Farnese had been duped into purchasing the grand-mastership of an order of Saint John supposedly set up by the emperor Constantine. The pope and the Austrian emperor swallowed the bait as well, and Farnese was assigned for the use of his order the beautiful church of Santa Maria della Steccata in Parma. Maffei demonstrated that the order must be bogus, since all such orders were of medieval date, a fact which did not save his book from being placed on the index of prohibited literature.

Maffei let it be known to the canon librarian of the cathedral in Verona that he was very anxious to discover the fate of the manu-scripts it had once possessed. One morning in 1712 the librarian found them; they had been piled on the top of a cupboard in order to avoid damage from flooding, and then had been entirely forgot-ten. The news was taken at once to Maffei's house, and he rushed over to the cathedral in his night clothes and slippers. When he set eyes on the books, a wonderful collection mostly of very early date, he thought that he must be dreaming, but the dream proved to be a reality and it was not long before he was studying the manuscripts in his own home. The result of this study was a very important theoretical improvement in the understanding of Latin book hands. Mabillon had divided them into five independent categories, Gothic, Langobardic, Saxon, Merovingian, and Roman. But he had said nothing about any possible relation between them. Maffei hit on the fact that the explanation of the diversity of Latin scripts in the early Middle Ages must be that in late antiquity there were certain basic types, majuscule, minuscule, and cursive, and when the Roman Empire broke apart variations of these scripts arose independently. It was this flash of insight which made palaeography a subject with a clear theoretical basis. The only major advance subsequently is the one associated with the name of Ludwig Traube (1861–1907), whose great contribution was to show that manuscripts, apart from being the primary sources for the texts of classical and medieval literature, can be treated as documents illustrating the history of medieval culture. A manu-script which may be proved utterly useless as a copy of an author's text may none the less be of the greatest value in another way, since if it can be assigned with certainty to its place of origin, or better still, if the scribe of it can be identified with certainty, it will tell us something about the intellectual history of the Middle Ages.

VI. DISCOVERIES OF TEXTS SINCE THE RENAISSANCE

(a) *Palimpsests*

The recovery of an unknown ancient text produces a special sense of excitement and one which the learned world was rarely in a position to experience in the centuries following the Renaissance. But a new series of discoveries, less glamorous but by no means unrewarding, began with the realization that some classical texts still lay hidden in the lower script of palimpsests. Although such palimpsests had long existed in some of the best-known European libraries, in Paris and Rome, Milan and Verona, they were not really exploited until the nineteenth century, when the great discoveries of Mai and Niebuhr conferred an aura of romance on the humble rescript and allowed it to make a spectacular entry into the story of classical scholarship.

The first palimpsest text to be brought to the notice of the public was an early and important manuscript of the Greek Bible, the fifth-century codex Ephraemi (Paris gr. 9, lower script), dicovered by Jean Boivin, the sub-librarian of the Royal Library in Paris, in 1692. The first new classical text to emerge from a palimpsest was again Greek and likewise discovered at Paris, by J. J. Wettstein in 1715–16, though he failed to attribute it correctly: the sixth-century codex Claromontanus of the Pauline Epistles (Paris gr. 107) had at some stage been patched up by the insertion of two leaves from a fifth-century manuscript of Euripides' *Phaethon*, which was then in part reused. This manuscript, supplemented in 1907 by a papyrus of the third century B.C. (P. Berol. 9771), gives us all we have of Euripides' play. Other scholars of the eighteenth century succeeded in anticipating some of the later discoveries, but their ignorance of the chemical means later used to restore faded writing or their reluctance to employ such aids meant that they failed to realize the full significance of their finds. Scipione Maffei had discovered some of the Verona rescripts, including both the palimpsested part and the one unpalimpsested leaf of Gaius' *Institutes* (Verona XV (13)), but it was not until 1816 that the text was correctly attributed. In the middle of the century Dom Tassin, one of the Maurist authors of the *Nouveau traité de diplomatique*, a revised and improved version of Mabillon's work, suggested that one of the primary scripts of a manuscript rewritten at Corbie (Paris lat. 12161) contained a fragment of the then completely unknown writer Fronto. His anticipation of Mai's discovery is hardly more remarkable than the fact that the sixth-century fragment which he had detected was not properly appreciated until 1956, almost exactly two centuries later, when it was identified by Bernard Bischoff as a fragment of one of Fronto's epistles (*Ad Verum* 2.1). In 1772 P. J. Bruns discovered the substructure of Vat. Pal. lat. 24, a rich patchwork of ancient codices, and from it he edited a fragment of Livy Book 91. In the following year G. Migliore extracted from the lower scripts of the same manuscript two fragmentary texts which he took to be Cicero but which were in fact the remains of the *De amicitia* and *De vita patris* of Seneca, later re-edited by Niebuhr and Studemund.

So considerable steps had been taken, faltering though they were at times, to salvage palimpsested texts before the dramatic second decade of the nineteenth century. Then, owing to a combination of circumstances, there was a great leap forward. The main contributory factors were the untiring and almost ruthless energy of Angelo Mai (1782–1854) and his good fortune in being appointed successively librarian of the Ambrosian and of the Vatican, the two libraries which housed the particularly rich collection of palimpsests from Bobbio. He was also the first to make successful use of reagents, which facilitated the detection of palimpsested texts, made the writing more legible, and aided identification; a great measure of his success must be attributed to this. In the space of a few years, beginning in 1814, he published a whole series of new texts, including fragments of some of Cicero's speeches and the *scholia Bobiensia* (Ambros. S.P. 11.66, *olim* R. 57 sup.), the letters of Fronto (S.P. 9/1, 6, 11, *olim* E. 147 sup.), and, from the great Ambrosian palimpsest of Plautus (S.P. 9/13–20, *olim* G. 82 sup.), what remains of the hitherto unknown *Vidularia*. In 1819 he moved from Milan to the Vatican and towards the end of that year crowned his achievements by finding the text for which men like Roger Bacon and Petrarch had passionately searched and which even the most optimistic scholars had given up as lost for ever, the *De republica* of Cicero (Plate X). He published the *editio princeps* in 1822.

Others were quick to enter the palimpsest field, many of them more careful and better scholars than Mai, who had been hasty and uncritical and not over-scrupulous; but he had creamed the collection. One of them was the great German historian Barthold Georg Niebuhr (1776–1831), who arrived in Rome as the Prussian ambassador in 1816, having made on his way to the capital the only find to rival the more spectacular discoveries of Mai. At Verona he succeeded in reading with the use of a reagent the lower script of the Gaius palimpsest, in parts *ter scriptus*, and so made possible the eventual publication in 1820 of the first edition of the complete *Institutes*. Though his greater acumen made relations with Mai somewhat strained, he did contribute to Mai's edition of the *De republica*.

No account of the decipherment and publication of palimpsests, however brief, could omit the name of Wilhelm Studemund (1843–89), who devoted years of an active scholarly life and finally his sight to the patient and meticulous transcription of palimpsest texts. The best known are his transcripts of Gaius (1874) and the Ambrosian Plautus (1889); the latter bears the touching inscription, taken from Catullus 14, *ni te plus oculis meis amarem*. The work of such later scholars was hampered by the earlier employment of reagents, which stained and sometimes corroded the parchment, often with disastrous results. The first reagent to be known was gallic acid and this was the one used by Mai, sometimes with a heavy hand; later scholars used potassium bisulphate or the recipe of a Turin chemist Giobert, which consisted of successive applications of hydrochloric acid and potassium cyanide. They were all harmful in some degree (but infinitely more slowly than might have been expected of such deadly compounds) and had the result that manuscripts so treated are rarely susceptible to the safer and more advanced techniques possible today, especially that of ultra-violet photography, which were perfected in particular by Alban Dold at the Palimpsest Institute of the Abbey of Beuron, in south-west Germany. Consequently the editions and transcripts of the nineteenth century retain their value.

Early in the present century J. L. Heiberg found in Constantinople a palimpsest copy of Archimedes which yielded two works of note (Metochion of the Holy Sepulchre, MS. 355). One, *On floating bodies*, was known already in the Latin translation by William of Moerbeke, but the other, *Method*, was entirely new and of great significance for the history of mathematics, since it showed that Archimedes devised a procedure similar to the integral calculus. Two other fairly recently discovered palimpsests may be worth notice. One is in Jerusalem (Patriarchate MS. 36), and contains part of several Euripidean plays, written probably in the middle of the eleventh century. It is the earliest surviving book with a substantial portion of Euripides' works, but despite its date it does not improve the text much. The other is in Leiden (B.P.G. 60 A), and yields parts of some Sophoclean plays. It is the twin brother of the famous Laurentian codex, written at much the same date.

(b) *Papyri*

Until the end of the last century our knowledge of ancient texts depended almost entirely on copies made during the Middle Ages, whereas manuscripts dating back to the later centuries of the ancient world formed only a tiny proportion of the total number known. From the Renaissance onwards such discoveries as were made of new texts, or more commonly, better manuscripts of texts already known, usually consisted in the unearthing of neglected medieval manuscripts. The only significant exception was the recovery of the charred remains of papyrus rolls from the excavations of Herculaneum; these contained the abstruse writings of the Epicurean philosopher Philodemus. But a remarkable change was brought about when the archaeologists working in Egypt brought to light quantities of ancient books, often generically known as papyri even though a substantial minority of them are in fact written on parchment. The biggest finds were made at Oxyrhynchus in the Fayum by B. P. Grenfell and A. S. Hunt. For the first time scholars could consult a mass of ancient books, which are on average about a thousand years older than the textual witnesses that they had had to rely on before. Discoveries and their publication have continued ever since. Even though the papyri of literary content are outnumbered by documents of various kinds in the ratio of perhaps ten to one, there are many early manuscripts of known texts and a significant number which add to the stock of extant Greek literature. Not all these texts are complete or of the highest quality as literature, but among them are such important books as Aristotle's *Athenian constitution* (P. Lit. Lond. 108), the *Odes* of Bacchylides (P. Lit. Lond. 46), and substantial fragments of Sophocles' satyr-play the *Ichneutae* (P. Oxy. 1174), Euripides' *Hypsipyle* (P. Oxy. 852), Menander's *Dyscolus* virtually complete (P. Bodmer 4), *Epitrepontes* and *Samia* (P. Cairo inv. 43227), and *Sicyonius* (P. Sorbonne 72, 2272, 2273). The authors best represented, however, are those of the schoolroom, and against the handful of really interesting papyri must be set the hundreds of Homer that have survived. Other fascinating discoveries include many important biblical papyri, the most notable being the scrap measuring two and a half by three and a half inches from the Gospel of Saint John that can be dated to the early second century (P. Rylands 457), and the unsavoury documents of ancient racial prejudice known as the *Acts of the pagan martyrs*.

Nearly all the papyri come from Egypt, though there are a few from Dura-Europos on the Euphrates and Nessana in the Negev desert. The vast majority of the Egyptian papyri have been found in a district some way from the capital. The number and variety of the literary finds are rather surprising, since one might not expect to find such evidence of wide reading in a country district. The survival of the papyri was made possible because in the villages refuse, including waste paper, was thrown on to huge rubbish dumps, which rose high enough to make their contents immune from any effects of moisture from the annual inundation or irrigation; with the dryness of the climate the papyri often avoided further damage. A few of them come not directly from the rubbish dumps, but from tombs, like Timotheus' *Persae* (P. Berol. 9875), or from cartonnage, the casing in which mummies were enclosed. This substance was made from layers of papyrus stuck together rather like papier mâché, and unwanted papyri were evidently bought up in quantity to make it. Many of these were damaged books no longer of any use to their owners, and we owe our knowledge of Menander's *Sicyonius* and a hundred lines of Euripides' *Antiope* (P. Lit. Lond. 70) to this fortunate habit of the Egyptian undertakers.

(c) *Other manuscript discoveries*

Since the end of the Renaissance there has been no great stream of discoveries of unknown texts except among the papyri. But for a long time research in manuscript collections was far from systematic, with the result that from time to time it was possible for a fortunate scholar to uncover an ancient text of more than trivial importance, and it is worth recording here the most notable examples.

In 1743 Prosper Petronius, working in the Vatican library, lit upon a unique codex of Theophrastus' *Characters*, which is still the only known witness to the text of nos. 29 and 30 (Vat. gr. 110), and thereby completed the text of this attractive and influential little book. Later in the century a much greater discovery was made in Venice. In 1788 Villoison published the marginal scholia to the *Iliad* found in the codex now known as Venetus A (Marc. gr. 454). They contained a vast fund of new information about the Alexandrian critics of Homer, and this information stimulated F. A. Wolf to write *Prolegomena ad Homerum*, one of the most important books in the whole history of classical scholarship (1795). While Robert Wood, in his *Essay on the original genius of Homer*, had already seen in 1767 that the usual picture of a literate Homer writing down his poems could not be a complete explanation of the present form of the Homeric poems, it was left to Wolf to demonstrate, with the help of the newly found scholia, that the textual problems in Homer were not of the same type as in other authors, and that an explanation for this state of affairs could be provided on the assumption that the text of Homer was not written down until the time of Solon or Pisistratus. Wolf's book marked the beginning of serious discussion of what is traditionally called the Homeric Question.

From the history of Greek scholarship in the nineteenth century it is worth mentioning the discovery of the verse fables by Babrius, found by M. Mynas in a manuscript on Mount Athos that is now in the British Museum (Add. 22087). Sometimes, however, hopes of discovery were deceived. In 1823 the famous Italian poet Giacomo Leopardi, who was also the best Italian classical scholar of his day, found in the Vatican what seemed to be a new piece of classical Attic prose. But the absence of a title in the manuscript and the lack of adequate works of reference conspired to delude his hopes; the text turned out to be a relatively common work of patristic literature written in the best imitation Attic, i.e. Atticist Greek; it was the address of Saint Basil to his nephews on the merits of reading classical literature.

In Latin there is less to record, since most of the great finds of modern times have been made in palimpsests as described above. A significant exception is Petronius' *Cena Trimalchionis*, which, although known for a fleeting moment in the Renaissance, was first printed at Padua in 1664. In 1899 an Oxford undergraduate examining an eleventh-century copy of Juvenal in Beneventan script (Canonici class. lat. 41) found that in satire VI it contained thirty-four additional verses, and though the text is extremely corrupt the balance of opinion now favours the view that they are genuine. And it may be just worth mentioning that an unknown letter of Saint Cyprian came to light not long ago in Holkham lat. 121, and though the letter itself is of no consequence its source at one remove may be a manuscript from Monte Cassino, a possibility which once again shows how important that one religious community was for the transmission of texts. Another recent find is the collection of Latin poems known as the Epigrammata Bobiensia, because the manuscript is a Renaissance apograph of a Bobbio codex (Vat. lat. 2836). Some of the authors represented are Augustan or of the first century, while nos. 2–9 are by Naucellius, a prominent literary figure of the end of the fourth century.

(d) *Epigraphic texts*
While books in their various forms have provided the main vehicle for the transmission of the vast legacy which the Greeks and Romans committed to writing, the large and increasing collections of inscriptions are themselves monuments to the enormous number of texts which have reached us inscribed on bronze,

stone, and the like. The valuable contribution which epigraphy and numismatics can make to the illumination of ancient life was appreciated as early as the Renaissance and is in general beyond the scope of this book, but some of the texts which have been preserved by these means should be mentioned, for they are in some cases extensive, of major importance, or useful in that they augment or complement or correct the purely literary tradition.

An obvious example is the *Res gestae Divi Augusti*, a document of crucial importance for the study of Augustus and the early principate. This is the record of his achievements which Augustus left behind him with the express wish that it be engraved on bronze and placed in front of his Mausoleum. Both the original manuscript, which he deposited with the Vestal Virgins, and the original inscription have perished without trace, but copies were set up in the provinces, sometimes with a Greek paraphrase for the benefit of the local population, and the bulk of the text can be recovered from three fragments discovered in Galatia, the largest one, which has been known since 1555, on the walls of a mosque in Ankara. Though it is a rather special and grandiose example, the *Res gestae* belong to the wider tradition of the *laudatio*, or obituary notice, and for obvious reasons this genre is particularly well represented by epigraphic texts, ranging from grandiloquent orations to humble and touching records of personal affection. A famous one is the so-called *Laudatio Turiae* (*ILS* 8393), the funeral oration of a Roman matron of the late first century B.C., a substantial piece of writing. But even stones, as the ancients never tire of telling us, have their own mortality, and much of this stout matron's virtuous career would have been lost to fame had not the pen finally come to the aid of the chisel; for of the six fragments which have turned up in various parts of Rome since the seventeenth century, three have disappeared and now survive only in manuscript copies, which we mainly owe to the Jesuit scholar Jacques Sirmond and J. M. Suárez, the librarian of Cardinal Barberini (Paris lat. 9696, Vat. lat. 9140).

The bronze tablet at Lyons (*ILS* 212) which preserves the speech which the emperor Claudius made to the Senate in A.D. 48 advocating the admission of Gallic nobles is of literary as well as historical interest. For this text, discovered in 1524 and first printed by Lipsius, gives us the unique opportunity of being able to compare Claudius' actual speech, rambling and pedantic, with the taut literary adaptation which Tacitus provides (*Ann.* 11.24). The monument of Antiochus I of Commagene, which was discovered towards the end of the last century on the lofty slopes of an extinct volcano at Nemrud Dagh in eastern Turkey, has won itself an important place in literary history. Its florid text, as elevated in style as in its place of rest, has filled a crucial gap in our knowledge by providing the only example of the ornate 'Asianic' style of oratory which featured so largely in the rhetorical polemic of Cicero's day.

We owe a remarkable philosophical text to the philanthropic urge of Diogenes of Oenoanda, who was so impressed with the efficacy of the Epicurean philosophy that about the year A.D. 200 he had his exposition of the doctrines of Epicurus set up in the market-place of Oenoanda, in Lycia, for the benefit of his fellow citizens. Fragments of this unique text, forty metres long, which number almost a hundred and are still being discovered, lie scattered among the ruins of Oenoanda and provide editors with a jig-saw puzzle of truly monumental proportions. A remarkable feature of the inscription is the way in which its disposition in columns and concern for the convenience of the reader reproduce on an enlarged scale the conventions of the contemporary book. The earliest known example of a Christian hymn in the form characteristic of Byzantium comes from an equally un source: it is an inscription from a catacomb at Kertsc Crimea which can be dated to the year 491. It is part of th for baptism.

More informal contributions to our store of ancient l have been made by those who write on walls. These inclu inconsiderable body of original poetry, but often graffiti quotations from works which have already reached us orthodox channels. These are occasionally of interest t critics as evidence of indirect tradition. In this way a po the second century B.C. (Berlin ostrakon 4758) can find its the apparatus criticus of Euripides (*Hipp.* 616ff.) and the f with which *arma virumque cano* is scrawled on the Pompeii helps to prove that this, and not *ille ego qui quond* true beginning of the *Aeneid*. A notable example is a distich of Propertius (3.16.13f.) found on a basilica at Pompeii. While the manuscript tradition is united in reading

> Quisquis amator erit, *Scythicis* licet *ambulat* oris,
> nemo *deo* ut *noceat* barbarus esse volet

the inscription (*CIL* iv. 1950) offers

> Quisquis amator erit, *Scythiae* licet *ambulet* oris,
> nemo *adeo* ut *feriat* barbarus esse volet

and is right in at least two of the four places in which it differs from the direct tradition.

VII. EPILOGUE

It is now time to draw together the threads of this rather selective account of the progress of scholarship between the end of the Renaissance and the beginning of what may be properly regarded as modern scholarship in the nineteenth century. Our purpose throughout this book has been to show how the existence of literary texts has been dependent both on material factors, such as the form of the book and the supply of writing materials, and on intellectual movements and changes in educational practice, and how the survival and quality of literary studies have been assisted by the gradual evolution of methods of scholarship. Once printing was established as the means of disseminating texts (and there was some resistance on the part of men such as Federigo duke of Urbino who declared that no printed book should ever form part of his library), one part of our story is at an end, since the survival of texts was assured. But it seemed worth while to pursue the history of scholarly method further, at least as far as the study of texts is concerned, and to highlight some of the developments which permitted a better and fuller use of the legacy of the past. The generally poor quality of the early printed editions shows how much remained still to be done for the theory of textual criticism, how the process of sifting manuscript resources had only just begun, how editing was hampered by a failure to appreciate the complexity of the study of classical civilization as a whole (*Altertumswissenschaft*). There were still obstacles to intellectual freedom, and much had still to be done to establish classical studies as an independent discipline; as late as 1777 F. A. Wolf had to put up a fight to be matriculated at Göttingen, not in the Faculty of Theology, but as a *studiosus philologiae*. To this end we have given a simple account of some of the critical phases in the history of scholarship and their leading figures; although the emphasis is on the editing of texts, we have given some idea of the achievements of these pioneers outside the literary field proper in order to suggest some of the ways in which textual studies have interacted with other parts of the discipline to the benefit of all.

In the present century the study of manuscripts has made a dramatic advance through the provision of moderately priced photography, so that scholars can now obey literally the advice of the Vice-Chancellor of Cambridge University who said, 'Let Mr. Porson collect his manuscripts at home.' With the modern conveniences of microfilm and quick and comfortable travel, it is easy to forget the difficulties which our predecessors faced. The systematic description of manuscripts has also become a branch of scholarship, and the official catalogues of the leading libraries are a source of primary material for the modern scholar that his predecessors generally lacked. Another very important contribution to scholarship has been the decreasing mobility of the manuscript collections. Most manuscripts of Latin and Greek texts are now owned by institutions that may be confidently expected to retain them in perpetuity. But at least up to the end of the last century manuscripts were almost as likely to travel as they had been in the unsettled days of the Middle Ages and Renaissance. In our account we have occasionally alluded to these movements, and some others are explained in the notes to the index of manuscripts. They form a minor but not entirely insignificant facet of the history of culture and scholarship. The accumulation of the primary source material needed to provide the best attainable texts of the ancient authors is now well advanced and parallel to this process is the accumulation and evaluation of the objects, whether inscriptions, documentary papyri, or works of art, unearthed by the archaeologists and serving to throw light on the history, art, and material culture of the ancient world. The interaction between these various fields, the promotion of which was one of the great contributions of German scholarship in the nineteenth century, is the basis of the modern concept of the study of antiquity as a whole and promises a rich and continuing supply of themes as long as classical studies retain their place as an intellectual discipline.

6. TEXTUAL CRITICISM

I. INTRODUCTORY

The foregoing chapters have attempted to give some idea of the ways in which the Greek and Latin classics were handed down through the Middle Ages to the modern world, and to outline some of the more important historical and cultural phenomena which affected the transmission of these texts. The business of textual criticism is in a sense to reverse this process, to follow back the threads of transmission and try to restore the texts as closely as possible to the form which they originally had.

Since no autograph manuscripts of the classical authors survive, we are dependent for our knowledge of what they wrote on manuscripts (and sometimes printed editions) which lie at an unknown number of removes from the originals. These manuscripts vary in their trustworthiness as witnesses to the original texts; all of them have suffered to some degree in the process of transmission, whether from physical damage, from the fallibility of scribes, or from the effects of deliberate interpolation. Any attempt to restore the original text will obviously involve the use of a difficult and complex process, and this process falls into two stages.

The first stage is recension (*recensio*). The object of recension is to reconstruct from the evidence of the surviving manuscripts the earliest recoverable form of the text which lies behind them. Unless the manuscript tradition depends on a single witness, it is necessary (1) to establish the relationships of the surviving manuscripts to each other, (2) to eliminate from consideration those which are derived exclusively from other existing manuscripts and therefore have no independent value (*eliminatio codicum descriptorum*), and (3) to use the established relationship of those which remain (ideally expressed in the form of a *stemma codicum* or family tree) to reconstruct the lost manuscript or manuscripts from which the surviving witnesses descend. When the most primitive state of the text which is recoverable from the manuscripts has been reconstructed, the second main stage of the critical process begins. The transmitted text must be examined and the critic must decide whether it is authentic or not (*examinatio*); if not, his duty is to emend it (*emendatio*), if this can be done with a reasonable degree of certainty, or to isolate the corruption. The task is often complicated by the presence of two or more variant readings, each with a claim to be the transmitted text. The whole of this second stage is sometimes still given its traditional, though misleading, name—*emendatio*.

II. THE DEVELOPMENT OF THE THEORY OF TEXTUAL CRITICISM

The invention of the printed book, and in particular the appearance of the first printed editions of Cicero in 1465, meant that for the first time the future of classical texts was secure. But it had one unfortunate side-effect: the early printers, by the act of putting a text into print, tended to give that form of the text an authority and a permanence which in fact it rarely deserved. The *editio princeps* of a classical author was usually little more than a transcript of whatever humanist manuscript the printer chose to use as his copy, a replica in print of the current manuscript article. The repetition of this text, with only minor changes, from one edition to another soon led to the establishment of a vulgate text; and while there was nothing to prevent one from improving the vulgate by piecemeal emendation, the forces of inertia and conservatism made it difficult to discard it in favour of a radically new text.

Emendation continued to do its work, as it had done in every age; and although the critic's basic equipment—common sense and judgement and taste—were natural rather than acquired gifts, the development of some of the more useful principles of emendation and the rapid progress of classical scholarship in general enabled him to make a sharper attack on textual corruption. But emendation cannot be used to the greatest effect until recension has done its work, and scholars right up to the nineteenth century were in most cases obliged to exercise their critical gifts, which were often of the highest order, not upon the transmitted text as it is properly understood, but upon an entrenched vulgate. This they tried to emend, not only by conjecture, but also by the use of such manuscripts as they could find. There were some very remarkable discoveries, but more often the new manuscripts were no better than those on which the vulgate had originally been based. For in the days when libraries were largely uncatalogued, travel difficult, photography unknown, and palaeography in its infancy, this was a hit or miss process. Worse still, when good manuscripts were found, their usefulness was limited because their aid was sought only when the vulgate was manifestly unsatisfactory.

The first step towards more scientific textual criticism was the rejection of the vulgate text as the basis for discussion and with it the illogical conservatism which regarded the use of manuscripts as a departure from the tradition rather than a return to it. In this, as in other departments of criticism, the first impulse came from New Testament studies, where the problem was more obvious: the wealth of manuscript evidence left little scope for conjectural emendation and the task of choosing the truth from the variant readings was hampered by the almost divine sanction which was attributed to the *textus receptus*. In 1721 Richard Bentley, known to classical students more for the untrammelled boldness of his conjectures, projected an edition of the New Testament based exclusively on the ancient manuscripts and the Latin Vulgate. The conservative attitude of theologians prevented the project from being realized until Lachmann's edition of 1831, but the attack on the *textus receptus* was renewed a few years later by J. J. Wettstein, and in the course of a few decades the same radical approach had percolated to the field of classical philology, where Johann August Ernesti and Friedrich August Wolf restated in the firmest terms the need to make the manuscripts the basis of any critical text.

The relentless accumulation of manuscript evidence through the seventeenth and eighteenth centuries accentuated the need to work out a valid method of sorting the grain from the chaff. Many scholars contributed to the elaboration of the stemmatic theory of recension; this had been formulated in all its essentials by the middle of the nineteenth century and, although his own contribution is much slighter than had been supposed, it is still associated with the name of Karl Lachmann. For all its limitations, it revolutionized the editing of classical texts. There were glimmerings of the genealogical method as early as the humanist age. Politian, as we have seen, saw that manuscripts which derived from an older surviving exemplar were of no value, and effectively applied the principle of *eliminatio* to some of the manuscripts of Cicero's

Letters. In 1508 Erasmus postulated a single archetype from which all the surviving manuscripts of a text descended; and although his notion of an archetype was less precisely defined than ours, he was able to explain how easy it is for all the manuscripts to be wrong. The notion of the medieval archetype seems to have been first entertained by Scaliger, who in 1582 tried to prove from the nature of the corruptions in the manuscripts of Catullus that they were derived from a common parent written in pre-caroline minuscule. Scaliger was right. The Catullus archetype must have been an ‹Irish MS. (written on the continent)›

Scaliger was far ahead of his time. No great advance was made towards a theory of recension until the eighteenth century and then the impetus came, once again, from New Testament scholarship. In the thirties J. A. Bengel perceived that the manuscripts of the New Testament could be classified on a genealogical basis. More than that, he spoke of the day when they would be reduced to what he called a *tabula genealogica*, and saw clearly the potentialities of his *tabula* as an instrument for the critical evaluation of variants. His genealogical approach was adopted with varying success by classical scholars of the late eighteenth and early nineteenth centuries, and brought to fruition in a brilliant burst of scholarship in the 1830's. In 1830 Lachmann, preparing the way for his edition of the New Testament, gave a more detailed formulation of the rules which Bengel had expounded for the choice of variants; in 1831 Carl Zumpt, in his edition of the *Verrines*, drew what appears to have been the first *stemma codicum* which the world had seen, and gave it the name which has won general acceptance; the great editions published by Ritschl and Madvig over the next few years refined and established the method. The most famous of all stemmata, that of Lucretius, was constructed by Jacob Bernays in 1847, and it remained for Lachmann, in his edition of 1850, to apply his rules for the mechanical application of the stemma and to give a classic demonstration of the validity of the hypothetical archetype by reconstructing its physical form and telling his astounded contemporaries how many pages it had, and how many lines to the page.

III. THE STEMMATIC THEORY OF RECENSION

The classic statement of the theory of stemmatics is that of Paul Maas. In practice the stemmatic theory has serious limitations, as Maas was well aware, since its successful operation depends on the tradition being 'closed'; these limitations are discussed below. The essentials of the theory are as follows:

See p.193

(*a*) *The construction of a stemma.* Of fundamental importance in stemmatics are the errors which scribes make in copying manuscripts; for these errors provide the most valid means of working

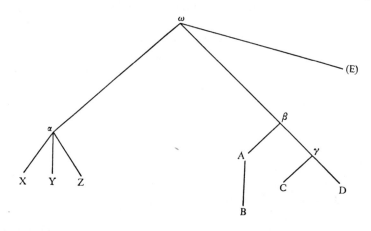

out the relationships of the manuscripts. Special attention is paid to errors of omission and transposition. For stemmatic purposes these errors can be divided into (*a*) those which show that two manuscripts are more closely related to each other than to a third manuscript (conjunctive errors), and (*b*) those which show that one manuscript is independent of another because the second contains an error or errors from which the first is free (separative errors). Care is taken to see that these errors are 'significant', i.e. not such mistakes as two scribes are likely to make independently, or such as a scribe could easily remove by conjecture. On this basis the interrelationships of the various manuscripts and manuscript groups are worked out step by step until, ideally, a stemma of the whole manuscript tradition has been reconstructed.

(*b*) *The application of the stemma.* The mechanical application of the stemma to reconstruct the reading of the archetype is best illustrated by a hypothetical stemma, as shown above. ω represents the archetype; the intermediate lost manuscripts from which the survivors descend are indicated, as is customary, by Greek letters. The extant manuscripts are eight in number (ABCDEXYZ); for the sake of the illustration, it is assumed that E is a fragment available only for a small part of the text.

1. If B is derived exclusively from A, it will differ from A only in being more corrupt. The first stage, therefore, is to eliminate B.
2. The text of γ can be inferred from the agreement of CD or from the agreement of one of them with an outside witness (A or α).
3. The text of β can be inferred from the agreement of ACD or of AC against D or of AD against C or from the agreement of either A or γ with α.
4. The text of α can be inferred from the agreement of XYZ or of any two of them against the third or from the agreement of one of them (provided the other two disagree with each other) with β.
5. When the texts of the two hyparchetypes (α and β) have been reconstructed, the readings peculiar to the individual witnesses ACDXYZ can be eliminated from consideration (*eliminatio lectionum singularium*).
6. If α and β agree, they may be assumed to give the text of the archetype (ω). If they disagree, either of the two readings may be the text of the archetype. It is the task of *examinatio* to decide which of these two variants is authentic.
7. If at some point in the text we have the evidence of a third independent branch of the tradition (E), then the principle of two against one will operate and the text of the archetype will only be in doubt if all three disagree or if two of them are likely to have fallen into the same error independently.

The application of these principles is sometimes a simple matter. The relationship of the manuscripts may be made clear by one or more glaring faults. Particularly striking examples are afforded when a book has suffered physical damage which is reflected in the copies made from it, whether directly or at more than one remove.

The first scholar to use this form of argument was Politian, in his discussion of Cicero's letters, but the utility of the method remained unappreciated by other scholars for a very long time. In the tradition of Lucretius important inferences were made by Lachmann from physical damage that must have taken place in a lost book. It is evident that at one time there was a copy with twenty-six lines to the page. Some leaves of this fell out and were incorrectly replaced, thus causing serious dislocation of the text in some surviving copies. A more far-reaching conclusion can be drawn from the manuscripts of Arrian's work on Alexander's expedition to India. There are about forty of these, and all have a substantial gap in the text at one point. As a rule this lacuna occurs in the middle of a page and the scribes have copied the text without noticing its existence. But in one manuscript (Vienna, hist. gr. 4) it occurs between the end of one verso page and the beginning of the next recto page, and further investigation shows that there is one leaf missing at this point. All other manuscripts evidently descend from this book after it had suffered mutilation In this case, therefore, the archetype is preserved. Another preserved archetype is the Oxford Epictetus (Auct. T. 4.13, Plate V); here a smudge of dirt has obscured a few words of text, which are missing from all other copies.

But such methods of inference cannot be applied in the majority of traditions. In general it may be possible to establish a few facts about the relation of the later manuscripts of an author from minor textual omissions, but for the main outline of the stemma it will be necessary to classify and arrange the manuscripts by reference to a series of significant errors.

IV. LIMITATIONS OF THE STEMMATIC METHOD

The apparent simplicity and finality of the stemmatic method as outlined above is deceptive. Though it often answers the editor's problem of selecting the right manuscript or manuscripts for his text, there are circumstances in which its utility is restricted. The theory assumes that readings and errors are transmitted 'vertically' from one manuscript to another, that is to say directly from one book to the copies that are made from it. But it has become increasingly evident as scholars have pursued more detailed in-

quiries that the tradition of many texts, including some of the
highest interest and importance, cannot be elucidated by the
application of the stemmatic theory. In these cases the manuscripts
cannot be assigned to classes or families characterized by groups
of errors because there has been contamination or 'horizontal'
transmission. Readers in ancient and medieval times did not necessarily copy a text from a single exemplar; as their texts were
often corrupt, they compared different copies, entering in their
own manuscripts good readings or interesting variants as they
found them. In some traditions—an example is Xenophon's
Cyropaedia—the process was undertaken so often that the tradition
has been hopelessly contaminated by the date of the earliest extant
manuscripts. Scholarly activity naturally led to this result, and in
many manuscripts the process can be observed, since variant readings are quoted in the margins or between the lines. It follows
that the texts most commonly read, including those prescribed for
the school syllabus, are most likely to show serious contamination.
But the tradition of more recondite authors is not exempt from
this feature, as the example of Diogenes Laertius shows.

A further difficulty in the theory lies in its assumption that all
surviving manuscripts can be traced back to a single archetype,
datable to the late ancient world or early middle ages. In practice
thorough examination of manuscript variants has often suggested
that this is not so, but that the tradition is 'open'. It may be
possible to account for almost all the variants on the assumption
of a stemma leading back to an archetype, but some readings
refuse to fit the pattern, and if they are apparently ancient readings
(a question of judgement arises here), another source has to be
postulated for them. This source may be one or more manuscripts
representing a different branch of tradition, which ceased to be
copied as a whole but was consulted by scholars for some readings;
these readings became variants within the main tradition, whether
incorporated into its 'archetype' or at a later stage (see pp. 53–54).
The plays of Aeschylus and Euripides which came to be prescribed
for school reading probably went through this process.

Occasionally the facts are even more puzzling. In 1899 an
Oxford manuscript of Juvenal (Canonici class. lat. 41) was found
to contain thirty-four lines in satire VI that appear nowhere else,

except that two of them are quoted by a scholiast. The passage has been regarded as spurious, but it is probable that interpolators would have lacked the powers or the motive to insert it; on the other hand if it is genuine, how are we to explain its survival in an otherwise mediocre copy and in only one of some five hundred manuscripts? A similar puzzle arises in the letters of Saint Cyprian. Recent work revealed the existence in a single copy (Holkham lat. 121) of a letter hitherto unknown and yet beyond all reasonable doubt genuine. Here too the tradition is copious and contaminated. No satisfactory explanation has yet been devised, but one feature is common to both cases: the Juvenal manuscript was written at Monte Cassino, while the Cyprian manuscript is very closely related textually to another book from the same monastery, which possessed so many unique texts.

One final complicating factor is the possibility that the ancient author himself made corrections or alterations to his original text after publication. Sometimes these would be extensive enough to justify us in speaking of a second edition. Under the conditions of the ancient publishing trade a second edition was much less likely to supplant its predecessor than in the modern world. Cicero's attempts to revise or eliminate errors in his works did not affect all the copies from which our archetypes descended (see p. 23). The two versions circulated side by side throughout antiquity with horizontal transmission taking place. Where a stemma cannot now be worked out this may be the reason. One or two examples can also be given in which authors' revisions are visible but have not affected the stemma so seriously. At Martial 10.48.23 it looks as if the name of a charioteer stood in the first edition of the book, but for the second edition, prepared after his death, the no longer topical name was replaced by a word indicating the team to which he belonged. A possible explanation of the incoherence of a scene in Aristophanes' *Frogs* (1437–53) is that some of the lines come from a revised version of the play. Similarly Galen (15.624) attributes the confused state of one of Hippocrates' works to marginal additions and revisions by the author.

V. AGE AND MERIT IN INDIVIDUAL MANUSCRIPTS

The notion of a best manuscript is sometimes found in discussions of textual problems, and there was a time when an appeal to the authority of the *codex optimus* was the normal or the most common way of discriminating between variant readings. But this procedure has rightly been criticized, since it was frequently used without regard to stemmatic method, and in any case it involves an error of logic. One cannot hope to identify the best manuscript of an author until one has considered the readings of all the significant manuscripts at all the points where they diverge; significant manuscripts are those extant or reconstructed books which the stemmatic method, in so far as it is applicable, proves to be of use for constituting the text.

When this has been done it is possible to draw up lists of passages in which the various manuscripts individually offer the reading which is best for literary, linguistic, historical or other reasons, and the manuscript which has the largest tally of such readings to its credit has a right to be termed the best manuscript. The utility of the term is often limited, particularly if there are one or more other manuscripts which have an almost equal number of good readings. In textual traditions where the term may reasonably be employed its use is confined to passages where there is a variety of readings among the manuscripts and there are no grounds for preferring one of these readings to another. Since the best manuscript is that which gives the greatest number of correct readings in passages where there are rational grounds for decision, it is more likely than the others to give the correct reading in passages where no such grounds exist. It is this argument from probability which justifies the appeal to the best manuscript in the circumstances indicated.

Here it is necessary to mention a variation of the faulty argument referred to above. This consists of an appeal to the authority of the oldest manuscript, usually implying that the antiquity of a manuscript guarantees its merit; conversely manuscripts of the Renaissance are dismissed as unimportant merely because of their date. There is of course no doubt that in general a certain relation exists between the age of a manuscript and the quality of the text

that it offers, since it is a reasonable supposition that a late manuscript is separated from the original text by a larger number of
intervening transcripts, each of which is to be presumed more
corrupt than its predecessors. In many textual traditions investigation will show that the oldest manuscript is the best. But there are
some exceptions which serve to show that the generalization must
not be carelessly applied. A general argument may be drawn from
the evidence of the papyri; though these are many centuries earlier
than the medieval manuscripts, they do not as a whole offer
markedly superior texts, and one of the most famous and important,
containing Menander's *Dyscolus* (P. Bodmer 4), is astonishingly
corrupt. Medieval manuscripts yield a number of instructive
examples. Several manuscripts of Greek authors which date from
the Palaeologan Renaissance (see p. 68) are of much the same value
to editors as the more famous manuscripts of the same texts that
are as much as three centuries earlier (e.g. Vienna supp. gr. 39 of
Plato, Paris gr. 1734 of Thucydides, Laur. 32.16 and Wolfenbüttel
Aug. 2996 of Apollonius Rhodius). A more extreme example is
the sixteenth-century Vienna manuscript of the minor works of
Xenophon (phil. gr. 37), which is clearly at least equal in importance
to the other witnesses, being the unique source of many correct
readings. The same phenomenon can be observed among Latin
texts. Here one outstanding example is the Renaissance copy of
Lucretius *l* 31 (Laur. 35.31), the unique source of many correct
readings, all apparently the work of a clever humanist. A slightly
different case is the notorious Leiden Tacitus (B.P.L. 16 B) which
offers a few good and many specious readings. As a result of the
discovery of these late manuscripts that are of interest to the editor
and textual critic a principle has been established, which is usually
expressed by the formula *recentiores, non deteriores*. Printed editions
too can have a similar importance; indeed some of the letters of
Cicero and Pliny are preserved only in print.

  These late manuscripts pose a problem for the editor; what is
the source of their good readings? In some cases it is clear beyond
any reasonable doubt that they represent a branch of tradition that
cannot otherwise be traced; the good readings are such that they
could not possibly have been invented by a scholar of the Middle
Ages or Renaissance. The copy of Xenophon mentioned above is a

case in point: it supplies words missing from the text, in some places where the gap had not even been demonstrated beforehand. But often it is not so easy to come to a conclusion; Renaissance scholars were capable of acute conjectures, at least in Latin texts, and it is often impossible to say with any certainty whether or not a particular conjecture would have been within their powers. The same considerations apply to Byzantine scholars, but recent investigations have tended to suggest that their ability in conjectural restoration of a text was rather more limited than has sometimes been assumed in the past.

VI. INDIRECT TRADITION

Apart from ancient and medieval books (and occasionally translations into other languages) the editor and critic sometimes has another source of help in the secondary or indirect tradition. This is the term applied to quotations of one author by another, who may on occasion preserve the correct reading when all the ordinary manuscripts of the author quoted are in error. There are one or two famous examples of this phenomenon. In Vergil's fourth *Eclogue* (62–3) the manuscripts give

> cui non risere parentes,
> nec deus hunc mensa, dea nec dignata cubili est.

But Quintilian (9.3.8; though his MSS. too are corrupt) evidently read *qui* at the beginning of the relative clause, which led to the necessary conjecture:

> qui non risere parenti.

And it is not only ancient authors whose quotations hint at the right text. Some good manuscripts that are now lost survived until late in the Middle Ages and were consulted by scholars of that period. A striking case has already been mentioned in another connection: Eustathius quotes Sophocles *Antigone* 1165–8 complete, whereas all manuscripts of Sophocles omit 1167 (see p. 61). It is interesting to note that this same quotation of the passage occurs in the late ancient author Athenaeus (c. A.D. 200) (280c, 547c); Athenaeus was known to Eustathius and could have been his source for the quotation, but the manner in which he introduces the lines rather suggests the opposite. Another medieval source of correct quotations is the *Suda* lexicon (see p. 58).

It should not be supposed, however, that secondary tradition is an unfailing source of correct readings. Ancient and medieval writers were even less inclined than their modern counterparts to follow the advice of Dr. Routh and verify their references. Quotations were usually made from memory and there were good reasons for this practice. Ancient books of the roll type did not facilitate quick reference, and when the codex form was adopted readers still could not count regularly on such aids as page numbering, chapter division, and line numbering, which are part of every modern text. These considerations must be borne in mind in cases where the manuscripts of an author offer one reading, and there is an acceptable but not absolutely certain alternative in the secondary tradition. Either reading may be what the author wrote. But in the majority of cases editors will probably be right to follow the primary tradition; the divergent reading of a quotation is likely to be right only if the purpose of the quotation was to emphasize or illustrate the divergent words or phrases, whereas if the divergence is incidental to the quotation it is probably due merely to lapse of memory.

The difficulty of enunciating firm principles may be shown by a few examples:

(*a*) Aristophanes, *Acharnians* 23: the MSS. have οὐδ' οἱ πρυτάνεις ἥκουσιν, ἀλλ' ἀωρίαν|ἥκοντες κτλ. The *Suda* lexicon quotes the line with the reading ἀωρίᾳ, in the article which is devoted to this word. In principle there is some reason to hope that this might be an accurate quotation, but the dative is less idiomatic than the accusative in this type of adverb and for that reason is rejected by the editors.

(*b*) In the same play at 391–2 the MSS. offer:

εἶτ' ἐξάνοιγε μηχανὰς τὰς Cιcύφου,
ὡc cκῆψιν ἀγὼν οὗτοc οὐκ εἰcδέξεται.

These lines are quoted in the *Suda* article on Sisyphus, but with two differences: in the first line εἶτα is replaced by ἀλλὰ, and in the second εἰcδέξεται by προcδέξεται. Since the quotation is not intended to illustrate either of these words, there is not much reason to trust its accuracy. Yet on other grounds ἀλλὰ may well be right, and προσδέξεται is as likely to be right as the rather puzzling εἰσδέξεται.

(c) Lucretius 3.72 is given in the MSS. as:

> crudeles gaudent in tristi funere fratres.

Macrobius quotes the line in a passage where he is comparing Lucretius and Vergil (6.2.15), and gives the variant *fratris*. This is clearly superior, but the quotation was not made to illustrate any single word in the line.

(d) In the same book at 676 the MSS. have:

> non, ut opinor, id a leto iam longius errat.

The grammarian Charisius (p. 265, Barwick[2]) quotes the line with the variant *longiter*, and says that it was his purpose to exemplify the form by this quotation. For this reason editors usually, though not invariably, adopt the reading.

VII. SOME OTHER BASIC PRINCIPLES

The critic may find himself in a position where he has to choose between two readings that are equally acceptable in respect of the sense and the linguistic usage of his author, but feels that it is unsafe or impossible to argue from the merits of the manuscripts. In such situations there are two maxims that are frequently invoked, *utrum in alterum abiturum erat* and *difficilior lectio potior*. The first of these is a general principle, and the basis of it can be easily explained. Given the tendency of scribes to corrupt texts it is reasonable to suppose that careless copying or a desire to simplify a difficult passage encouraged certain types of alteration. The maxim *difficilior lectio potior* is strictly speaking no more than an application of this general principle. It embodies the notion that if one of the available readings is more difficult to understand, it is more likely to be the correct reading. The justification of this view is that scribes tended, sometimes consciously, sometimes inadvertently, to remove from the text the rare or archaic linguistic forms that were no longer readily understood, or to simplify a complex process of thought that they could not master. Alternative terms to describe these activities are interpolation and trivialization. Many references to the maxim *difficilior lectio* will be found in commentaries, and there is no doubt of its value. But it has probably been overworked, for there is a temptation to use it as a defence of anomalous syntax or usage; in such cases the more difficult reading may be more difficult because it is wrong.

VIII. CORRUPTIONS

In order to extract the truth from the manuscript evidence the scholar needs to have some acquaintance with the various types of corruption that occur. The primary cause of these was the inability of scribes to make an accurate copy of the text that lay before them. The majority of errors were involuntary, but at the end of this section we refer to an important category of which this is not true. Although it seems surprising at first sight that the concentration of the scribes should have failed so often, anyone may soon verify for himself by experiment how difficult it is to make an entirely accurate copy of even a short text. If due allowance is made for the length of time during which copying by hand was the only means of transmission, it is perhaps remarkable that more ancient texts were not reduced to an unintelligible condition. Many different pitfalls lay in the path of the scribe if he once allowed his attention to wander. Some of the possibilities are indicated in the list below. They are to be regarded as a small selection divided into rough and ready categories. It must be emphasized that scribal errors have never been made the subject of a statistical study, and so it is not possible to establish with any degree of precision the relative frequency of the various types. Another important warning is that the assignment of an error to a class is not always as easy as it might appear. Cases arise in which it is possible to attribute a mistake to one of several causes or to a combination of them. A third consideration to be borne in mind is that not all causes of error were active at all times. A case in point is that the use of some abbreviations which were liable to cause difficulty to scribes can be set within chronological or geographical limits.

A. Mistakes induced by any feature of ancient or medieval handwriting may be taken as a first class of error. It might be supposed that this class is much more numerous than any other, but the careful study of an apparatus criticus casts doubt on this view. Typical causes of error within this class are (i) the lack of division between words in many manuscripts, (ii) a close similarity of certain letters in a script which results in their being confused, (iii) the misreading of an abbreviation; apart from ordinary signs representing syllables or common short words there was a special method of abbreviation for certain key terms of Christian theology; these are known as *nomina sacra*, and are frequent in both Greek *[in Irish]* and Latin texts. In both languages abbreviations are so numerous and complex that the study of them forms a subject in itself (Plate V). (iv) Since numerals were represented by letters in both languages they were often incorrectly transmitted, a fact which is a serious hindrance to students of economic and military history. Perhaps one may add here (v) the confusion of two words of similar shape or spelling even when there is no immediate cause of confusion in the forms of the individual letters.

(i) 1. Petronius, *Cena* 43.
   Quid habet quod queratur? *abbas secrevit.*
   ab asse crevit   Scheffer. (Cf. also G (i).)

   2. Aeschylus, *Eumenides* 224.
   δίκας δ' ἐπ' ἄλλας τῶνδ' ἐποπτεύσει θεά.
   δὲ *Παλλὰς* Sophianus.

(ii) The following letters are commonly confused in Latin scripts:
   In capitals: ILT EF PT PF PC BR HN OQ COG and such combinations as M NI.
   In uncials: ILT FPR CEOGU and such combinations as U CI. Characteristic of uncial, as opposed to capital, is the confusion of EU (now rounded in form) with the group COG.
   In minuscule: *au oe cld nu sf ct* and various letters or combinations of letters made of one or more downstrokes (minims), e.g. the letters in *minimum*. The confusion of *pr rn ns* is characteristic of insular script; in Visigothic the peculiar *t*, and in Beneventan both the *t* and the *a* cause difficulty (see Plate XIV).

1. Seneca, *Epist.* 81.25.

Manifestum etiam *contuenti* discrimen est.

coniventi codd. recc.

2. Lucretius ii.497.

quare non est ut credere possis
esse infinitis distantia *femina* formis.

semina O[c]

Groups of letters liable to be confused with each other in Greek
script are:

In uncials: *ΑΔΛ ΕΘΟC ICK ΓΤ.*

In minuscule: *βϰμ μν α ευ.*

1. Aristotle, *Poetics* 1462 b 3.

λέγω δ' οἷον εἴ τις τὸν Οἰδίπουν θείη τὸν Cοφοκλέους ἐν
ἔπεϲιν ὅϲοιϲ ἢ ἰδίαϲ.

ἢ ἰδίαϲ MSS.: ἡ 'Ιλιάϲ a humanist corrector (confusion of Δ and
Λ).

2. Julian, *Epist.* 23.

δόϲ μοί τι κατὰ τοὺϲ μελικτὰϲ εἰπεῖν ῥήτοραϲ.

μελικτὰϲ Aldine edition: μελητὰϲ VL: μελίτουϲ N: βελτίϲτουϲ
Jackson. β and μ are very similar in minuscule; here the corruption is aided by the uncial confusion of IC and K.

(iii) 1. Curtius Rufus, vi.11.30.

Intellego non prodesse mihi quod praesentis sceleris *expressum.*

expers sum   codd. recc.

The symbols for *per pro prae* (usually p p p̄) are one example of
the many *notae* which are open to misinterpretation.

2. Seneca, *epist.* 76.7.

Quare *autem* unum sit bonum quod honestum dicam.

autem] ħ V: hoc M: om. P: in b. The manuscript V has preserved
the insular abbreviation for *autem* which has been the undoing of
MPb.

3. Scholium on Aristophanes, *Knights* 505.

τοῦτο πρῶτον τὸ δρᾶμα δι' αὐτοῦ καθῆκε, τὰ δ' ἄλλα δι'
ἑτέρων ἄπων.

ἀπων V: προσώπων ΕΓΘΜ. In V's exemplar there were two compendia, α (= προ) and ∼ (= ω).

4. Aeschylus, *Eumenides* 567–8.

†ἤ τ᾽ οὖν διάτορος† Τυρσηνικὴ
σάλπιγξ βροτείου πνεύματος πληρουμένη.

οὖν seems to conceal the *nomen sacrum* οὐρανόν (ουνον), which has been further corrupted.

(iv) 1. Cicero, *Att.* i.13.6.

Messalla consul Autronianam domum emit HS CXXXIIII. Other MSS. offer CXXXVII or CXXXIII or XXXIII. HS 13,400,000 is an astronomical price for a house. A plausible emendation is |XXXIII| = 3,300,000 (Constans), but certainty is in the circumstances unattainable.

2. Thucydides, iii.50.1.

τοὺς δ᾽ ἄλλους ἄνδρας οὓς ὁ Πάχης ἀπέπεμψεν ὡς αἰτιωτάτους ὄντας τῆς ἀποστάσεως Κλέωνος γνώμῃ διέφθειραν οἱ Ἀθηναῖοι (ἦσαν δὲ ὀλίγῳ πλείους χιλίων), καὶ Μυτιληναίων τείχη καθεῖλον καὶ ναῦς παρέλαβον.

χιλίων MSS.; but this number seems too large for the ringleaders of a revolt in Mytilene, and τριάκοντα has been suggested instead. χιλίων would be written ͵Α (in uncials), τριάκοντα Λ' (cf. A (ii) above).

(v) 1. Seneca, *Epist.* 102.22.

Tempus hic ubi inveni relinquam, ipse me diis reddam.
corpus   Pincianus.

2. Pindar, *Pythians* 4.90.

καὶ μὰν Τιτυὸν βέλος Ἀρτέμιδος θήρευσε κραιπνόν.

κραιπνόν correctly most MSS.: τερπνόν C.

B. Other corruptions arose out of changes in spelling and pronunciation. For instance in late Latin the sounds *ae* and *e* became identical, while *b* came to be sounded as a fricative and was confused with *v*. In Greek several vowels and dipthongs were reduced to the single sound of iota, as in the modern language. Error resulting from this change is known as iotacism. Beta became fricative as in modern Greek, and so did upsilon in diphthongs.

The distinction between omicron and omega was lost. The diphthong alpha-iota became identical with epsilon. Orthographical errors are of extreme frequency, but the majority of them are of no consequence for the establishment of the text and are not recorded in the apparatus.

1. Quintilian 6.3.93 (quoting Domitius Afer).

   Pane et aqua *bibo.*

   vivo   Haupt. (Most MSS. inevitably have *panem et aquam bibo.*)

2. Diogenes Laertius, *Vitae philosophorum* ix.10.

   (ἔφη) ἡμέραν τε καὶ νύκτα γίνεςθαι καὶ μῆνας καὶ ὥρας αἰτίους καὶ ἐνιαυτοὺς ὑετούς τε καὶ πνεύματα καὶ τὰ τούτοις ὅμοια κατὰ τὰς διαφόρους ἀναθυμιάσεις.

   αἰτίους BP: ἐτείους F.

C. Omissions constitute a third large class of error. Here again subdivision is possible. Sometimes we find (i) omission of not more than a few letters; if this occurs in a passage where the scribe has written a sequence of letters only once when they should be repeated, the term haplography is used. This mistake arises if the scribe is moving ahead too quickly with his task, and an extended form of the same mistake is sometimes referred to as (ii) *saut du même au même.* Here the scribe, finding the same word twice within a short space, copies the text as far as its first occurrence; then looking back at the exemplar to see what he must copy next he inadvertently fixes his eye on the second occurrence of the word and proceeds from that point. As a result the intervening words are omitted from his copy. Mistakes are also caused if two words in close proximity have the same beginning or ending; the technical terms for these are homoearcton and homoeoteleuton. The same fault of eyesight was responsible for similar errors which it is convenient to list as a slightly different category, (iii) the omission of a whole line of text. This error is often found in the manuscripts of the poets, and its informative value to scholars trying to establish a stemma is obvious. Examples can be found in prose texts also. It should be added, however, that a large number of omissions occur for no apparent reason except the carelessness of the scribe; this is particularly common with small words.

(i) 1. Lucretius, iii.135.

Quidquid ⟨id⟩ est, habeant; tu cetera percipe dicta.

id suppl. *l* 31.

2. Aristophanes, *Acharnians* 221–2.

μὴ γὰρ ἐγχάνοι ποτὲ
μηδέ περ γέροντας ὄντας ἐκφυγὼν Ἀχαρνέας.

ὄντας is omitted by most MSS., but is clearly necessary.

(ii) 1. Cicero, *Att.* vii.9.4.

Praeteriit tempus non legis *sed libidinis tuae, fac tamen legis*; ut succedatur decernitur; impedis et ais 'habe meam rationem'.

sed . . . legis C: om. Ω.

2. Aristophanes, *Acharnians* 692–5.

ταῦτα πῶς εἰκότα, γέροντ' ἀπο (λέ-
cαι πολιὸν ἄνδρα περὶ κλεψύδραν,
πολλὰ δὴ ξυμπονήcαντα καὶ θερμὸν ἀπο-)
μορξάμενον ἀνδρικὸν ἱδρῶτα δὴ καὶ πολύν.

The MS. A omitted the section enclosed in parentheses.

(iii) 1. Seneca, *de ira* 3.7.1.

tenerique iam visa cum ipso cadunt ita fit ut frequenter inrita sit eius voluntas

These words form one line of the Ambrosianus: they are omitted by a number of the later manuscripts, which in this way reveal their derivation from A.

2. The omission of Sophocles *Antigone* 1167 in all the manuscripts has been mentioned already in connection with Eustathius and the importance of the secondary tradition. A stemma of the Sophocles manuscripts is facilitated by the omission of *Oedipus Tyrannus* 800 from the famous Medicean MS. (Laur. 32.9) and its twin brother, the Leiden palimpsest (Leiden, B.P.G. 60 A).

D. A fourth group may be termed errors of addition. The simplest of these are no more than the repetition of a few letters or syllables, which is referred to as (i) dittography. More substantial is the addition to the text of explanatory or illustrative material. The most frequent type in this category is (ii) the addition of a gloss. Most Greek manuscripts have a number of brief interlinear notes explaining rare or difficult words. These glosses were easily added to the text in the course of transcription. In poetry a simple addition of this kind may be immediately obvious because of the violence it does to the metre; but sometimes the word used as a gloss had the same metrical value as the word in the text and replaced it without impairing the metre, and examples of this process are not easy to detect. The detection of (iii) glosses in a prose text is often of the greatest difficulty. Many passages contain explanatory phrases which are not strictly required for the sense but offer no offence to grammar or syntax. These phrases present problems which may remain insoluble. Two texts which scholars have recently discussed in detail in the light of these questions are Petronius' *Satyricon* and Cicero's *Tusculan Disputations*. (iv) A rare but interesting corruption is the addition to a text of a parallel passage originally written in the margin of a book by a learned reader. This may happen in verse or prose. Cases are known from Greek tragedy, and Galen (17(1).634) noticed that it had happened in one of the Hippocratic treatises.

(i) 1. Seneca, *Epist.* 78.14.

> Quod acerbum fuit ferre, *retulisse* iucundum est.

> tulisse   Bartsch.

2. Song quoted by Athenaeus 694d.

> γελάceιac, ὦ Πᾶν, ἐπ' ἐμαῖc
> εὐφροcύναιc ταῖcδ' ἀοιδαῖc, ἀοιδέ, κεχαρημένοc.

> εὐφροcύναιc A: εὔφροcι Wilamowitz
> ἀοιδαῖc ἀοιδέ A: ἀοιδαῖc Hermann

(ii) 1. Aeschylus, *Agamemnon* 549.

> καὶ πῶc; ἀπόντων τυράννων ἔτρειc τινάc;

> So F: Triclinius restored the metre by substituting κοιράνων for τυράννων.

2. Plautus, *Truculentus* 278.

> Cumque ea noctem in stramentis pernoctare perpetim [totam].

The Ambrosian palimpsest gives both the gloss (*totam*) and the word which has been glossed (*perpetim*); the Palatine family give the correct text.

(iii) 1. Seneca, *Epist.* 42.4.

Eadem velle [subaudi si] cognosces: da posse quantum volunt.

The words *subaudi si* ('understand *si*'), corrupted to *subaudis* and worse in the MSS., were put in the margin to help the reader with the paratactic conditional sentence and then incorporated into the text.

2. Diogenes Laertius, *Vitae philosophorum* v.76.

λέγεται δ' ἀποβαλόντα αὐτὸν τὰς ὄψεις ἐν 'Αλεξανδρείᾳ κομίcαcθαι αὖθιc παρὰ τοῦ Cαράπιδοc.

ἀποβαλόντα BP: τυφλωθέντα F, which is a gloss.

(iv) 1. In the margin of the Medicean Aeschylus at *Persae* 253 the line Sophocles *Antigone* 277 has been written. In copies of M this line has been incorporated into the Aeschylean text.

2. Vergil, *Aen.* ii.76.

ille haec deposita tandem formidine fatur.

Sinon is about to explain himself. This line is omitted in P and added at the foot of the page in M by a later hand. It is a doublet of iii.612, where it is in place, and has been added here because of the similarity between this passage and that in book iii.

E. Errors of transposition are another well-known class. (i) Transposition of letters is common. (ii) In poetry verses are often copied in the wrong order. (iii) In all kinds of text word order is subject to fluctuation. The number of variants of this kind is large enough to suggest that inferences about the word order of Latin and Greek prose should be made with great care.

In Greek texts of both verse and prose there were special causes leading to corruption of word order during the middle ages. (iv) One of these affected the text of tragedy. A common metre in Byzantium was a twelve-syllable line rather like the classical iambic line but subject to different rules, the most important being that the penultimate syllable must carry an accent (at this date a stress accent). As a result some scribes altered, probably unconsciously, lines of tragedy in order to make them conform to this rule. The process is known as *vitium Byzantinum.* (v) In Byzantine prose there was a rule affecting the order of words; in general it was necessary that the last two stressed syllables of a sentence should be separated by two or four unstressed syllables (in special cases by none or six). The effect of this is sometimes visible in manuscripts of classical prose writers.

(i) 1. Lucretius, iii.170.

> Si minus offendit vitam vis horrida *leti*
> ossibus ac nervis disclusis intus adacta . . .

> teli Marullus.

2. Aeschylus, *Agamemnon* 1205.

> βαρύνεται γὰρ πᾶς τις εὖ πράccων πλέον.

So Triclinius' autograph; but F has the correct reading ἁβρύνεται.

(ii) This extremely frequent error may be found exemplified in the text of any author.

(iii) 1. Seneca, *Epist.* 117.24.

> Deos vitam et salutem roga.

So Bθ. Other manuscripts read *vitam roga et salutem* or *salutem et vitam roga*. Manuscript authority and rhythm (double cretic) decide.

2. Pindar, *Nemeans* 7.37.

> ἵκοντο δ᾽ εἰc Ἐφύραν πλαγχθέντεc.

So the MSS.; Boeckh restored metrical responsion by reading πλαγχθέντεc δ᾽ εἰc Ἐφύραν ἵκοντο.

(iv) Aeschylus, *Agamemnon* 1106.

> ἐκεῖνα δ᾽ ἔγνων. πᾶca γὰρ πόλιc βοᾷ.

So M, correctly, but F and Triclinius have βοᾷ πόλιc.

(v) Plutarch, *de curiositate* 13 (522).

> ὁμοίωc οὐδ᾽ Ἀλέξανδροc εἰc ὄψιν ἦλθε τῆc Δαρείου γυναικὸc
> ἐκπρεπεcτάτηc εἶναι λεγομένηc.

So most MSS.: the Λ-family alter to give a Byzantine clausula: τῇ Δαρείου γυναικὶ εὐπρεπεcτάτῃ λεγομένῃ τυγχάνειν.

F. In a sixth group one may include errors induced by the context. (i) The inflection of a word may be wrongly assimilated to that of an adjacent word. (ii) The scribes allowed themselves to be influenced by words or phrases that they had recently copied or were just about to copy.

(i) 1. Catullus, xxxiv. 17.

> tu cursu dea *menstrua*/metiens iter annum
> rustica agricolae bonis/tecta frugibus exples.

menstruo   B. Guarinus.

2. Euripides, *Helen* 1243.

> κενοῖϲι θάπτειν ἐν πέπλοιϲ ὑφάϲμαϲιν.

πέπλοιϲ L: πέπλων Scaliger.

(ii) 1. Seneca, *Epist.* 114.9.

> Ubi luxuriam late felicitas fudit, *luxus* primum corporum esse diligentior incipit.

cultus   Muretus.

2. Euripides, *Rhesus* 776–7.

> ἤπυϲα δ' αὐτοῖϲ μὴ πελάζεϲθαι ϲτρατῷ,
> κλῶπαϲ δοκήϲαϲ ϲυμμάχων πλάθειν τινάϲ.

At 776 V has πλάθειν for πελάζεϲθαι by anticipation.

G. Some mistakes betray the influence of Christian thought. As all readers in the Middle Ages were more or less devout Christians it would be very surprising if they had succeeded in copying thousands of manuscripts without committing mistakes of this kind.

1. Petronius, *Cena* 58.

> Sathana tibi irata sit curabo.

Sathana H: Athana   Heinsius. (Cf. also D (i). As the previous sentence ends with *habeas*, this could be a case of dittography.)

2. Aristophanes, *Knights* 1302–4.

> οὐδὲ πυνθάνεϲθε ταῦτ', ὦ παρθένοι, τὰν τῇ πόλει;
> φαϲὶν αἰτεῖϲθαί τιν' ἡμῶν ἑκατὸν εἰϲ Καρχηδόνα,
> ἄνδρα μοχθηρὸν πολίτην, ὀξίνην Ὑπέρβολον.

Καρχηδόνα RVΦ: Χαλκηδόνα Γ² and a scholiast.

Carthage is more likely to be right than Chalcedon, a city of little importance in the Athenian empire but well known to every orthodox Greek in the Middle Ages because of the famous church council held there in A.D. 451.

H. There is also a class of mistakes that derives from the deliberate activity of the scribe. As has been seen above, ancient and medieval readers tried to emend passages that they found difficult or corrupt, and their attempts were sometimes misguided or ill-informed. A typical example is that Triclinius mutilated some Euripidean lyrics because he knew that metrical responsion ought to be restored, but was not well enough acquainted with the language of classical poetry to make the correct emendations. Such faulty corrections are often referred to as interpolations, though the term is not quite apt. Deliberate alteration on a larger scale can be seen in attempts to bowdlerize. This process was not as widespread, however, as might be expected. It seems that schoolmasters of late antiquity and the Middle Ages were not as anxious to suppress obscene or otherwise embarrassing passages as more recent editors have been. The excisions found in some modern school editions of Aristophanes do not seem to be anticipated in medieval manuscripts. But there are manuscripts of Herodotus which omit the account of sacred prostitution at 1.199, and there is a family of Martial manuscripts in which some of the blatant obscenities have been replaced by less offensive words. Another type of interpolation, for which scribes were not responsible, is that made by the actors in the texts of Greek tragedy (see pp. 14–15).

1. Juvenal, viii.148.
   Ipse rotam adstringit sufflamine mulio consul.

In some manuscripts this has been, not unnaturally, corrupted to *sufflamine multo*. At this point deliberate interpolation steps in and restores the metre: other manuscripts read *multo sufflamine*.

2. Tacitus, *Annals* 13.39.1.
   Et Corbulo, ne irritum bellum traheretur utque Armenios ad sua defendenda cogeret, exscindere parat castella.

So M. In the Leiden Tacitus interpolation has run riot, producing specious nonsense:

> Et Corbulone irritum bellum trahente ut Armenios ad sua defendenda cogeret exinde repetit castella.

3. Euripides, *Electra* 435–7.

> ἵν' ὁ φιλάδελφος ἔπαλλε δελ-
> φὶς πρώραις κυανεμβόλοι-
> σιν εἰλισσόμενος.

So the first hand in L; Triclinius used his knowledge of strophic responsion and the quotation of this passage at Aristophanes *Frogs* 1314ff. to make one good alteration (φίλαυλος), but then committed a bad error (κυανεμβόλοις εἰειλισσόμενος).

4. Plutarch, *de curiositate* 7 (518).

> φέρε γὰρ ʽHρόφιλον ἢ ʼEρασίστρατον ἢ τὸν ʼAσκληπιὸν αὐτόν, ὅτ'
> ἦν ἄνθρωπος, ἔχοντα τὰ φάρμακα καὶ τὰ ὄργανα, κατ' οἰκίαν παριστ-
> άμενον ἀνακρίνειν, μή τις ἔχει σύριγγα περὶ δακτύλιον ἢ γυνὴ
> κάρκινον ἐν ὑστέρᾳ.

The *Δ*-family here alter δακτύλιον to δάκτυλον and delete ἐν ὑστέρᾳ.

The diversity of the causes of error brings with it a consequence of great importance to the critic. He cannot approach his task in the belief that any one class of error is predominant. In practice many scholars appear to have assumed that errors arising from palaeographical causes are the commonest; certainly this is the conclusion to be drawn from the numerous and often elaborate palaeographical justifications that accompany proposed emendations. The only safe method is to follow the rule explicitly enunciated by Haupt, and reiterated by Housman: 'the prime requisite of a good emendation is that it should start from the thought; it is only afterwards that other considerations, such as those of metre, or possibilities, such as the interchange of letters, are taken into account. . . . If the sense requires it I am prepared to write *Constantinopolitanus* where the MSS. have the monosyllabic interjection *o*.' In order to drive home their lesson Haupt and Housman quoted an extreme example. In fact when a critic has decided on grounds of sense how a corrupt passage might be restored, he considers various possibilities in the light of the types of error listed above, and is influenced by them in his choice between different restorations of the text. When really serious corruption has taken place it may well be necessary to print between obeli (††) the text of the archetype and indicate in the apparatus the best conjectures; in such passages certainty is unattainable even with the critic's sharpest weapons.

IX. CONCLUSION

In this account of the function and methodology of textual criticism we have described some of the principles and criteria which have been most commonly and most usefully employed by those who attempt to reverse the process of transmission and restore the words of the ancients as closely as possible to their original form. In order to reduce to the length of a chapter a subject which normally fills a book and even then is no more than a guide, we have confined our account to basic and well-tried techniques. This will inevitably give the impression that textual criticism is a tidier and more cut-and-dried process than it proves to be in practice. While general principles are undoubtedly of great use, specific problems have an unfortunate habit of being *sui generis*, and similarly it is rare to find two manuscript traditions which respond to exactly the same treatment.

One omission is obvious. While giving space to the limitations of the stemmatic theory, we have not explored the complicated and sometimes controversial methods which have been devised to deal with contaminated traditions. The more open a tradition is, the less fruitful the stemmatic approach is likely to be, and other methods must be tried. These range from empirical, common-sense approaches which accept the necessities of an imperfect world, to elaborate statistical techniques which aim at more objective results. In some cases it is possible to adopt a flexible modification of the genealogical method. The manuscripts are classified as far as is possible into broad groups and the editor chooses his readings eclectically, persuaded more by their intrinsic merit than by considerations of affiliation and authority and taking care to balance these factors to suit the nature of the tradition. But if contamination has gone so far that, in the words of Housman, 'the true line of division is between the variants themselves, not between the manuscripts which offer them,' various approaches may be adopted which all tend to concentrate on the variants themselves rather than on the manuscripts which carry them. These may involve sophisticated mathematical techniques, which are particularly tempting at the present time, now that the development of computers and allied mechanical and electronic devices have made them more feasible. We have given no account of distributional and statistical methods, which would be a study in itself, nor of their automatization, which is at an experimental stage and already generating a body of literature not readily intelligible to most students of the humanities. It is not yet clear whether elaborate mechanized techniques, however valid as a theoretical study, will yield practical results which justify the labour and expense entailed or are markedly superior to those produced by traditional means and 'nature's own computer, located between the ears of the investigator.' In any case their future seems to lie more in the biblical and patristic fields and with vernacular languages than with classical texts, where the material is more easily controlled and not usually unmanageable by traditional methods accompanied by the limited use of scientific aids. Ultimately, the basic essential equipment is taste, judgement, common sense, and the capacity to distinguish what is right from what is wrong in a given context; and these remain the perquisite of human wit. But where the tradition is large and complex, computers can be usefully employed in building up a provisional picture of the interrelationship of texts. Outside the field of recension, machines can be used, if great caution is observed, in stylistic studies, and they have already proved their worth for information retrieval and in the making of concordances; and the fruits of these activities have a real bearing on the editing of texts.

NOTES

I

The growth of the book trade in classical Athens is described by E. G. Turner, *Athenian books in the fifth and fourth centuries* B.C., London 1952. The exact period at which it becomes legitimate to speak of a trade is uncertain, but it is worth emphasizing that Xenophon, *Anabasis* 7.5.14, speaks of books (βίβλοι γεγραμμέναι) as forming part of the cargo of ships wrecked off Salmydessos on the north coast of Thrace; the inference seems inescapable that books were an article exported (from Athens?) to the cities of the Euxine coast as early as the year 399 B.C. If this is so, our inability to extract more precise information from the passages of Eupolis and Plato cited in the text is of little importance.

On the form and appearance of books in Greece from the classical period until the end of the Roman Empire the reader should consult E. G. Turner, *Greek papyri*, Oxford 1968, and his companion volume, *Greek manuscripts of the ancient world*, Oxford 1971, which offers a well-chosen album of plates with commentary.

The supply of papyrus was precarious in the classical period, if we can trust the evidence of the letter from Speusippus to Philip of Macedon (p. 50 in L. Köhler's ed., *Philologus Supplement-Band* 20, Leipzig 1928); the text indicates a shortage of papyrus c. 342 B.C. owing to the Persian occupation of Egypt. But though this letter is now regarded as genuine by many authorities, its status is not entirely above suspicion.

The use and gradual refinement of punctuation are still debated; apart from Turner's book cited above see R. Pfeiffer, *History of classical scholarship*, Oxford 1968, pp. 178–81; his view is essentially shared by R. Renehan, *Greek textual criticism, a reader*, Cambridge, Mass., 1969, pp. 76–7; but see the reservations expressed by N. G. Wilson, *CR* 19 (1969), 371, and note that the passages cited by Renehan do not all prove as much as he thinks. Perhaps the best view is that of H.-I. Marrou, *Histoire de l'éducation dans l'antiquité*, Paris 1965[6], p. 602 n. 30, that books with full punctuation never passed into general use but were confined to teachers and pupils (though Marrou appears to be making this suggestion about books in the Roman period). An interesting example of a conjecture that finds part of its justification in the absence of punctuation from ancient texts is given by H. Lloyd-Jones, *The justice of Zeus*, Berkeley 1971, p. 193 n. 23.

II

The standard work on Alexandrian scholarship is R. Pfeiffer, *History of classical scholarship: from the beginnings to the end of the Hellenistic age*, Oxford 1968, reviewed by N. G. Wilson, *CR* 19 (1969), 366–72. This is the first volume of a work that will replace Sir J. E. Sandys, *History of classical scholarship*, vols. 1–3, Cambridge 1903–8 (some volumes subsequently revised), reprinted 1958, which is still of considerable use as a reference book. On the Museum and library see P. M. Fraser, *Ptolemaic Alexandria*, Oxford 1972, chapter 6.

The monograph of Lloyd W. Daly, *Contributions to a history of alphabetization in antiquity and the Middle Ages*, Brussels 1967 (= Collection Latomus, vol. 90), is of interest; since it is there shown that Zenodotus and Callimachus used the principle of alphabetical order in some of their writings, one may conjecture that the same principle was employed to some extent in the arrangement of the library in the Museum.

The so-called 'wild' papyri of Homer were re-edited by S. R. West, *The Ptolemaic papyri of Homer*, Cologne 1967.

G. P. Goold, *TAPA* 91 (1960), 272–91, expressed extreme scepticism about the idea that copies of Homer in the old Athenian alphabet found their way into the Alexandrian library; but his conclusion if right does not necessarily apply to all other authors.

The primary sources about the use of the critical signs are corrupt and confused, but the facts were reasonably well sorted out by A. Gudeman in *RE*, s.v. Kritische Zeichen.

The statistics of Aristarchan emendations generally adopted in the text of Homer come from T. W. Allen's edition of the *Iliad*, Oxford 1931, vol. 1, pp. 199–200; on pp. 201–2 similar calculations are given for readings ascribed to Zenodotus and Aristophanes. Subsequent publications will not have altered the figures substantially.

On Aristarchus' principle of interpreting Homer from Homer see N. G. Wilson, *CR* 21 (1971), 172.

The actors' interpolations are discussed by D. L. Page, *Actors' interpolations in Greek tragedy*, Oxford 1934; on the passage mentioned in the text see A. M. Dale, *Wiener Studien*, 69 (1956), 103–4 (= *Collected papers*, Cambridge 1969, pp. 126–7), and M. D. Reeve, *GRBS* 13 (1972), 263–4.

H

III

For the archaeological discoveries at Pergamon see E. Akurgal, *Ancient civilisations and ruins of Turkey*, Istanbul 1970², pp. 79–80.

Didymus' commentary on Demosthenes was edited by H. Diels and W. Schubart, Berlin 1904; for the exact definition of the type of literature to which it belongs see F. Leo's review in *NGG* (1904), 254–61 (= *Kleine Schriften*, vol. 2, pp. 387–94), but note also the reservations of S. West, *CQ* N.S. 20 (1970), 288–96.

IV

The Latin book does not receive very much specific treatment in the standard works on books in the ancient world, since it is similar in all essentials to its Greek counterpart, and the bulk of our evidence comes from Egypt, where there was comparatively little interest in Latin. The degree of punctuation enjoyed by a reader in the classical period is as much in dispute for Latin books as for Greek, owing to the extremely limited palaeographical evidence and the ambiguous nature of statements casually made by our literary authorities. The view that Latin books, down to the end of the first century A.D., were provided with more in the way of punctuation and aids to the reader than was customary in antiquity, was propounded by R. P. Oliver, *TAPA* 82 (1951), 241–2, and has been further developed by E. O. Wingo, *Latin punctuation in the classical age*, The Hague etc., 1972. For a more sceptical view, see G. B. Townend, *CQ* N.S. 19 (1969), 330–3. In general, see R. W. Müller, *Rhetorische und syntaktische Interpunktion*, Diss. Tübingen 1964. The Roman contribution to the development of the codex is discussed in VIII.

Pending the appearance of R. Pfeiffer's second volume in the *History of classical scholarship*, there is no full and comprehensive account of scholarship during the Roman period. The primary material can be found in G. Funaioli, *Grammaticae Romanae fragmenta*, vol. 1, Leipzig 1907, and its continuation, A. Mazzarino, *Grammaticae Romanae fragmenta aetatis Caesareae*, vol. 1, Turin 1955. Brief accounts are given by F. Leo, *Geschichte der römischen Literatur*, vol. 1, Berlin 1913, pp. 355–68; G. Funaioli, *Studi di letteratura antica*, vol. 1, Bologna 1946, pp. 206ff. Much can also be derived from Leo's *Plautinische Forschungen*, Berlin 1912², and G. Pasquali's *Storia della tradizione e critica del testo*, Florence 1952².

The history of the text of Plautus in antiquity throws some much needed light on the beginnings of Roman scholarship, murky though that story sometimes is: cf. W. M. Lindsay, *The ancient editions of Plautus*, Oxford 1904; F. Leo, *Plautinische Forschungen*, pp. 1–62; Pasquali, *Storia della tradizione*, pp. 331–54. The date of the alternative ending of the *Andria* of Terence has been most recently discussed by O. Skutsch, *RhM* 100 (1957), 53–68. There is a good account of the history of the text of the dramatic poets in ancient times, with particular reference to Ennius, in H. D. Jocelyn, *The Tragedies of Ennius*, Cambridge 1967, pp. 47–57.

On the *Anecdoton Parisinum* and the critical activity of Aelius Stilo and his circle see S. F. Bonner, *Hermes*, 88 (1960), 354–60.

Attention focuses on Atticus because of the wealth of information in Cicero's letters, in contrast to our ignorance of the book trade at Rome before his time. His precise role has been discussed by R. Sommer, *Hermes*, 61 (1926), 389–422; see further R. Feger, *RE*, Suppl. 8 (1956), 517–20, K. Büchner in *Geschichte der Textüberlieferung der antiken und mittelalterlichen Literatur*, vol. 1, Zürich 1961, p. 328. The evidence is conveniently presented (and interpreted with predictable bias) by J. Carcopino, *Les Secrets de la correspondence de Cicéron*, vol. 2, Paris 1947, pp. 305–29. The nature of 'publication' in antiquity and the concept of 'edition', so different from ours, have been discussed by H.-I. Marrou, *VCh* 3 (1949), 208–24; H. L. M. Van der Valk, *VCh* 11 (1957), 1–10; B. A. van Groningen, *Mnem.* Ser. 4, 16 (1963), 1–17.

For a general account of the book trade in Rome, see T. Kleberg, *Buchhandel und Verlagswesen in der Antike*, Darmstadt 1967, pp. 22–68.

v

The gnomic quality of *Aen.* 10.284 and the danger of drawing any general conclusion from it have been pointed out to us by Sir Roger Mynors.

The importance of Probus in the history of scholarship is highly controversial. The exaggerated esteem of earlier scholars, such as Leo (*Plautinische Forschungen*, pp. 23ff.), has given way to a much more cautious assessment: cf. Pasquali, *Storia della tradizione*, pp. 339ff.; N. Scivoletto, *GIF* 12 (1959), 97–124; K. Buchner in *Geschichte der Textüberlieferung*, pp. 335–9. See also R. Hanslik in *RE*, 8 A.1 (1955), 195–212, and, for a detailed consideration of the crucial chapter in Suetonius, A. Grisart, *Helikon*, 2 (1962), 379–414. The reputation of Hyginus has similarly declined; for a critical view of his Vergilian textual criticism, see G. P. Goold, *HSCP* 74 (1970), 161–2, and J. E. G. Zetzel, ibid. 77 (1973), 237–8.

VI

A general account of the second-hand book trade in Rome is given by T. Kleberg, 'Antiquarischer Buchhandel im alten Rom', *Annales Acad. Reg. Scient. Ups.* 8 (1964), 21–32. J. E. G. Zetzel, in the article cited above, has cogently demonstrated that many of the imposing volumes reported to exist in the second century and later were forged by alert entrepreneurs to meet the demand of antiquarian enthusiasts, and that Lampadio's Ennius and Tiro's Cicero and some of the more 'authentic' copies of Vergil should be numbered among such fakes. This is an understandable phenomenon, as easily paralleled in antiquity as at other times (cf. p. 7), and a testimony to the strength of the archaic revival, if not to the expertise of the antiquarian scholars. At the same time one should perhaps not be too sceptical about the existence of early texts at this period. Evidence which the Elder Pliny provides for the previous century is less suspect in that it predates the change in literary fashion and therefore the motive for forgery on a large scale: he claims (*NH* 13.83) to have seen documents written by the Gracchi, adding that autographs of Cicero, Augustus, and Vergil were common. He may be referring primarily to letters and similar documents. The theory that the collection of Ciceroniana bought by the bookseller Dorus (Seneca, *Ben.* 7.6.1) was part of Atticus' legacy is pure conjecture, based on a philosophical *exemplum*.

An accurate text of the subscription to the *De lege agraria* was first given in *Codices Vaticani Latini: Codices 11414–11709*, rec. J. Ruysschaert, Vatican 1959, pp. 93–5, and is printed as it stands in Poggio's. manuscript except for the expansion of *Dom* to *Domitium* and the emendation *oratio XXIIII* for *oratio eximia*. The last is due to Zetzel, who discusses the textual problem posed by the subscription and its significance in general, op. cit., 226–30.

VII

For the audacious fraudulence of the author of the *Historia Augusta*, see Sir Ronald Syme, *Ammianus and the Historia Augusta*, Oxford 1968, and in particular p. 9.

VIII

The now classic account of the codex is that of C. H. Roberts, *Proc. Brit. Acad.* 40 (1954), 169–204. See further E. G. Turner, *Greek papyri*, pp. 6ff.; T. C. Skeat, 'Early Christian book-production: papyri and manuscripts', *Cambridge history of the Bible*, vol. 2, ed. G. W. H. Lampe,

Cambridge 1969, pp. 54–79. On the dating of the fragment *De bellis Macedonicis*, cf. J. Mallon, *Emerita*, 17 (1949), 1–8.

IX

Aspects of the conflict between paganism and Christianity in the fourth century are discussed in the essays edited by A. Momigliano, *The conflict between paganism and Christianity in the fourth century*, Oxford 1963; of special relevance is the contribution by H. Bloch, pp. 193–218. Alan Cameron has redated the *Saturnalia* of Macrobius and put it into a new perspective, *JRS* 56 (1966), 25–38. For the Christianization of the senatorial class, see P. Brown, *JRS* 51 (1961), 1–11.

For a more general treatment of the confrontation between the two cultures, see M. L. W. Laistner, *Christianity and pagan culture in the later Roman Empire*, Ithaca, N.Y., 1951 (Cornell Paperbacks 1967); *Thought and letters in Western Europe, A.D. 500–900*, London 1957², pp. 25–53. A real assessment of the attitudes and practice of the two most influential figures of the fourth century, Jerome and Augustine, has been made possible by the detailed studies of H. Hagendahl, *Latin Fathers and the classics* (Studia Graeca et Latina Gothoburgensia, vol. 6), Göteborg 1958; *Augustine and the Latin classics* (Studia Graeca et Latina Gothoburgensia, vol. 20), Göteborg 1967.

On the question of style and taste, see C. E. Chaffin in *The classical world* (Literature and Western Civilization, ed. D. Daiches and A. Thorlby), London 1972, pp. 461–86.

X

Many editions of the subscriptions have been projected, but we are still dependent on the fundamental work of Otto Jahn, 'Über die Subscriptionen in den Handschriften römischer Classiker', *Berichte über die Verhandlungen der Sächsischen Gesellschaft der Wissenschaften, Phil.-hist. Classe*, 3 (1851), 327–72. Much of the historical detail is filled in by H. Bloch, in Momigliano, *The conflict*.

Whether the Asterius subscription in the Medicean Vergil is an autograph or not has long been in dispute; for a negative view, see e.g. O. Ribbeck, *Prolegomena critica ad P. Vergili Maronis opera maiora*, Leipzig 1866, p. 223. W. Clausen provides a warning against attaching too much importance to the revision of the gentleman amateurs who feature so often in the subscriptions, *Hermes*, 91 (1963), 252f. For the imperial fora as intellectual centres, see H.-I. Marrou, *Mélanges d'archéologie et d'histoire de l'École française de Rome*, 49 (1932), 94–110.

CHAPTER 2

I

In general see Sandys, *History of classical scholarship*. The ancient grammarians' contributions to syntax are noted by J. Wackernagel, *Vorlesungen über Syntax*, Basle 1950². There is no satisfactory modern treatment of Atticism and its effects on scholarship and literature; the basic reference book is still W. Schmid, *Der Attizismus in seinen Hauptvertretern*, Stuttgart 1887–96.

II

On the Christians and education see H.-I. Marrou, *Histoire de l'éducation*, pp. 451–71. The early Christian apologists are well presented by H. Chadwick, *Early Christian thought and the classical tradition*, Oxford 1966. W. Jaeger, *Early Christianity and Greek paideia*, Harvard 1961–Oxford 1969, is a good introduction to another side of the question. A sketch of the influence of the Church on scholarship, mainly in the Byzantine period proper, will be found in N. G. Wilson, *Antike und Abendland*, 16 (1970), 68–77.

Various views have been taken of Saint Basil's intention in his so-called twenty-second homily (it is in fact addressed to his nephews). Marrou, p. 462, emphasizes that it does not consist of a recommendation to study the classical authors; its advice is rather that, given the existing curriculum of pagan texts, there are ways of ensuring that these do the pupil good instead of harm. On the other hand it is probably wrong to see in Basil no more than a grudging recognition; the tone of the treatise is not unfriendly.

On Apollinaris it should be added that he also recast the Gospels and Epistles in the form of Platonic dialogues (Socrates, *Hist. eccl.* 3.16).

The burning of books is discussed by C. A. Forbes, *TAPA* 67 (1936), 114–25. The documents relating to ecclesiastical censorship in the twelfth century are nos. 1003 and 1008 in V. Grumel, *Regestes des actes du patriarcat de Constantinople*, Istanbul 1947.

III

On the closure of the philosophical school at Athens see A. D. E. Cameron, *Proc. Camb. Phil. Soc.* 195 (1969), 7–29, and R. C. McCail, ibid. 196 (1970), 79–82.

On the school at Gaza and the formation of scholia see the tentative hypothesis advanced by N. G. Wilson, *CQ* 17 (1967), 244–56 and 18 (1968), 413.

Wilamowitz's theory of the selection of plays for use in schools was put forward in his *Einleitung in die griechische Tragödie* (vol. 1 of his edition of Euripides' *Herakles*), 1895[2] and subsequently reprinted, pp. 175–80, 196–8. Its main features had been anticipated by T. Barthold in a Bonn dissertation of 1864.

The evidence that Menander was still being read in the school at Gaza may be found in J. Irmscher's essay in *Menanders Dyscolos als Zeugnis seiner Epoche*, ed. F. Zucker, Berlin 1965, p. 209. (The article by A. Dain on the survival of Menander in *Maia*, 15 (1963), 278–309, contains an error and a dubious interpretation on this point.) J.-M. Jacques, *Bull. Assoc. G. Budé* (1959), 200–15, has shown that Menander may have been read in Byzantium as late as c. 600 by the historian and epistolographer Theophylactus Simocatta.

The history of the other schools or universities of late antiquity is much more obscure. Some idea of the law school at Beirut may be had from the attractive picture in M. L. Clarke, *Higher education in antiquity*, London 1971, pp. 116–17 (with further references). For Alexandria the best guide is H. D. Saffrey, *REG* 67 (1954), 396–410.

IV

A recent review of the use of local vernacular languages in the eastern provinces is given by R. MacMullen in *AJP* 87 (1966), 1–16.

Oriental versions of the New Testament are discussed by B. M. Metzger, *The text of the New Testament*, Oxford 1968[2], pp. 67–84, 265–8, and K. Aland (ed.), *Die alten Uebersetzungen des Neuen Testaments, die Kirchenväterzitate und Lektionare*, Berlin 1972.

Syriac translations of Greek texts are listed by A. Baumstark, *Geschichte der syrischen Literatur*, Bonn 1922. On the schools of Nisibis and Edessa one may consult A. Vööbus, *History of the school of Nisibis*, Louvain 1965. For studies of particular authors see e.g. A. Baumstark, *Jahrbücher für classische Philologie*, Supp.-Band 21 (1894), 357–524, *Aristoteles bei den Syrern*, Leipzig 1900, G. Uhlig's edition of Dionysius Thrax, Leipzig 1883, pp. xliv–xlvi, M. Aubineau's edition of Gregory of Nyssa, *De virginitate* (= Sources Chrétiennes, vol. 119), Paris 1966, pp. 223–5, M. D. Macleod–L. R. Wickham, *CQ* 20 (1970), 297–9.

The best introduction to Arabic translations and Hunain ibn Ishaq is by R. Walzer, *HSCP* 63 (1958), 217–31, where further bibliography will be found There is also quite a useful bibliographical survey by F. Gabrieli, *Al-Andalus*, 24 (1959), 297–318. For a recent and instructive illustration of the difficulties to be overcome and the gains to be expected from the use of an Arabic version, see R. Kassel, *Der Text der aristotelischen Rhetorik*, Berlin 1971, pp. 88–92, 125–6, 141–2.

Joseph Needham, *Science and civilization in China*, vol. 1, Cambridge 1954, p. 219, draws attention to a fascinating episode in the life of the great Arab physician and alchemist Rhazes, who dictated some of the works of Galen to a Chinese scholar visiting Baghdad.

For Armenian translations see M. Leroy, *Ann. Inst. de phil. et d'hist. orient.* 3 (1935), 263–94, who gives the reference to Callimachus; there does not seem to be a more recent survey of the field. For some recent work on the Armenian version of Plato see W. S. M. Nicoll, *CQ* 16 (1966), 70–4.

It may be worth adding that occasionally one has to reckon with a translation into another Oriental language (Hebrew or Persian), but these cases are very much rarer, and the number of them discovered so far did not seem to justify a mention of them in the main text.

V

Byzantine scholarship from its beginnings to the middle of the tenth century is dealt with by P. Lemerle, *Le Premier Humanisme byzantin*, Paris 1971. Since this will evidently be the standard work for some time to come, we refer the reader to it without listing earlier contributions to the subject, and we only mention here a few articles in English that have remained unknown to the author and some matters of palaeography that require comment.

(1) p. 119: L. says that minuscule script brought with it accentuation, word-division, and punctuation. However, in the earliest minuscule only the last of these three features is found.

(2) p. 168: L. says that MS. Vat. gr. 1 of Plato's *Laws* was written for Arethas by John the Calligrapher, who was the scribe of his copies of Plato and Aristides. But the scribe is certainly not John the Calligrapher, and M. Ch. Astruc, as quoted by L. in n. 73, is probably right in saying that the marginalia are not in the hand of Arethas. For a further note on this MS. (and a general account of Byzantine libraries) see N. G. Wilson, *GRBS* 8 (1967), 53–80.

(3) On Photius it may be as well to say that the new early dating of the *Bibliotheca*, though ingenious, is not without its difficulties; see N. G. Wilson, *GRBS* 9 (1968), 451–6. On the nature of the circle or club of which Photius was the central figure see the postscript to the same writer's article on books and readers in Byzantium in *Dumbarton Oaks Papers* (forthcoming). As to the absence of poetry from the *Bibliotheca* (except from one codex), it should be noted that in letter 150 Photius shows knowledge of Aristophanes' *Plutus*, which he is likely

to have encountered in the school curriculum; and a close reading of his works might well reveal acquaintance with a number of other poetic texts, most probably known to him for the same reason.

(4) p. 215: there is no strong reason for associating MS. Paris gr. 1807 with Arethas; on palaeographical grounds it is likely, but not certain, that the book was written before Arethas began to form his library.

VI

The identification of scribes, and very rarely scriptoria, through features of handwriting or book production, is one of the chief means by which our knowledge of Byzantine scholarship advances. Autographs of the leading scholars are still being recognized, and our knowledge of scriptoria is making slow progress. For the methods involved see J. Irigoin, *Scriptorium*, 12 (1958), 208–27 and 13 (1959), 177–209. The objection of principle raised by B. Hemmerdinger, *BZ* 56 (1963), 24, remains a serious difficulty, but need not be held to invalidate all the results of this method of inquiry (known in some circles as codicology). A successful application of the method may be seen in Irigoin's identification of a group of manuscripts of the Greek historians all written with thirty-two lines to the page: *Annuaire de l'école pratique des hautes études*, 1968–9, section IV, pp. 137ff.

There is no satisfactory study of Psellus (the article by E. Kriaras in *RE* leaves a good deal to be desired). What is said in our text may need to be substantially revised in due course. Psellus' literary interests can be seen for instance in his short essays comparing the novels of Achilles Tatius and Heliodorus and the verse of Euripides with that of George of Pisidia, a Byzantine versifier of the seventh century; but since neither of these texts is available in an adequate edition judgement must be reserved.

Anna Comnena's circle was unearthed by R. Browning, *Proc. Camb. Phil. Soc.* 188 (1962), 1–12.

For Eustathius see R. Browning on the patriarchal school in *Byzantion*, 32 (1962), 167–202, 33 (1963), 11–40. This is the appropriate place to mention that though the school is well attested as an institution in the twelfth century, the evidence for its existence at other periods is very weak (see H. G. Beck, *Polychronion, Festschrift Dölger*, pp. 69ff.); yet it may be hypercritical to deny its existence at any time other than the twelfth century. Eustathius' commentary on the *Iliad* is now being edited from the surviving autograph manuscript by M. van der Valk (vol. 1, Leiden 1971, with prolegomena of considerable value for assessing Eustathius' sources and methods of scholarship). The superior text of Sophocles' *Antigone* possibly comes from a reading of Athenaeus, who quotes the passage; but this does not diminish Eustathius' merit in recalling as he read that the Sophoclean text, as he knew it, was faulty at that point. His work on Aristophanes was brought to light by W. J. W. Koster–D. Holwerda, *Mnemosyne*, 7 (1954), 136ff., 8 (1954), 196ff.

On Tzetzes see C. Wendel in *RE*. His scholia on Aristophanes have been edited by L. Massa Positano, D. Holwerda, and W. J. W. Koster, Groningen 1960–4. The philological club is mentioned in his notes to *Frogs* 897.

For Michael Choniates see G. Stadtmüller, *Michael Choniates Metropolit von Athen*, Vatican City 1934. The incorrect name Acominatos is ingeniously explained by J.-L. Van Dieten, *Niketas Choniates, Erlaüterungen zu den Reden und Briefen nebst einer Biographie*, Berlin 1971, pp. 4–8. See also O. Lampsidis, *BZ* 64 (1971), 26–7.

Constantine Lascaris' statement about Diodorus Siculus is in Migne, *PG* 161.918: he had seen a complete copy in the emperors' library.

A general account of literature and learning in the kingdom of Nicaea is given by A. A. Vasiliev, *History of the Byzantine Empire*, Madison, Wis., 1952, pp. 548–63. On the contribution of southern Italy to Byzantine culture see J. Irigoin, *JÖBG* 18 (1969), 37–55; pp. 51–3 concern the thirteenth century.

Sketches of Palaeologan scholarship and related matters are given by Sir Steven Runciman, *The last Byzantine Renaissance*, Cambridge 1970, and D. M. Nicol, *Studies in church history*, 5 (1969), 23–57.

For Planudes see the article by C. Wendel in *RE*. Two further facts about his scholarship may be worth adding here to what is said in the text. In preparing his edition of Plutarch from a damaged exemplar he seems to have instructed his scribes to pay attention to the length of each lacuna. Less to his credit is that he bowdlerized the Greek Anthology and his translation of Ovid. The autograph of his text of Aratus has now been discovered in the Advocates Library in Edinburgh (MS. 18.7.15); see I. C. Cunningham, *Scriptorium*, 24 (1970), 367–8 with plate 24. Planudes' alterations to the text are found exactly as expected. The translations of Ovid's amatory works cannot be ascribed to him with the same degree of certainty as the other translations; on this side of his activity see W. O. Schmitt, *JÖBG* 17 (1968), 127–47, and E. J. Kenney, *Hermes* 91 (1963), 213–27.

On Triclinius see A. Turyn, *The Byzantine manuscript tradition of the tragedies of Euripedes*, Urbana, Ill., 1957, pp. 23ff., 32ff.; N. G.

Wilson, *CQ* 12 (1962), 32–47; G. Zuntz, *An inquiry into the transmission of the plays of Euripides*, Cambridge 1965, *passim*; A. Wasserstein, *JÖBG* 17 (1968), 153ff.

An observation about the Byzantine school curriculum may be added here. There are sporadic references in authors of widely differing dates to the *quadrivium* (τετραχτύς), but the evidence does not enable us to say whether the concepts of *trivium* and *quadrivium* were as influential in Byzantium as they were in the educational practice of Western Europe. See A. Diller, *Isis*, 36 (1945–6), 132, who points to the existence of these concepts in a work dating from A.D. 1008.

CHAPTER 3

I

Among the most relevant general works on the intellectual and cultural history of the Dark Ages mention should be made of P. Courcelle, *Les Lettres grecques en Occident de Macrobe à Cassiodore*, Paris 1948[2]; P. Riché, *Éducation et culture dans l'Occident barbare, vi[e]–viiie siècles* (Patristica Sorbonensia, vol. 4), Paris 1962; B. Bischoff, 'Scriptoria e manoscritti mediatori di civiltà dal sesto secolo alla riforma di Carlo Magno', *Settimane di studio del Centro italiano di studi sull' alto medioevo*, 11 (Spoleto 1963), 479–504, reprinted in his *Mittelalterliche Studien*, vol. 2, Stuttgart 1967, pp. 312–27; also the works earlier cited by Laistner and Marrou. The fundamental work is E. A. Lowe, *Codices latini antiquiores*, vols. 1–11 with Supplement (Oxford 1934–71), now complete except for further indexes to be published and containing facsimiles and descriptions of all Latin manuscripts prior to the ninth century (abbreviated *CLA*).

Martin of Braga's *Formula vitae honestae*, dedicated to the Suevic king Mir and written between 570 and 579, is an adaptation of a lost work of Seneca, probably the *De officiis* (cf. E. Bickel, *RhM* 60 (1905), 505–51). Unlike his *De ira*, a carefully constructed mosaic of borrowings from Seneca's treatise of that name, which survives in only one medieval manuscript, the *Formula* was an extremely popular work in the Middle Ages and later. Often entitled *De quattuor virtutibus cardinalibus*, it was commonly attributed, with perspicacity if not a sense of poetic justice, to Seneca. For further information see C. W. Barlow, *Martini episcopi Bracarensis opera omnia*, New Haven, Conn., 1950.

For bibliographical material on Cassiodorus see the important article by A. D. Momigliano, 'Cassiodorus and the Italian culture of his time', *Proc. Brit. Acad.* 41 (1955), 207–45, reprinted (with a more select bibliography) in his *Secondo contributo alla storia degli studi classici* Rome 1960, pp. 219–29, and *Studies in historiography* (London 1966, paperback 1969), pp. 181–210. The theory that the oldest Bobbio manuscripts came from Vivarium was advanced by R. Beer in *Anz. Akad. der Wiss. in Wien, Phil.-Hist. Kl.* 48 (1911), 78–104. For some of the important stages in its demolition see E. A. Lowe, *CQ* 19 (1925), 205 (= *Palaeographical papers 1907–1965*, ed. L. Bieler, vol. 1, Oxford 1972, p. 198), and *CLA* 4 (1947), xx–xxvii; G. Mercati, *Prolegomena* to the facsimile edition of the palimpsest of Cicero's *De republica*, Vatican 1934, pp. 1–174; P. Courcelle, *Les Lettres grecques*, pp. 357–88, who has made the most positive contribution to the problem (but cf. Bischoff, *Karl der Grosse*, p. 44 n. 17). For a survey of the question see the important review of *CLA* 4 by H. Bloch in *Speculum*, 25 (1950), 277–87. *Cassiodori Senatoris institutiones*, ed. R. A. B. Mynors, Oxford 1937, provides a critical text of the *Institutiones* and valuable indexes.

A full-length study of Isidore and his classical sources is provided by J. Fontaine, *Isidore de Seville et la culture classique dans l'Espagne wisigothique*, 2 vols., Paris 1959. It seems dangerous to draw firm conclusions about the classical content of the episcopal library at Seville from Isidore's *Versus in bibliotheca* (ed. C. H. Beeson, *Isidor-Studien* (Quellen und Untersuchungen zur lateinischen Philologie des Mittelalters, 4.2, Munich 1913), pp. 157–66). The remarkable story of the dissemination of his works has been most recently and authoritatively treated by B. Bischoff, 'Die europaische Verbreitung der Werke Isidors von Sevilla', *Isidoriana. Estudios sobre San Isidoro de Sevilla en el XIV centenario de su nacimiento*, León 1961, pp. 317–44, reprinted in *Mittelalterliche Studien*, vol. 1, Stuttgart 1966, pp. 171–94.

A celebrated manuscript long attributed to the sixth century, the Morgan Pliny (Pierpont Morgan Library M.462) has been recently redated to the late fifth century (*CLA* XI.1660).

For the facts and figures about early palimpsests, which can be supplemented from the volumes of *CLA*, see E. A. Lowe, 'Codices rescripti', *Mélanges Eugène Tisserant*, vol. 5, Vatican 1964 (Studi e Testi, 235), 67–112, reprinted in *Palaeographical papers*, vol. 2, pp. 480–519.

II

The extent to which the early Irish knew the classics is as controversial as many Irish problems, and the scope of their classical knowledge has doubtless been exaggerated at times. The controversy tends to turn on the rather subjective question of whether Columban's familiarity with classical poetry, evidenced for instance in his *Carmen ad Fedolium*, was acquired at home or on the continent. The negative view has recently been put by E. Coccia, 'La cultura irlandese precarolina—miraculo o mito?', *Studi medievali*, 3rd ser. 8 (1967), 257–420. For a judicious defence of Irish classical culture see L. Bieler, 'The classics in Celtic Ireland', *Classical influences on European culture A.D. 500-1500*, ed. R. R. Bolgar, Cambridge 1971, pp. 45–9. The works of Columban have been recently edited by G. S. M. Walker, *Sancti Columbani opera* (Script. Lat. Hiberniae, vol. 2), Dublin 1957, who however makes some exaggerated statements about classical culture in Ireland: see the review by M. Esposito, *C&M* 21 (1960), 184–203. There are two valuable articles on the scholarly activity of the Irish by B. Bischoff, 'Il monachesimo irlandese nei suoi rapporti col continente', *Settimane di studio del Centro italiano di studi sull' alto medioevo*, 4 (Spoleto 1957), 121–38, and 'Wendepunkte in der Geschichte der lateinischen Exegese im Frühmittelalter', *Sacris Erudiri, Jaarboek voor Godsdienstwetenschappen*, 6 (1954), 189–279; both are reprinted in *Mittelalterliche Studien*, vol. 1, pp. 195–205, 205–73. For a handsome introduction to early Irish culture, see L. Bieler, *Irland, Wegbereiter des Mittelalters*, Olten etc. 1961 (English edition, *Ireland, Harbinger of the Middle Ages*, Oxford–London 1963).

For a survey of the books known to the English scholars of this period, see J. D. A. Ogilvy, *Books known to the English* (Mediaeval Academy of America Publications, no. 76), Cambridge, Mass., 1967. Bede's classical sources are thoroughly studied by M. L. W. Laistner, 'Bede as a classical and a patristic scholar', *Tr. Royal Hist. Soc.*, 4th ser. 16 (1933), 69–94, and 'The library of the Venerable Bede', in *Bede: his life, times, and writings*, ed. A. H. Thompson, Oxford 1935, pp. 237–66; both are reprinted in his collected essays, *The intellectual heritage of the early Middle Ages*, ed. Chester G. Starr, Ithaca, N.Y., 1957, pp. 93–116, 117–49. On Bede see also R. W. Southern, *Medieval humanism and other studies*, Oxford 1970, pp. 1–8.

Alcuin's lines on the contents of the library at York are to be found in his *Versus de sanctis Euboricensis Ecclesiae*, 1535ff., ed. E. Dümmler, *MGH, Poetae latini aevi Carolini*, vol. 1, Berlin 1880–1, pp. 203–4.

III

W. Levison's *England and the continent in the eighth century*, Oxford 1946, remains the authoritative work on the missionary activity of the Anglo-Saxons: see especially pp. 132–73.

We owe the brilliant identification of Virgil of Salzburg as the author of the *Cosmographia* to H. Löwe, *Ein literarischer Widersacher des Bonifatius, Virgil von Salzburg und die Kosmographie des Aethicus Ister* (*Abhandl. der Akad. der Wissenschaften und der Literatur in Mainz*, 11), 1955. For further details about the tradition of Pomponius Mela see p. 94 and the notes to VIII.

IV

One of the difficulties of assessing the part played by the Irish and the English in the transmission of classical texts is the imprecise nature of the term 'insular tradition'. This may be postulated in a variety of circumstances: when one or more manuscripts of a text were actually written in Britain, or written in insular script on the continent, or associated with some Irish or Anglo-Saxon foundation, or showing traces, more or less conjectural, that a lost exemplar belonged to one of these categories. The route which the flow of cultural life followed from Italy to Britain and then back again to the continent is very much the *romantische Strasse* for the transmission of texts and it can be dramatically documented for some biblical traditions, as in the case of the Fulda and Echternach Gospels and, still more clearly, the codex Amiatinus (Laur. Amiat. 1), where the part played by England in the story is beyond doubt. This great Bible was written at Wearmouth or Jarrow as part of Ceolfrid's project to produce three pandects of the Bible and was almost certainly used by Bede himself, but much of its decoration was modelled on that of the lost *codex grandior* of Cassiodorus, written at Vivarium and brought from Rome to Northumbria by Ceolfrid as one of the fruits of his journey with Benedict Biscop in 678; he was taking the Amiatinus to Rome, as a present for the pope, when he died at Langres in 716 (cf. R. L. S. Bruce-Mitford, *Journal of the British Archaeological Association*, 3rd ser. 32 (1969), 1–25). Unfortunately, it is not easy to substantiate such romantic journeys for classical texts and some of the hastily posited insular traditions once fashionable have evaporated, such as the insular pre-archetype of Lucretius, a text which does not appear to have reached England before the late fifteenth century.

For the manuscripts of Pliny, Justinus, and Servius, see *CLA* X.1578, IX.1370, *Suppl.* 1806.

V

The educational aims of Charlemagne are fully and explicitly set out in the mandate which he sent to Baugulf, abbot of Fulda, between 794 and 800. This document has been edited and fully discussed by L.

Wallach in *Speculum*, 26 (1951), 288–305, reprinted in his *Alcuin and Charlemagne*, Ithaca, N.Y., 1959, rev. ed. 1967, pp. 198–226. Of particular interest is Wallach's demonstration, from the thought and style of the mandate, that Alcuin had taken a hand in its composition. For the educational role of the Palace School, see F. Brunhölzl, 'Der Bildungsauftrag der Hofschule', in *Karl der Grosse, Lebenswerk und Nachleben*, vol. 2, *Das geistige Leben*, ed. B. Bischoff, Düsseldorf 1965, pp. 28–41.

VI

This brief account of the history of the national hands and the development of Caroline minuscule, complex and at points controversial, has been simplified to accord with the scope and nature of this volume. For the Beneventan manuscripts, which are of most interest to classical scholars, see E. A. Lowe, *The Beneventan script*, Oxford 1914, and 'A new list of Beneventan manuscripts', *Collectanea Vaticana in honorem Anselmi M. Card. Albareda*, vol. 2, Vatican 1962 (Studi e Testi, 220), pp. 211–44. The introductory matter from both of these has been reprinted in *Palaeographial papers*, vol. 1, pp. 70–91, and vol. 2, pp. 477–9. S. Prete (*Observations on the history of textual criticism in the medieval and Renaissance periods*, Collegeville, Minn., 1971, p. 16 n. 46) has drawn attention to two Visigothic manuscripts of classical authors. There appear to be at least three: a ninth-century manuscript of Ausonius, actually written by Spanish emigrants at Lyons (Leiden, Voss. lat. F. 111), an eleventh-century Terence (Madrid Vitr. 5.4), and a Lucan of the late eleventh or early twelfth century (Vat. Ottob. lat. 1210 + Vat. Pal. lat. 869). The possibility of lost exemplars in pre-Caroline minuscule may have been underplayed: for another view see S. Timpanaro, *Maia*, 22 (1970), 288.

VII

For the key to the Palace Library see B. Bischoff, 'Die Hofbibliothek Karls des Grossen', in *Karl der Grosse*, pp. 42–62. It is noteworthy that the compiler of the book-list, an Italian, was interested in jotting down the titles of only the classical books in the collection. For Hadoard and the Corbie manuscripts, see B. Bischoff, 'Hadoardus and the manuscripts of classical authors from Corbie', *Didaskaliae. Studies in honor of Anselm M. Albareda*, ed. S. Prete, New York 1961, pp. 41–57, reprinted (in German) in *Mittelalterliche Studien*, vol. 1, pp. 49–63.

The survey of the classical books in Carolingian libraries is mainly

derived from such catalogues as survive or deduced from the manuscript traditions of the individual texts concerned. The information
from the catalogues, though in places out of date, is conveniently
assembled in M. Manitius, *Handschriften antiker Autoren in mittelalterlichen Bibliothekskatalogen* (Zentralblatt für Bibliothekswesen, Beiheft
67), Leipzig 1935. See also B. Bischoff, 'Panorama der Handschriften-
überlieferung aus der Zeit Karls des Grossen', *Karl der Grosse*, vol. 2,
pp. 233–54.

VIII

The true identity of the 'Saxon' corrector, which has teased generations,
was finally revealed by B. Bischoff in the catalogue to the 1965 Charlemagne Exhibition at Aachen: cf. *Karl der Grosse, Werk und Wirkung*,
Aachen 1965 (= *Charlemagne, œuvre, rayonnement et survivances*, Aix-
la-Chapelle 1965), pp. 202–3. For further information on Dungal, see
Bischoff, 'Die Bibliothek im Dienste der Schule', *Settimane di studio
del Centro italiano di studi sull' alto medioevo*, 19 (Spoleto 1972), 410–12.
For Hadoard, see the notes to VII; also C. H. Beeson, 'The Collectaneum of Hadoard', *CPh* 40 (1945), 201–22. Walafrid Strabo's scrap-
book is identified and described by Bischoff in 'Eine Sammelhandschrift
Walafrid Strabos (Cod. Sangall. 878)', *Aus der Welt des Buches, Festschrift Georg Leyh* (Zentralblatt für Bibliothekswesen, Beiheft 75),
Leipzig 1950, pp. 30–48; this article is reprinted and enlarged in
Mittelalterliche Studien, vol. 2, pp. 34–51, the addenda including the
discovery of Walafrid's role in the Horace tradition. For the Seneca
excerpt, see L. D. Reynolds, *The medieval tradition of Seneca's letters*,
Oxford 1965, pp. 92–3 and Plate 1; for Columella, Å. Josephson,
Die Columella-Handschriften, Uppsala 1955, pp. 39–41.

For a general study of Lupus see P. E. von Severus, *Lupus von
Ferrières, Gestalt und Werk eines Vermittlers antiken Geistesgutes an das
Mittelalter im 9. Jahrhundert*, Münster in Westf. 1940. C. H. Beeson
has edited a facsimile of the manuscript of the *De oratore* written by
Lupus: *Servatus Lupus as scribe and text critic* (Mediaeval Academy of
America Publications, no. 4), Cambridge, Mass., 1930. For an up-to-
date list of the other books which he has annotated or corrected see
E. Pellegrin, 'Les Manuscrits de Loup de Ferrières', *BEC* 115 (1957),
5–31. His scholarly interests are vividly illustrated by his letters,
edited by L. Levillain, 2 vols., Paris 1927–35. See also M. L. W.
Laistner, *Thought and letters*, pp. 252ff.

For Theodulfus' Bible see G. Pasquali, *Storia della tradizione*, p. 155
n. 2.

We now have a good edition of Heiric's *florilegium*: R. Quadri, *I 'Collectanea' di Eirico di Auxerre* (Spicilegium Friburgense, 11), Fribourg 1966. The whole story of the transmission of the collection of texts which include Mela and Julius Paris, one of the most fascinating of all since it can be traced almost continuously from antiquity to the Renaissance, has been told by Gius. Billanovich, in 'Dall' antica Ravenna alle biblioteche umanistiche', *Annuario dell' Università Cattolica del S. Cuore-Milano*, 1955–7, pp. 71–107; an earlier version appeared in *Aevum*, 30 (1956), 319–53.

IX

For Ratherius and the text of Livy's first decade, see Gius. Billanovich, 'Dal Livio di Raterio (Laur. 63,19) al Livio del Petrarca (B.M. Harl. 2493)', *IMU* 2 (1959), 103–78. The early history of the Catullus tradition and Ratherius' part in it remains as puzzling as the epigram by Benvenuto Campesani (cf. p. 112) which should have thrown some light on it. For different views see B. L. Ullman, *Studi in onore di Luigi Castiglioni*, vol. 2, Florence 1960, pp. 1031f.; G. Billanovich, op. cit., pp. 164–5.

The fundamental article on the history of Livy's text, and in particular the third and fourth decades, is Gius. Billanovich, 'Petrarch and the textual tradition of Livy', *Journal of the Warburg and Courtauld Institutes*, 14 (1951), 137–208. For the early history of the fourth decade see pp. 183ff.; also A. H. McDonald, in the preface to the Oxford Text of Livy XXXI–XXXV (= vol. 5), pp. x ff.

The manuscript containing Ovid's *Ars amatoria* in early Welsh minuscule is a very remarkable book: R. W. Hunt, *Saint Dunstan's classbook from Glastonbury* (Umbrae Codicum Occidentalium, 4), Amsterdam 1961.

X

For Monte Cassino and its manuscripts see the notes to VI. On the whole, it seems to have kept its manuscripts to itself during the Middle Ages. With the exception of the *Dialogues* of Seneca, what one may call the 'Cassinese texts' did not begin to circulate until the Renaissance. A facsimile of the Tacitus was published by E. Rostagno, *Codices graeci et latini photographice depicti*, vol. 7, pars 2, Leiden 1902. It and the Apuleius have been discussed at length by Lowe: *CQ* 14 (1920), 150–5 (= *Palaeographical papers*, vol. 1, pp. 92–8), and *Casinensia*, Monte Cassino 1929, pp. 257–72 (= *P.P.* 1.289–302). For Seneca and Monte

Cassino, see L. D. Reynolds, *CQ* N.S. 18 (1968), 355–72; for Juvenal, J. G. Griffith, *Hermes*, 91 (1963), 104ff.

XI

For general accounts see C. H. Haskins, *The Renaissance of the twelfth century*, Cambridge, Mass., 1927: G. Paré, A. Brunet, P. Tremblay, *La Renaissance du douzième siècle*, Paris 1933; C. Brooke, *The twelfth century Renaissance*, London 1969. England is put into its context by R. W. Southern, 'The place of England in the twelfth century Renaissance', *Medieval Humanism and Other Studies*, Oxford 1970, pp. 158–180, which is based on an earlier paper printed in *History*, 45 (1960), 201–16. See also R. W. Hunt, 'The deposit of Latin classics in the twelfth-century renaissance', *Classical influences*, pp. 51–5. On John of Salisbury, H. Liebeschütz, *Mediaeval humanism in the life and writings of John of Salisbury*, London 1950; J. M. Martin, 'John of Salisbury and the classics', summarized in *HSCP* 73 (1969), 319–21; on William of Malmesbury, H. Farmer, 'William of Malmesbury's life and works', *Journal of Ecclesiastical History*, 13 (1962), 39–54.

The *florilegium Gallicum* has been discussed in relation to the classical texts it contains by B. L. Ullman in a series of articles in *Classical Philology*, 23–7 (1928–32); for a summary see the last, pp. 1–42. Also A. Gagnér, *Florilegium Gallicum*, Lund 1936. It was used by the author of another important twelfth-century *florilegium*, the *Moralium dogma philosophorum* (ed. J. Holmberg, Uppsala 1929), and in the thirteenth century by Vincent of Beauvais (cf. p. 102).

XII

The *Biblionomia* of Richard de Fournival was edited by L. Delisle, *Le Cabinet des manuscrits de la Bibliothèque nationale*, vol. 2, Paris 1874, pp. 518–35. For recent contributions to the subject of his library and its transmission to the Sorbonne, see: P. Glorieux, 'Études sur la "Biblionomia" de Richard de Fournival', *Recherches de Théologie ancienne et médiévale*, 30 (1963), 205–31; R. H. Rouse, 'The early library of the Sorbonne', *Scriptorium*, 21 (1967), 47–51, and 'The "A" text of Seneca's tragedies in the thirteenth century', *Revue d'Histoire des Textes*, 1 (1971), 93–121. A further and important article by Rouse is forthcoming in vol. 3 of the *Revue d'Histoire des Textes*. Valuable pioneering work was done by B. L. Ullman, who identified Fournival's Propertius with the extant Voss. lat. Q. 38 and established some links between his library and that of Corbie: cf. in particular 'The library of the Sorbonne in the fourteenth century', *The septicentennial celebration of the founding of the Sorbonne College in the University of Paris*, Chapel Hill, N.C., 1953, pp. 33–47, reprinted in *Studies in the Italian Renaissance*, Rome 1955, pp. 41–53. Ullman's identification of the Propertius has been confirmed by Rouse's researches and his discovery that a number of Fournival's books, including the Propertius and the Seneca, were written by the same scribe. Corbie is just twelve miles from Amiens and a likely source for some of his classical manuscripts, but the evidence is circumstantial: Rouse argues for Paris. Another interesting manuscript which belonged to Fournival is the oldest surviving copy of Aristippus' translation of the *Phaedo* (see p. 106); this is Paris lat. 16581, probably the parent of Petrarch's manuscript (cf. *Plato latinus*, vol. 2: *Phaedo*, ed. L. Minio-Paluello, London 1950, pp. xi f.).

The relevant Tibullus *florilegium* is Venice, Marc. Z.L. 497, of the eleventh century: cf. F. Newton, *TAPA* 93 (1962), 259ff. For the most recent comprehensive study of the manuscript tradition of Seneca's *Tragedies*, see R. H. Philp, *CQ* N.S. 18 (1968), 150–79; for the history of the A-text, Rouse, op. cit.

The medieval tradition of the *Dialogues* is discussed by L. D. Reynolds, *CQ* N.S. 18 (1968), 355–72. The early history of this text belongs entirely to Italy and is particularly interesting for that reason. The whole essential process, from the copying of the archetype through contamination and correction to the appearance of a vulgate, took place in Italy, in a period—between the end of the eleventh and the middle of the thirteenth century—in which such a lively interest in the classics has rarely been assumed.

The activities of the English friars have been illuminated and brought into focus by Beryl Smalley, *English friars and antiquity in the early fourteenth century*, Oxford 1960.

XIII

For the ninth-century translators see P. Lemerle, *Le Premier Humanisme byzantin*, pp. 13–16. He underestimates the possibility of some knowledge of Greek at Saint Gall; see L. Bieler's introduction to the facsimile of the Basle Psalter (MS. A.VII.3), published as vol. 5 of Umbrae Codicum Occidentalium, Amsterdam 1960, esp. p. xix.

Burgundio of Pisa is discussed by E. M. Buytaert in the preface to his edition of *St. John Damascene, de fide orthodoxa, versions of Burgundio and Cerbanus*, Saint Bonaventure 1955. James of Venice is dealt with by L. Minio-Paluello, *Traditio*, 8 (1952), 265–304.

Basic information on the twelfth-century translators and much else can be found in C. H. Haskins, *Studies in the history of medieval science*,

Cambridge, Mass., 1927², pp. 141–241. E. Grant, *Speculum*, 46 (1971), 656–79, casts serious doubt on the idea that Hero's *Pneumatica* were known in Latin as early as the twelfth century.

Grosseteste's copy of Pseudo-Dionysius was recognized by R. Barbour, *Bodleian Library Record*, 6 (1958), 401–16.

Moerbeke's activity can be studied in the various volumes of the *Aristoteles Latinus* series and a convenient résumé of the current state of knowledge is given by B. Schneider, *Die mittelalterlichen griechisch-lateinischen Uebersetzungen der Aristotelischen Rhetorik*, Berlin 1971, pp. 5–9. Moerbeke's translations were very popular; there are 98 surviving manuscripts of his *Rhetoric*, and Dante shows that he knew the work in this version.

In general medieval translations were made word for word, and a sign of their unidiomatic character is that from 1266 onwards Moerbeke felt impelled to reproduce the Greek definite article by using the French 'le'; the lack of an article in Latin had made it impossible to deal properly with many abstract expressions.

On matters related to this section two papers by B. Bischoff may be recommended: 'The study of foreign languages in the Middle Ages' (*Speculum*, 36 (1961), 209–24) and 'Das griechische Element in der abendländischen Bildung des Mittelalters' (*Byzantinische Zeitschrift*, 44 (1951), 27–55; both are now reprinted (the first in an enlarged form) in his *Mittelalterliche Studien*, vol. 2, pp. 227–45 and 246–75.

CHAPTER 4

I

The first important discussions of the origin of the term 'humanist' appeared almost simultaneously: P. O. Kristeller, 'Humanism and scholasticism in the Italian Renaissance', *Byzantion*, 17 (1944–5), 346–74, and A. Campana, 'The origin of the word "humanist"', *Journal of the Warburg and Courtauld Institutes*, 9 (1946), 60–73. For recent bibliography and further discussion, see R. Avesani, 'La professione dell' "umanista" nel cinquecento', *IMU* 13 (1970), 205–323.

The wider problem of the origin of Italian humanism and its place in the context of the Renaissance is beyond the competence of this book, but some of the more general studies which have influenced the shape of this chapter may be conveniently mentioned here: P. O. Kristeller, various essays and lectures collected together in *Studies in Renaissance thought and letters*, Rome 1956, and *Renaissance thought*, vols. 1–2, New York 1961–5; Kenneth M. Setton, 'The Byzantine background to the Italian Renaissance', *Proc. Amer. Philosoph. Soc.* 100 (1956), 1–76; F. Simone, *Il Rinascimento francese*, Turin 1961 (updated English version by H. Gaston Hall, *The French Renaissance*, London 1969); Beryl Smalley, *English friars*, pp. 280–98; B. L. Ullman, *Studies in the Italian Renaissance*, Rome 1955; R. Weiss, *The dawn of humanism in Italy*, London 1947, *The spread of Italian humanism*, London 1964, and *The Renaissance discovery of classical antiquity*, Oxford 1969.

Though in many respects out of date, the fundamental works on the rediscovery of classical texts remain those of R. Sabbadini: *Le scoperte dei codici latini e greci ne' secoli xiv e xv*, 2 vols., Florence 1905–14, reprinted with author's additions and corrections and an appreciation by E. Garin, Florence 1967; *Storia e critica di testi latini*, Catania 1914, of which a second edition has now been produced (Medioevo e Umanesimo, no. 11, Padua 1971) with new indexes and a full bibliography of Sabbadini's works.

II

The first real indication of the strength of Paduan prehumanism was given by Gius. Billanovich in *I primi umanisti e le tradizioni dei classici latini*, Fribourg 1953. The evidence for the wide knowledge of Latin poetry shown by members of this circle is set out by Guido Billanovich, '*Veterum vestigia vatum*', *IMU* 1 (1958), 155–243. Their poetry is still not properly edited or easily accessible; for a bibliography see Guido Billanovich, ibid., p. 181. Mussato's *Ecerinide* was edited by L. Padrin, Bologna 1900, and texts pertaining to the study of Seneca's *Tragedies* at Padua have been edited, with full discussion of this topic, by A. Kh. Megas, Ὁ προουμανιστικὸς κύκλος τῆς Πάδουας (*Lovato Lovati-Albertino Mussato*) καὶ οἱ τραγωδίες τοῦ *L. A. Seneca*, Thessalonica 1967 (English summary, pp. 229–33). For a good account of Lovato, see R. Weiss, *Italian Studies*, 6 (1951), 3–28. Geremia da Montagnone is dealt with by Weiss, *Il primo secolo dell' umanesimo*, Rome 1949, pp. 15–20, and Ullman, 'Hieremias de Montagnone and his citations from Catullus', *CPh* 5 (1910), 66–82, reprinted in *Studies*, pp. 81–115. For Benvenuto Campesani, see Weiss, *Bollettino del Museo Civico di Padova*, 44 (1955), 129–44.

III

The study of Petrarch's manuscripts and his work on the text of classical authors is proceeding at such a pace and covers so much ground that it was necessary to be very selective in this section and concentrate on the most important examples. For Petrarch's contribution to the tradition of Livy and Mela, see the articles by Giuseppe Billanovich cited on p. 231; for Propertius, B. L. Ullman, 'The manuscripts of Propertius', *CPh* 6 (1911), 282–301, *Studies*, pp. 181–92. Good discussions of Petrarch's list of favourite books are provided by Ullman, 'Petrarch's favourite books', *TAPA* 54 (1923), 21–38 (reprinted in *Studies*, pp. 117–37), and H. Rüdiger, in *Geschichte der Textüberlieferung*, 1. 526–37; it was Ullman who first demonstrated the precise significance of the list. A. Petrucci, *La scrittura di Francesco Petrarca* (Studi e Testi, 248), Vatican 1967, provides a list of Petrarchan manuscripts and a most useful bibliography. The pioneering work of P. de Nolhac, *Pétrarque et l'humanisme*, 2nd ed., vols. 1–2, Paris 1907, should not be forgotten, though inevitably out of date in many respects.

The importance of Avignon emerges from the study of any text which passed through it. The significance of its role in channelling manuscripts to Italy was pointed out by Ullman in 1941 (*Philological Quarterly*, 20 (1941), 213–17 = *Studies*, pp. 29–33) and recent studies of individual texts have dramatically substantiated his theory. For broader discussions of Avignon as a cultural centre, see F. Simone, *Il Rinascimento*, pp. 9–24; W. Braxton Ross, 'Giovanni Colonna, historian at Avignon', *Speculum*, 45 (1970), 533–45.

Billanovich, *I primi umanisti*, pp. 29–33, deals with the rediscovery of the Monte Cassino manuscripts and Zanobi da Strada's part in it.

IV

We are fortunate in having a recent full-length study of Coluccio by B. L. Ullman: *The humanism of Coluccio Salutati* (Medioevo e Umanesimo, no. 4), Padua 1963. His book on *The origin and development of the humanistic script*, Rome 1960, should also be consulted.

V

The fantastic tale of Poggio's discoveries is still best followed in Sabbadini, though the details need to be checked against recent work on the individual texts concerned. See also A. C. Clark, *Inventa Italorum* (Anecdota Oxoniensia, Classical Series, Part 11), Oxford 1909. Poggio's expedition to Cluny in the spring of 1415 remains dubious: cf. T. Foffano, *IMU* 12 (1969), 113–28. The works by Ullman cited in the preceding section contain important material, particularly on Poggio's contribution to the development of the new script, and manuscripts in Poggio's hand continue to turn up. One of the most important recent identifications was that of Poggio's autograph copy (Vat. lat. 11458) of the eight Cicero speeches which he found in 1417, made by A. Campana: cf. *Codices Vaticani Latini*, vol. 8 (1959), pp. 93ff. The detailed work of C. Questa on Poggio's contribution to the textual tradition of the twelve plays of Plautus permits some assessment of his philological ability: *Per la storia del testo di Plauto nell' umanesimo* 1: *La 'recensio' di Poggio Bracciolini*, Rome 1968. The standard biography is that of E. Walser, *Poggius Florentinus: Leben und Werke*, Leipzig 1914; a new one is needed.

The discovery that the best copy of the lost vetus Cluniacensis is the handiwork of Nicholas of Clémanges was made by Gilbert Ouy (cf. *Annuaire de l'école pratique des hautes études* (IVᵉ Section. Sciences hist. et philol.), 1965–6, 259); his work on the manuscripts of Nicholas of Clémanges has still to be published.

The traditional view that the humanists did not possess a complete text of Quintilian until Poggio's discovery of the Saint Gall manuscript (now Zürich, Stadtbibl. 288) in 1416 is not invalidated, as some have thought, by Sabbadini's attempt to prove that Nicholas of Clémanges possessed the whole text (*Le scoperte*, 2. pp. 84–5; *Storia*, pp. 283–4). Nicholas could indeed have found a complete Quintilian north of the Alps, had he looked in the right places, but the evidence adduced by Sabbadini does not prove more than that he had access, as did other early humanists, to a *mutilus* plus the excerpt from book 10 (1.46–107) which circulated separately or in conjunction with the incomplete text: cf. P. S. Boscoff, *Speculum*, 27 (1952), 71ff.; M. Winterbottom, *CQ* N.S. 17 (1967), 339 n. 5. But startling evidence that there was a complete Quintilian in Italy as early as the first half of the fourteenth century is provided by Winterbottom, *Problems in Quintilian, Bulletin of the Institute of Classical Studies*, Supplement 25 (London 1970), pp. 20–1.

The evidence for the survival of the Murbach Velleius into August 1786 was published by A. Allgeier in *Miscellanea Mercati*, 6 (Studi e Testi, 126,) 1946, 457ff.

VI

E. J. Kenney has written a penetrating article on the limitations of humanist philology and the problems of its assessment: 'The character of humanist philology', *Classical influences*, ed. Bolgar, pp. 119–28.

We now have a detailed study of the building up of one of the richest and most influential of the Renaissance libraries: B. L. Ullman and P. A. Stadter, *The public library of Renaissance Florence: Niccolò Niccoli, Cosimo de' Medici and the Library of San Marco* (Medioevo e Umanesimo, no. 10,) Padua 1972.

The *Opera omnia* of Valla have been reprinted with a preface by E. Garin and other material, 2 vols., Turin 1962. A different recension of his *Adnotationes in Novum Testamentum* from that printed by Erasmus has been discovered and edited by A. Perosa, Florence 1970. Good examples of his work on Latin texts are provided by Livy and Quintilian. For Livy see Gius. Billanovich, *Journal of the Warburg and Courtauld Institutes*, 14 (1951), 137ff., *IMU* 1 (1958), 245–64 (with M. Ferraris) and 265–75; for Quintilian, M. Winterbottom, *CQ* N.S. 17 (1967), 356ff.

A good idea of the range of Politian's activities is given by the catalogue of an exhibition held at the Biblioteca Laurenziana in 1954 (*Mostra del Poliziano*, a cura di A. Perosa, Florence 1955). See also *Il Poliziano e il suo tempo, Atti del IV convegno internazionale di studi sul Rinascimento*, Florence 1957; I. Maier, *Les Manuscrits d'Ange Politien* (Travaux d'humanisme et Renaissance, no. 70), Geneva 1965. The Greek epigrams were edited by A. Ardizzoni, Florence 1951; the *Miscellanea* will be edited with an important commentary by A. Perosa in the near future. The recently discovered Centuria has now been published as *Angelo Poliziano, Miscellaneorum Centuria Secunda*, ed. critica per cura di V. Branca–M. Pastore Stocchi, vols. 1–4, Florence 1972. On his contribution to the development of the stemmatic method, see S. Timpanaro, *La genesi del metodo del Lachmann*, Florence 1963, especially pp. 4–6. Whether Politian used the Vaticanus of Valerius Flaccus and the lost copy of Statius' *Silvae* is disputed and depends very much on one's opinion of his accuracy as a collator. For two views on the former question see W. Wolfgang Ehlers, *Untersuchungen zur handschriftlichen Überlieferung der Argonautica des C. Valerius Flaccus* (Zetemata 52), Munich 1970, pp. 102ff., E. Courtney, *CR.* N.S. 22 (1972), 216f.; for the latter, M. Pastore Stocchi, 'Sulle *curae statianae* del Poliziano', *Atti del Istituto Veneto, Classe di scienze morali*, 125 (1966–7), 39–74.

VII

The primary sources for this section, together with an extensive discussion, will be found in A. Pertusi, *Leonzio Pilato fra Petrarca e Boccaccio*, Venice–Rome 1964 (pp. 62ff. deal with his copy of Homer). F. Di Benedetto, 'Leonzio, Omero e le "Pandette" ', *IMU* 12 (1969), 53–112, has shown that Leonzio Pilato owned the Florentine Pandects and translated into Latin the Greek quotations of the *Digest*. Petrarch's copy of Plato has been identified as Paris gr. 1807 by A. Diller, *CP* 59 (1964), 270–2.

For Chrysoloras see G. Cammelli, *Manuele Crisolora*, Florence 1941. The way that most humanists had to learn Greek is made clear by R. Sabbadini, *Il metodo degli umanisti*, Florence 1922, pp. 17–27, who cites a letter of Ambrogio Traversari about his own experience and a latter of Aldus to Alberto Pio referring to the use of these methods by Ermolao Barbaro, Pico della Mirandola, and Politian. G. Cammelli, *Demetrio Calcondila*, Florence 1954, p. 7, quotes a letter of Giovanni Antonio Campano in which he complains that he has not yet been able to learn Greek for want of a tutor.

On the discovery of manuscripts in general see R. Sabbadini, *Le scoperte dei codici latini e greci ne' secoli xiv e xv*, reprinted with additions, Florence 1967.

VIII

A short and up-to-date account of Bessarion is given by L. Labowsky in the *Dizionario biografico degli Italiani*. The fundamental work is L. Mohler, *Kardinal Bessarion als Theologe, Humanist und Staatsmann*, Paderborn 1923–42; in the third volume, sub-titled *Aus Bessarions Gelehrtenkreis*, pp. 70–87, will be found the pamphlet expounding his views on the status of the Vulgate translation. His palaeographical researches are outlined in his letter to Alexios Lascaris Philanthropenos. See also J. Gill, *The council of Florence*, Cambridge 1959. To mark the quincentenary of his donation to Venice an exhibition was mounted; the catalogue, which contains also a text of his act of donation, was published as *Cento codici Bessarionei*, a cura di T. G. Leporace e E. Mioni, Venice 1968.

For Valla's *Adnotationes* see the edition by A. Perosa cited above (vi) and in particular p. xxxiv n. 64.

The relevant bibliography on Politian has been given in the notes to section vi.

IX

The authorities on the early printing of Greek are R. Proctor, *The printing of Greek in the 15th century*, Oxford 1900, reprinted 1966, and V. Scholderer, *Greek printing types 1465–1927*, London 1927; see also a paper by the latter on 'Printers and readers in Italy in the fifteenth century', *Proc. Brit. Acad.* 35 (1949), 1–23. The great reduction in book prices brought about by the new invention is made clear by Giovanni Andrea De Bussi, bishop of Aleria, in his preface to the Rome edition of Saint Jerome's letters printed in 1468; he says (fol. 1ᵛ) that books are now available at one fifth of the price that they used to command. But this boast naturally applied to Latin and vernacular texts only. Knowledge of Greek remained for some time a rarity; one may wonder if the frequent tags and quotations of it in the writings of Erasmus, who could count on a very wide readership, imply that the situation had changed for the better in the first two or three decades of the sixteenth century.

On Aldus and Musurus one may consult D. J. Geanakoplos, *Greek scholars in Venice*, Cambridge, Mass., 1962, reprinted 1973 with the title *Byzantium and the Renaissance*. It does not, however, discuss the scholarship of either man in sufficient detail to permit us to form an estimate of their capacities as textual critics, and here further research is required. The favourable judgement on Musurus' edition of Hesychius comes from K. Latte's edition, vol. 1, Copenhagen 1953, p. xxxiii; the addition to the text of Moschus is dealt with by W. Bühler in his edition (Hermes Einzelschriften 13), Wiesbaden 1960, p. 14; fresh light was thrown on the Aristophanes scholia by N. G. Wilson, *CQ* 12 (1962), 32–47 (Musurus' contribution is less substantial than was once believed).

For the history of the Marciana library, which was very badly housed and difficult of access for more than half a century after Bessarion's donation, see J. Valentinelli, *Bibliotheca manuscripta ad S. Marci Venetiarum, Codd. Mss. Latini*, vol. 1, Venice 1868, pp. 10–55.

X

Erasmus' classical scholarship has not been the subject of a properly informed study; one must await the publication of the next volume of Professor Pfeiffer's *History of classical scholarship*. In the meantime one may refer to his paper in *Historisches Jahrbuch*, 74 (1955), 175–88 (= *Ausgewählte Schriften*, Munich 1960, pp. 218–21): this deals with Erasmus' concept of the relation between classical and theological scholarship. Pfeiffer cites a revealing aphorism: incorrect punctuation, a tiny detail in itself, is enough to give rise to heresy (*tantula res gignit haereticum sensum*). P. S. Allen, *Proc. Brit. Acad.* 11 (1924), 349–68, argues that Erasmus' chief services to learning were in editing patristic texts, mainly of Latin Fathers (his attempts to assemble material for an edition of Chrysostom never made enough progress for printing to begin). See also the essay of M. M. Phillips in *Erasmus*, ed. T. A. Dorey, London 1970, pp. 1–30.

For the preparation of the Alcalá Bible and Erasmus' New Testament see the summary in B. M. Metzger, *Text of the N.T.*, pp. 96–103. Erasmus' use of manuscripts for his edition and its subsequent revised impressions has to be worked out from various sources, including his letters and passing remarks in his commentaries on the New Testament (the idea of a systematic exposition of the manuscripts used for an edition is relatively modern). The facts stated in the text depend on P. S. Allen's introduction to letter 373 in vol. 2 of *Opus epistolarum Desiderii Erasmi Roterodami*, Oxford 1906–54, pp. 164–6. Allen's account seems to be reliable, with the possible exception of his statement about the Leicester codex. With regard to the Vatican codex B (Vat. gr. 1209), Erasmus had learned of its existence in 1521, and when he was reminded of its importance some years later by the Spanish humanist and theologian Sepúlveda he failed to respond as he should have done. In his reply to Sepúlveda he suggested that a Greek manuscript which supported some readings of the Vulgate had probably been tampered with, not realizing that the great age of B made this relatively implausible; and he advanced the exaggerated but not entirely unreasonable proposition that the only way to be sure of recovering the original Greek was to go back to the text as cited by patristic authorities of the third, fourth, and fifth centuries (letter 2905, written in 1534).

A good way of approaching the *Adagia* is to read M. M. Phillips, *The 'Adages' of Erasmus*, Cambridge 1964; on pp. 65–9 there is an account of the polemic arising from Erasmus' stay in Aldus' house. His stay is also described by D. J. Geanakoplos, *Greek Scholars in Venice*; see especially pp. 273–5 for the question of the so-called Erasmian pronunciation of Greek.

For further orientation and bibliography, P. Petitmengin, 'Comment étudier l'activité d'Érasme éditeur de textes antiques', *Colloquia Erasmiana Turonensia*, vol. 1 (Paris 1972), pp. 217–22. See also E. Bloch, 'Erasmus and the Froben Press: the making of an editor', *Library Quarterly*, 35 (1965), 109–120.

On Seneca, L. D. Reynolds, *The Medieval Tradition of Seneca's Letters*, Oxford 1965, pp. 4–6, W. Trillitzsch, *Philologus*, 109 (1965), 270–93, M. M. Phillips, op. cit., 15–17.

CHAPTER 5

I

Erasmus' *Ciceronianus* has been edited with substantial prolegomena by A. Gambaro, Brescia 1965. He discusses the history of the controversy, but it is also worth consulting *'Attic' and baroque prose style: the anti-Ciceronian movement*, essays by Morris W. Croll, edited by Patrick-Evans-Wallace, Princeton, N.J., 1966 (paperback 1969). For the

Estienne family see especially E. Armstrong, *Robert Estienne, royal printer*, Cambridge 1954. Vettori's work on the Latin Aristotle is discussed by B. Schneider, *Die mittelalterlichen griechisch-lateinischen Uebersetzungen der Aristotelischen Rhetorik*, Berlin 1971, pp. 73–6. Robortello's scholarship has been discussed by A. Carlini, 'L'attività filologica di Francesco Robortello', *Atti dell' Accademia di Udine*, 7 (1967), 36ff. On Fulvio Orsini the standard work is still P. de Nolhac, *La Bibliothèque de Fulvio Orsini* (Bibl. de l'École des Hautes Études, 74), Paris 1887. For the Vatican edition of Saint Augustine see P. Petit-mengin, 'Le Saint Augustin de la typographie vaticane', *Recherches augustiniennes*, 4 (1966), 199–251. For Thomas James see N. R. Ker, 'Thomas James' collation of Gregory, Cyprian and Ambrose', *Bodleian Library Record*, 4 (1952), 16–32.

II

For the progress of studies on early French humanism one may consult, in addition to F. Simone, *Il Rinascimento francese*, and other works mentioned in the notes to the previous chapter: *Humanism in France at the end of the Middle Ages and in the early Renaissance*, ed. A. H. T. Levi, Manchester 1970; E. Ornato, *Jean Muret et ses amis Nicolas de Clamanges et Jean de Montreuil*, Geneva 1969.

Short accounts of Budé are provided by L. Delaruelle, *Guillaume Budé: les origines, les débuts, les idées maîtresses*, Paris 1907; J. Plattard, *Guillaume Budé et les origines de l'humanisme français*, Paris 1966. See also R. R. Bolgar, 'Humanism as a value system with reference to Budé and Vives', *Humanism in France*, pp. 199–215, and the Catalogue of the Budé Exhibition, *VIIIᵉ Congrès international Guillaume Budé*, Paris 1968.

There are not as many recent studies of individual French scholars of this period as one would wish. An exception is V. Hall, *Life of Julius Caesar Scaliger* (1484–1558) (*Trans. Amer. Philosoph. Soc.*, N.S. 40, Part 2), Philadelphia, Pa., 1950, and Mark Pattison's classic *Isaac Casaubon* (2nd ed., Oxford 1892) retains its value. For a brilliant demonstration that Julius Caesar Scaliger was plain Giulio Bordon, see M. Billanovich, 'Benedetto Bordon e Giulio Cesare Scaligero', *IMU* 11 (1968), 187–256.

For Turnebus's manuscript of Plautus, see W. M. Lindsay, *The codex Turnebi of Plautus*, Oxford 1898. The significance of Joseph Scaliger's work on Catullus has been pointed out by Timpanaro, *La genesi del metodo*, pp. 9–10.

III

The study of the scholarship of the Netherlands is facilitated by some good articles in the *Biographie Nationale*, published by the Académie Royale des Sciences et des Lettres et des Beaux-Arts de Belgique (1866–1944, with later Supplements). Isaac Vossius qualifies for an entry in the *Dictionary of National Biography*. Also useful are L. Müller, *Geschichte der klassischen Philologie in den Niederlanden*, Leipzig 1869; G. Cohen, *Écrivains français en Hollande dans la première moitié du XVIIᵉ siècle*, Paris 1920.

It is not surprising, in view of the amount of time and effort expended on editing texts and producing critical miscellanea, that there should be a market for theoretical studies of textual criticism. Canter, who had been anticipated by Robortello, was succeeded in 1597 by a German scholar, Caspar Schoppe, whose *De arte critica* did for Latin texts what Canter had done for Greek; it also attempts a brief history of textual criticism by reviewing critics ancient and modern. Exactly a century later appeared the first edition of the more ambitious *Ars critica* of Jean Le Clerc.

Modius' search for manuscripts has been fully documented and discussed by P. Lehmann, *Franciscus Modius als Handschriftenforscher* (Quellen und Untersuchungen zur lateinischen Philologie des Mittelalters, 3.1), Munich 1908.

For two recent views on the Blandinius of Horace, see Pasquali, *Storia della tradizione*, pp. 381ff.; E. Fraenkel, *Horace*, Oxford 1957, pp. 97ff.

Lipsius' methods have been studied by J. Ruysschaert, *Juste Lipse et les Annales de Tacite: une méthode de critique textuelle au XVIᵉ siècle*, Louvain 1949. His work on Tacitus is assessed critically by C. O. Brink, 'Justus Lipsius and the text of Tacitus', *JRS* 41 (1951), 32–51; F. R. D. Goodyear, *The Annals of Tacitus*, vol. 1, Cambridge 1972, pp. 8–10.

N. Heinsius collated manuscripts of Ovid on such a scale that their identification and evaluation have been slow, despite the fact that the Heinsius material is available in Oxford and Berlin and that the manuscripts he used are still extant. The latest contributions of importance are H. Boese, 'Zu den Ovidkollationen des N. Heinsius', *Philologus*, 106 (1962), 155–73; F. W. Lenz, 'Die Wiedergewinnung der von Heinsius benutzten Ovidhandschriften II', *Eranos*, 61 (1963), 98–120. An article by M. D. Reeve is forthcoming (*RhM* 1974).

IV

Bentley is treated at considerable length here because of his position in both classical and biblical studies, and it did not seem possible to do justice to him without giving some details of his life and work. Sir R. C. Jebb, *Bentley*, London 1882, is a lively and entertaining account with bibliography. *The Epistola ad Joannem Millium* has been reprinted with an introduction by G. P. Goold, Toronto 1962 (note that the date of Malalas is incorrectly given as the eighth or ninth century).

The history of biblical scholarship is set out by B. Metzger, *The text of the New Testament*, pp. 95ff., but we have given here rather more detail of Bentley's *Proposals* and taken a different view of the importance of Richard Simon; on him one may consult the study of Jean Steinmann, *Richard Simon et les origines de l'exégèse biblique*, Desclée de Brouwer 1960, but there too the important details are not always fully brought out. The facts recounted in the text are drawn from chapters 29–33 of his *Histoire critique*, principally from 29.

V

For a convenient sketch of the history of palaeography one may consult L. Traube, *Geschichte der Paläographie*, printed in vol. 1 of his *Vorlesungen und Abhandlungen*, Munich 1909, pp. 13–80. David Knowles, *Great historical enterprises: problems in monastic history*, London 1963, pp. 33–62, gives an attractive short account of the achievements of the Maurists in scholarship, without giving quite as much detail as one might wish about palaeography. His essay on the Bollandists, ibid., pp. 1–32, should also be consulted for the life and work of van Papenbroeck; he was one of the continuators of Jean Bolland's great project for a comprehensive edition of the lives of the saints, *Acta Sanctorum*; an impressive series of volumes has been, and is still being, produced by a small team of Jesuits in Belgium, who despite some interruptions due to wars and revolutions have maintained an astonishing academic tradition over the centuries. See further P. Peeters, *L'œuvre des Bollandistes*, 2nd ed., Brussels 1961.

Traube and Knowles give all the essential guidance for further reading about the Maurists and Maffei. But on the latter one may also refer to an essay by A. Momigliano, 'Mabillon's Italian disciples', in *Terzo contributo alla storia degli studi classici e del mondo antico*, Rome 1966, pp. 135–52. Maffei's letters, in addition to the works mentioned by Traube, contain some statements about palaeography; see nos. 158 and 160 in the *Epistolario*, ed. C. Garibotto, Milan 1955, pp. 199–201, 203–4.

VI

(a) The first comprehensive account of Latin palimpsests is that of E. Chatelain, 'Les Palimpsestes latins', *Annuaire, École pratique des hautes études, Section des sciences hist. et philol.* 1904 (published 1903), pp. 5–42. This has now been largely superseded by E. A. Lowe, '*Codices rescripti*: a list of Latin palimpsests with stray observations on their origin', *Mélanges Eugène Tisserant*, vol. 5, Vatican 1964 (Studi e Testi 235), 67–112, reprinted in *Palaeographical papers*, 2. 480–519. S. Timpanaro provides an excellent account of both Angelo Mai and the early history of palimpsest discovery in 'Angelo Mai', *Atene e Roma*, N.S. 1 (1956), 3–34. For the new palimpsest fragment of Fronto, still absent from all editions, see B. Bischoff, 'Der Fronto-Palimpsest der Mauriner', *Sitz. Bayer. Akad. der Wiss., Phil.-Hist. Kl.* (1958), p. 2. Further information can be sought in the editions of the texts concerned.

(b) On papyri in general see the works by E. G. Turner, cited above on Chapter 1 (1). It is also worthwhile to read Sir H. I. Bell, *Egypt from Alexander the Great to the Arab conquest*, Oxford 1948, which is still an excellent introduction from a cultural and historical point of view.

The codex containing Menander's *Dyscolus* has given us in addition a substantial proportion of his *Aspis* and *Samia* (edited by C. F. L. Austin, Berlin 1969); the fragments of the latter overlap to some extent with those already known, with the result that in these passages we possess two uncommonly early witnesses to the text of a classical author.

Literary papyri, including the very small number of Latin texts among them, are listed with a bibliography by R. A. Pack, *The Greek and Latin literary texts from Greco-Roman Egypt*, Ann Arbor, Mich., 1965. For statistics showing how the main authors are represented at various dates see W. H. Willis, *GRBS* 9 (1968), 205–41.

(c) A history of the Homeric Question is given by Adam Parry in the introduction to the collected papers of his father Milman Parry, *The making of Homeric verse*, Oxford 1971, pp. xiii–xv.

Leopardi's disappointing experience is recounted by S. Timpanaro in *Differenze*, 9 (*Studi in memoria di Carlo Ascheri*), Urbino 1970, pp. 357–79.

Heiberg's find of Archimedes was announced in *Hermes*, 42 (1907), 235ff. On Juvenal VI and Saint Cyprian see J. G. Griffith, *Hermes*, 91 (1963), 104–14. For the new letter of Saint Cyprian see also M. Bévenot, *The tradition of manuscripts: a study in the transmission of St. Cyprian's treatises*, Oxford 1961. The Epigrammata Bobiensia were edited by

A. Campana and F. Munari, Rome 1955. More recent still is the recovery, from a strip of parchment used for binding, of 39 mutilated lines of Rutilius Namatianus: see M. Ferrari, 'Spigolature bobbiesi, I: In margine ai *Codices Latini Antiquiores*, II: Frammenti ignoti di Rutilio Namaziano', *IMU* 16 (1973), 1–31.

(d) Roberto Weiss, in *The Renaissance discovery of classical antiquity*, Oxford 1969, traces the beginnings of an interest in the tangible remains of antiquity. For the impact of inscriptions on literary texts, see the section 'Rapports avec la littérature' of the 'Bulletin epigraphique' of J. and L. Robert in the *Revue des études grecques*.

The *Res gestae* of Augustus, sometimes referred to as the *Monumentum Ancyranum*, has been frequently edited and it will suffice to mention the editions of J. Gagé, Paris 1935, and P. A. Brunt–J. M. Moore, Oxford 1967. The *Laudatio Turiae* has been edited with a translation and commentary by M. Durry, *Éloge funèbre d'une matrone romaine*, Paris 1950.

For the monument of Antiochus of Commagene and its importance for the history of ancient prose style, see K. Humann and O. Puchstein, *Reisen in Kleinasien und Nordsyrien*, Berlin 1890, and E. Norden, *Die antike Kunstprosa*, 2nd ed., Leipzig–Berlin 1909, vol. 1, pp. 140ff.

Diogenes of Oenoanda has been recently re-edited and studied by C. W. Chilton, *Diogenis Oenoandensis fragmenta*, Leipzig 1967; *Diogenes of Oenoanda: The Fragments*, Oxford 1971. There is an important article on the inscription by J. Irigoin, *Studi filologici e storici in onore di Vittorio De Falco*, Naples 1971, pp. 477–85; and for recent progress in the finding of new fragments, see M. F. Smith, *AJA* (1970), 51–62 and plates 11–16, ibid. (1971), 357–89 and plates 81–4.

For the early Christian hymn, see P. Maas, *Kleine Schriften*, Munich 1973, p. 315.

Pompeian graffiti have been collected and edited by E. Diehl, *Pompeianische Wandinschriften und Verwandtes*, 2nd ed. (Kleine Texte für Vorlesungen und Übungen 56), Berlin 1930. For the corpus of epigraphic poetry, see the relevant parts of the *Anthologia latina* edited by F. Bücheler and E. Lommatzsch, vols. 1–3, Leipzig 1930², 1897, 1926; E. Engström, *Carmina latina epigraphica*, Gothenburg 1911. The occurrence of *arma virumque* on ancient walls is documented by R. P. Hoogma, *Der Einfluss Vergils auf die Carmina Latina Epigraphica*, Amsterdam 1959, pp. 222f. The text of Propertius 3.16.13f. is discussed by M. E. Hubbard in 'Propertiana', *CQ* N.S. 18 (1968), 318f.

CHAPTER 6

Our account of stemmatic theory and the history of its evolution depends on P. Maas, *Textual criticism*, Oxford 1958, and S. Timpanaro, *La genesi del metodo del Lachmann*, Florence 1963, revised and translated into German under the title *Die Entstehung der Lachmannschen Methode*, Hamburg 1971. Timpanaro's second and third appendices are also important explorations of areas of stemmatic theory. Maas' exposition is so brief as to verge on the obscure, and some of the finer points of stemmatic theory require a full statement in order to make latent assumptions explicit. Timpanaro, *Maia*, 23 (1970), 289, pointed to one such assumption in the fourth of the inferences from our hypothetical stemma on p. 191, where we have added a parenthesis to meet the case: the agreement of one of the MSS. XYZ with β indicates the reading of α, *provided that* the readings of the other two of the MSS. XYZ disagree with each other; if they agree, as can happen, the tradition has been affected by contamination or emendation. L. Canfora, *Belfagor*, 23 (1968) 361-4, has directed attention to some other obscurities in Maas's presentation of the theory.

Limitations of the stemmatic method were emphasized by G. Pasquali, *Storia della tradizione e critica del testo*, 2nd ed., Florence 1952, and they have been urged more recently, but perhaps too passionately, by R. D. Dawe, *The collation and investigation of manuscripts of Aeschylus*, Cambridge 1964. We have tried to make it clear in our text that controversy on this subject is largely misplaced. Maas knew as well as anyone else that there is no simple answer to the problems of a contaminated tradition, but some critics have failed to notice his explicit statement on the matter. Others, perhaps unduly impressed by the wealth of examples in Pasquali's rather discursive but deservedly famous book, most of which is devoted to unusual traditions, have assumed that contamination is the rule rather than the exception, and that consequently Maas's theory is of no practical use. We doubt whether Pasquali could have wished to create this impression, and it must be stressed that in many traditions the amount of contamination that has taken place is not sufficient to prevent the useful application of stemmatic theory. It may be worth adding here that an interesting *eliminatio codicum* has recently been performed in the stemma of Aristotle's *Rhetoric*, where the tradition is not entirely free from contamination; see R. Kassel, *Der Text der Aristotelischen Rhetorik*, Berlin 1971, pp. 54-5.

I

G. B. Alberti, *SIFC* 40 (1968), 44–60, has observed that the term 'open tradition' has come to be used in more than one sense. Pasquali's original use meant that judgement rather than the application of automatic rules was needed in order to infer the readings of the archetype, and in this sense the word can obviously be applied to traditions in which there is no single archetype.

The facts about Saint Cyprian and Juvenal VI have been commented on above in Chapter 5, section (VI) c.

The standard work on second editions in antiquity is H. Emonds, *Zweite Auflage im Altertum*, Leipzig 1941. For the question of author variants in the case of Longus, and for a recent bibliography of the whole subject, see M. D. Reeve, 'Author's variants in Longus?', *Proc. Camb. Philol. Soc.*, 195 (1969), 75–85 (with a reply by D. C. C. Young, ibid. 197 (1971), 99–107); for Ovid, add A. S. Hollis, *Ovid, Metamorphoses Book VIII*, Oxford 1970, pp. x–xi, xxvii. A most instructive discussion of the problems raised by indirect tradition is offered by S. Timpanaro, *Maia*, 22 (1970), 351–9.

The principle of *difficilior lectio* seems to have been first expressly formulated as a criterion by Jean Le Clerc (Clericus) in his *Ars Critica*, vol. 2, Amsterdam 1697, p. 389: cf. S. Timpanaro, *La genesi*, p. 21.

Two other critical principles which are useful from time to time may be briefly mentioned here. One is the so-called geographical criterion, which appears in two forms. The first of these involves the notion of survivals on the periphery of a culture, and is an application of a notion that has been fruitful in comparative philology: if there is agreement in striking variants between manuscripts written in two or more peripheral areas of a culture, these readings are probably survivals from a very ancient state of the text. It is not often that we are in a position to know enough about the place of origin of the manuscripts in question, especially if they are Greek, to apply this criterion. The other form of the geographical criterion was worked out by critics of the New Testament, by which one or more manuscripts are assigned to a region, whether peripheral or not, and reference is still frequently made to the Western, Caesarean, and Alexandrian text or family of manuscripts.

Another useful principle in the criticism of prose authors is Wettstein's canon *brevior lectio potior*. This too was devised because of the problems of editing the New Testament, and in particular because of the many additional phrases and sentences found in the Western text, represented notably by the codex Bezae. On both these principles one should consult B. M. Metzger, *The text of the New Testament*.

Valuable advice on dealing with contaminated traditions is given by M. L. West, *Textual criticism and editorial technique* (Stuttgart 1973), pp. 37–46. This book is intended to replace to a great extent both Paul Maas's *Textkritik* and O. Stählin's *Editionstechnik*, 2nd ed., Leipzig 1914.

For other methods of recension, see H. Quentin, *Mémoire sur l'établissement du texte de la Vulgate*, Rome 1922, *Essais de critique textuelle*, Paris 1926; W. W. Greg, *The calculus of variants*, Oxford 1927; A. A. Hill, 'Postulates for distributional study of texts', *Studies in Bibliography, Papers of the Bibliog. Soc. Univ. Virginia* 3 (1950–1), 63–95; V. A. Dearing, *A manual of textual analysis*, Berkeley 1959. The rapidly increasing number of publications on the use of computers in textual and related studies presents a problem in that much of it demands a measure of familiarity with current mathematical theory. But a representative picture of methods and progress in this field may be obtained from Dom J. Froger, *La Critique des textes et son automatisation*, Paris 1968; H. Love, 'The computer and literary editing: achievements and prospects', in *The computer in literary and linguistic research*, ed. R. A. Wisbey, Cambridge 1971, pp. 47–56; B. Fischer, 'The use of computers in New Testament studies, with special reference to textual criticism', *JTS* N.S. 21 (1970), 279–308; W. Ott, 'Computer applications in textual criticism', *The computer in literary studies*, ed. A. J. Aitken, R. W. Bailey, N. Hamilton-Smith, Edinburgh 1973, pp. 199–223. Two practical demonstrations of the application of the methods of numerical taxonomy to the classification of manuscripts, intelligible to both literate and numerate, are given by J. G. Griffith: 'A taxonomic study of the manuscript tradition of Juvenal', *Mus. Helv.* 25 (1968), 101–38; 'Numerical taxonomy and some primary manuscripts of the Gospels', *JTS* 20 (1969), 389–406.

Our account of textual criticism may give the impression that once a text has been printed for the first time its form is static except where an editor deliberately alters it. In fact there is sometimes more error and fluctuation than might be supposed, as has been shown in a particular case by A. Severyns, *Texte et apparat: histoire critique d'une tradition imprimée*, Brussels 1962.

In conclusion we mention a small selection of books and articles on textual criticism which supplement the information given above:

(a) M. Bévenot, *The tradition of manuscripts: a study in the transmission of St. Cyprian's treatises*, Oxford 1961.

    A. C. Clark, *The descent of manuscripts*, Oxford 1918, reprinted 1969.

A. Dain, *Les Manuscrits*, 2nd ed., Paris 1964.

H. Fränkel, *Einleitung zur kritischen Ausgabe der Argonautika des Apollonius*, Göttingen 1964. The theoretical sections were translated into Italian under the title *Testo critico e critica del testo*, Florence 1969.

B. A. van Groningen, *Traité d'histoire et de critique des textes grecs*, Amsterdam 1963.

L. Havet, *Manuel de critique verbale appliquée aux textes latins*, Paris 1911.

A. E. Housman, *Selected prose*, ed. J. Carter, Cambridge 1961. (see also the complete prefaces to the editions of Juvenal, Lucan, and Manilius).

J. Jackson, *Marginalia scaenica*, Oxford 1955.

W. M. Lindsay, *An introduction to Latin textual emendation*, London 1896.

B. H. Streeter, *The Four Gospels*, Oxford 1936[5].

J. Willis, *Latin textual criticism* (Illinois Studies in Languages and Literature, 61), Urbana 1972.

(b) R. Browning, 'Recentiores non deteriores', *BICS* 7 (1960), 11–21.

W. Bühler, 'Gibt es einen gemeinsamen Archetypus der beiden Überlieferungsstränge von Tertullians Apologeticum?', *Philologus*, 109 (1965), 121–33.

W. Headlam, 'Transposition of words in MSS', *CR* 16 (1902), 243–56.

J. Irigoin, 'Éditions d'auteur et rééditions à la fin de l'antiquité (à propos du "Traité de la virginité" de Grégoire de Nysse), *Rev. phil.* 96 (1970), 101–6.

A. H. McDonald, 'Textual criticism', in *The Oxford Classical Dictionary*, 2nd ed., Oxford 1970.

R. Merkelbach, 'Interpolierte Eigennamen', *Zeitschrift für Papyrologie und Epigraphik*, 1 (1967), 100–2.

R. M. Ogilvie, 'Monastic corruption', *Greece and Rome*, 18 (1971), 32–4.

T. C. Skeat, 'The use of dictation in ancient book production', *Proc. Brit. Acad.* 38 (1952), 179–208.

D. C. C. Young, 'Some types of error in manuscripts of Aeschylus' *Oresteia*', *GRBS* 5 (1964), 85–99.
'Some types of scribal error in manuscripts of Pindar', *GRBS* 6 (1965), 247–73.

INDEX OF MANUSCRIPTS

Note: the number of collections, both public and private, which contain Greek and Latin manuscripts of direct importance for the subjects treated in this book, is very considerable. Guides to printed descriptions or handwritten catalogues are given for Greek by M. Richard, *Répertoire des bibliothèques et des catalogues des manuscrits grecs*, 2nd ed., Paris 1958, with a *Supplément*, Paris 1965, and for Latin by P. O. Kristeller, *Latin manuscript books before 1600*, 3rd ed., New York 1965. The history of manuscripts since their discovery in the Renaissance is in some cases very complicated. The formation of some of the major libraries has been made the subject of specialized monographs which are outside the scope of the present book. It would be useful if students were able to refer to a short account of the movements of manuscripts from the Renaissance to the present day, which would explain the names and present location of the various collections and would incidentally cast an interesting light on a section of European cultural history. At the moment there does not seem to be a study which precisely fills this need, but the chapter on the 'Nomenclature of manuscripts' in F. W. Hall, *A companion to classical texts*, is still valuable; and for a selective treatment of the subject see M. R. James, *The wanderings and homes of manuscripts* (Helps for Students of History no. 17), London 1919, G. Laurion, 'Les Principales Collections de manuscrits grecs', *Phoenix*, 15 (1961), 1–13.

A: MANUSCRIPTS

ATHOS
Almost all the monasteries on Mount Athos have a number of manuscripts; some of the collections are extremely large and have a nucleus of books acquired in the Middle Ages.
Lavra 184: 59
Vatopedi 747: 59

BAMBERG, Staatliche Bibliothek
Class. 35: 96

BASLE, Universitätsbibliothek
A.VII.3: 233
A.N.IV.1: 143

BERLIN, Deutsche Staatsbibliothek
This library is in East Berlin; during the Second World War the books were removed for safety, but some were lost and others are now provisionally held in West Berlin. A good many of the manuscripts come from the library of the nineteenth-century English eccentric Sir Thomas Phillipps. ~Collector of Gaelic (Irish) MSS inter alia.~
Diez B.66: 86
lat. fol. 252: 100
lat. qu. 364: 76

B: PAPYRI

After publication many papyri have been distributed to libraries or other
institutions which bore part of the cost of the excavations in Egypt. In such
cases they usually receive a shelf-mark in the library in question, in addition
to retaining their serial number in the original publication.

GENERAL INDEX

NOTES TO THE PLATES

I. Oxford, Bodleian Library, MS. gr. class a.1(P). 2nd cent. The papyrus known as the Hawara *Iliad*. The fibrous nature of the material is clearly visible.

II. Venice, Biblioteca Marciana, MS. gr. 454, fol. 41ʳ. 10th cent. This famous book from the collection of cardinal Bessarion is generally known as Venetus A of the *Iliad*.

Plates I and II illustrate the relation between the Alexandrian critical signs and the commentary. They both show the same passage of the *Iliad* (ii. 856ff.); the papyrus has the critical signs in the margin but no scholia, the manuscript has both. It is not surprising to find that the signs are not quite identical. A *diplē* seems to be the correct sign at 856, but the papyrus apparently has the *diplē periestigmenē*; the scholia have simply a geographical note about the Alizones and add that there was another Hodios in the Greek camp, but there is no indication of a difference between Aristarchus and Zenodotus here. At 858 the papyrus has a *diplē*, and the manuscript a note that the name Chromis is elsewhere given as Chromios. 859–61 are obelized in the papyrus, 860–1 in the manuscript, and the ground given in the latter is that in the battle by the river the death of Chromis is not related, whereas Homer is careful to record the death of any commander of a contingent; this is a good example of an argument that does not satisfy the modern reader. At 863 both books have a *diplē*, and the manuscript gives a geographical note on the use of the name Phrygia.

III. Oxford, Bodleian Library, MS. E. D. Clarke 39, fol. 113ʳ. A.D 895. Plato; the plate shows the opening of the *Sophist*. The text was written for Arethas by the scribe known as John the Calligrapher, who also prepared for Arethas a copy of Aelius Aristides (MSS. Laur. 60.3 and Paris gr. 2951). The marginal scholia are in Arethas' own hand; the first note begins: αὕτη ἡ ἐλαία οὐχ ὥc τινεc ὑπέλαβον τῆc Ἰωνίαc ἐcτιν ἀλλὰ τῆc Ἰταλίαc, εἴ τι δεῖ Cτράβωνι πείθεcθαι τῷ γεωγράφῳ.

IV. Oxford, Bodleian Library, MS. Auct. V. 1.51, fol. 94ʳ. Late 10th cent. Notes on the *Odyssey*. The plate shows the outline of the story of Book XI (the descent to the underworld), followed by the beginning of the vocabulary list for that book. Such aids were necessary for readers in the Middle Ages and their existence throws light on the school curriculum. This MS. is from the collection of Giovanni Aurispa and later belonged to the monastery of San Marco in Florence. The opening clause reads: ἀπαγγέλλει πῶς κατὰ τῆς Κίρκης ἐντολὰς λαβὼν εἰς ῞Αιδου κατῆλθεν.

V. Oxford, Bodleian Library, MS. Auct. T. 4.13, fol. 132ʳ. 11th cent. The archetype of the works of Epictetus. It is thought that Arethas possessed a manuscript of this text, of which the Oxford MS. is perhaps a direct copy. The script displays a certain number of abbreviations. The opening words read: ἐλεύθερος ἐστιν ὁ ζῶν ὡς βούλεται, ὃν οὔτ' ἀναγκάσαι ἔστιν οὔτε κωλῦσαι οὔτε βιάσασθαι.

VI. Oxford, Bodleian Library, MS. Barocci 109, fol. 167ʳ. 15th cent. This late copy of Aratus' *Phaenomena* is one of the few which have the lines interpolated by Planudes. The plate shows line 480 followed by the interpolation. The name Triclinius in the right-hand margin is thought to indicate his authorship of the scholium at the foot of the page explaining what Planudes had done. It reads as follows: ἰστέον δὲ ὅτι ἡ τοῦ Ἀράτου σφαῖρα οὐκ ἀκριβῶς ἔχει πρὸς τὴν θέσιν τῶν κύκλων ἐκτεθειμένα τὰ ζώδια. ἡ δὲ τοῦ Πτολεμαίου λίαν ἠκριβωμένως ἐκτίθεται. ταύτῃ γοῦν τῇ τοῦ Πτολεμαίου σφαίρᾳ ἑπόμενος ὁ σοφὸς Πλανούδης κατὰ τὴν ἐκείνης θέσιν ἐκδέδωκε τοὺς παρόντας στίχους, ἐναλ<λ>άξας ὅσα μὴ καλῶς εἴρηκεν ὁ ῞Αρατος. διὸ οἱ ἐντυγχάνοντες ταύταις καὶ μάλιστα τοῖς περὶ τούτων λεχθεῖσι παρὰ ἀμφοτέρων ἔχουσιν ἀκριβῆ τὴν περὶ τούτων κατάληψιν, ἀμφοτέρους [ἐπὶ τούτοις] εὑρίσκοντες ἐπὶ τούτοις συμφωνοῦντας.

VII. Oxford, Bodleian Library, MS. Holkham gr. 88, fol. 207ʳ. 15th cent. Aristophanes. This copy shows the text and scholia in the recension prepared about a century earlier by Demetrius Triclinius; it is the only known manuscript source for his scholia to four of the plays. Note in this plate Triclinius' scholium on metre at the foot of the page (beginning ἡ εἴσθεσις τοῦ παρόντος δράματος) and his misleading title to the main body of scholia, 'old scholia by Aristophanes the grammarian'.

VIII. The *editio princeps* of Aristophanes, Venice 1498, at the Aldine press. Text and scholia were prepared by Musurus, who had among his manuscript materials at least two copies of the Triclinian recension. In the style of type-face and arrangement of text and scholia there is a close resemblance to contemporary manuscripts. The marginal scholia, after the lemma ὀρθὴν κελεύεις, begin with the metrical note of Triclinius shown in the previous plate.

IX. Florence, Biblioteca Medicea-Laurenziana, MS. Laur. 39.1, fol. 8ʳ. This is the codex Mediceus of Vergil, written in Italy in the 5th century. It was corrected at Rome by Asterius, consul in 494, and later found its way to Bobbio. The script is rustic capital. The plate shows the end of the *Eclogues* (10.61–77). Abbreviations are few, here restricted to *B·* (*bus*) and *Q·* (*que*). Among the corrections, apparently by Asterius himself, we may note in line 62 the change from *DRUSUM* to *RURSUS* and *NABIS* to *NOBIS*, and in line 70 *HAES* corrected to *HAEC*. In line 63 the reading *RURSUSM* suggests a *duplex lectio* at an earlier stage in the tradition (*RURSUS/M*). In the space left vacant at the end of the *Eclogues* Asterius has added a subscription recording his work on the manuscript, rounded off with a poem in elegiacs. The subscription is written in a small hand and is somewhat defaced; the first part reads (the abbreviations are expanded and enclosed within brackets): *Turcius Rufius Apronianus Asterius v(ir) c(larissimus) et inl(ustris), ex comite domest(icorum) protect(orum), ex com(ite) priv(atarum) largit(ionum), ex praef(ecto) urbi, patricius et consul ordin(arius) legi et distincxi codicem fratris Macharii v(iri) c(larissimi) non mei fiducia set eius cui si et ad omnia sum devotus arbitrio XI Kal. Mai(as) Romae.*

X. Biblioteca Apostolica Vaticana, MS. Vat. lat. 5757, fol. 171ʳ. The famous palimpsest of Cicero's *De republica*. Originally a *de luxe* edition of Cicero, it was reused in the 7th century at Bobbio to copy a text of Augustine on the Psalms. The primary script is a bold uncial of the late 4th or early 5th century, the secondary script is a small uncial of [Irish] the 7th century. Here we have part of *De republica* 2.33. The lower text reads: *ENIM SERPIT/SED VOLAT IN/OPTIMUM STA/TUM INSTITU/TO TUO SERMO/NE REMP·POS /TUM NUMAE/ POMPILI NEPOS/EX FILIA REX/A POPULO EST/ANCUS MAR/CIUS CONSTITU/(TUS).*

XI. Paris, Bibliothèque Nationale, MS. lat. 5730, fol. 77ᵛ. This uncial manuscript of Livy's third decade was written in Italy in the first half of the 5th century and is the parent of all the complete extant manuscripts of this decade. A direct copy of it, written at Tours about the year 800, is shown on Plate XIII. For the history of this manuscript in the Carolingian Renaissance see p. 86. The parchment is so fine and thin that in places, as here, the writing shows through from the other side of the leaf. Both this plate and Plate XIII show the beginning of Book XXIII; in line 11 a second hand has 'corrected' *MOPSIORUM* to *COMPSINORUM*, and this further change in an already corrupt passage has established itself in the text of the copy (Plate XIII).

XII. Leiden, Bibliotheek der Rijksuniversiteit, MS. Voss. lat. F. 4, fol. 20ᵛ. This beautiful manuscript of the Elder Pliny, written in Anglo-Saxon majuscule, was produced in Northumbria in the first half of the 8th century. The plate shows the opening of Book IV of the *Naturalis Historia*, beginning: *tertius europe sinus acrocerauniis incipit montibus finitur helisponto amplectitur praeter minores simus* (i.e. *sinus*) $\overline{XIX}.\overline{XXV}$ *passuum*. The first three words are repeated in the margin in minuscule.

XIII. Biblioteca Apostolica Vaticana, MS. Vat. Reg. lat. 762, fol. 32ʳ. Caroline minuscule. This manuscript of Livy's third decade was written at Tours about the year 800 and copied directly from the 5th-century uncial manuscript shown on Plate XI. Both plates show approximately the same passage from the beginning of Book XXIII. The survival of both ancient exemplar and minuscule copy enable one to examine the mistakes which arise when a medieval scribe copies an ancient book, and the errors made in this transcription have been collected and studied (F. W. Shipley, *Certain sources of corruption in Latin manuscripts*, New York 1904). The words are divided for the most part, there is little punctuation, and abbreviations are few, e.g. *q̃*; (*que*), *b̃*; (*bus*), *p̄* (*prae*). Some cursive elements survive from earlier scripts, the open *a* which appears along with the other forms of the letter and the ligatures of *et*, *rt*, *st*. The open *a* disappeared in time, and the majuscule *N*, here used alongside the minuscule form, later had a more restricted use.

XIV. Florence, Biblioteca Medicea-Laurenziana, MS. Laur. 68.2, fol. 6ᵛ. This is the manuscript which has preserved for us *Annals* XI–XVI and the *Histories* of Tacitus. It was written at Monte Cassino during the latter half of the 11th century and provides an example of Bene-ventan script of the best period. The plate shows the last words of *Annals* XI and the beginning of XII. The end of Book XI is seriously corrupt and reads: *sed ex quis* (glossed with *quibus*) *deterrima orerentur tristitiis multis*.

XV. London, British Museum, MS. Harley 2493, fol. 101ᵛ. The history of this manuscript of Livy, written about the year 1200 and later in the possession of both Petrarch and Valla, is told on pp. 114–15. The plate shows one of the passages of Livy (21.46.3) used by Valla to discredit the scholarship of his rivals Panormita and Facio (see p. 126). The manuscript offers the corrupt *ex quo propinquo*. Valla points out that, while his rivals had failed to see anything wrong with the transmitted text, Petrarch had long since altered *ex quo* to *ex loco*, and Petrarch's correction can still be seen in the text. In the margin Valla has written his own conjecture *exque*, an emendation accepted by modern editors. One may note in passing the increased use of abbreviation at this period.

XVI. Florence, Biblioteca Medicea-Laurenziana, MS. Laur. 48.22, fol. 121^r. This manuscript contains Cicero's *Philippics* and *Catilinarians* and was written by Poggio in 1425. Here we have the end of *In Catilinam* IV.

PLATE I

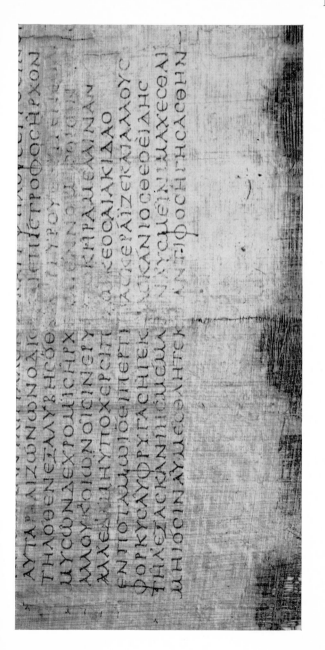

PLATE II

PLATE III

PLATE IV

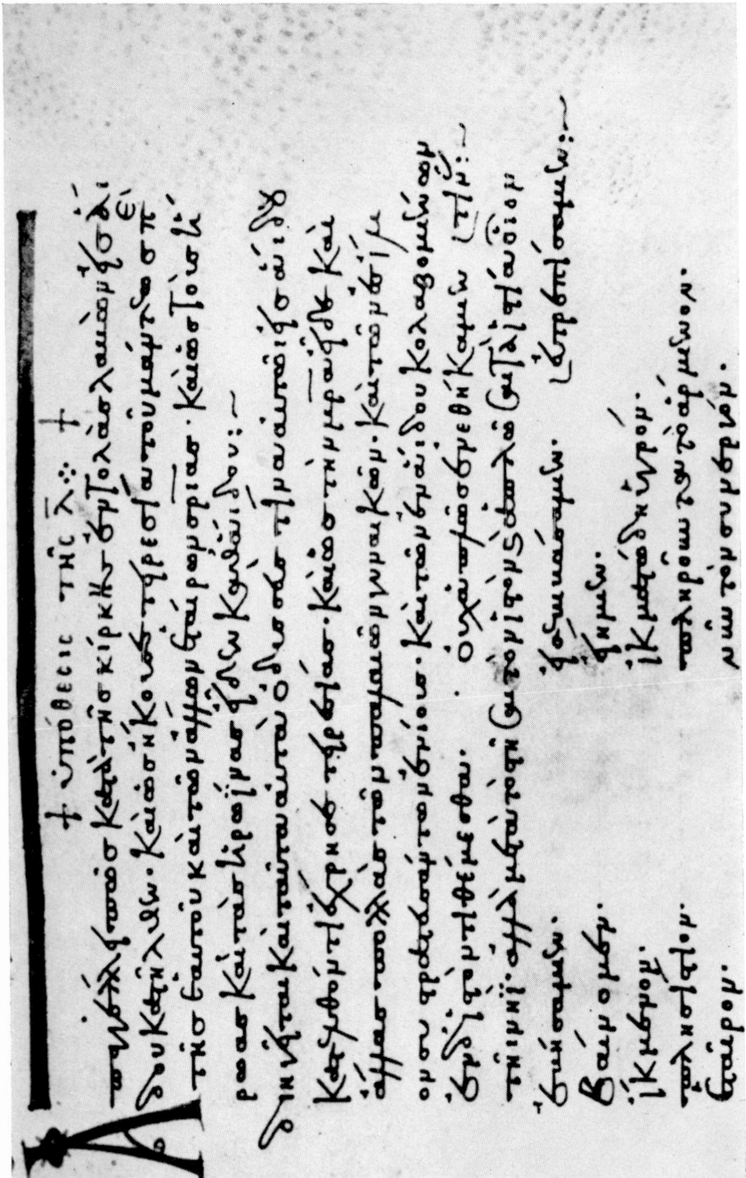

PLATE V

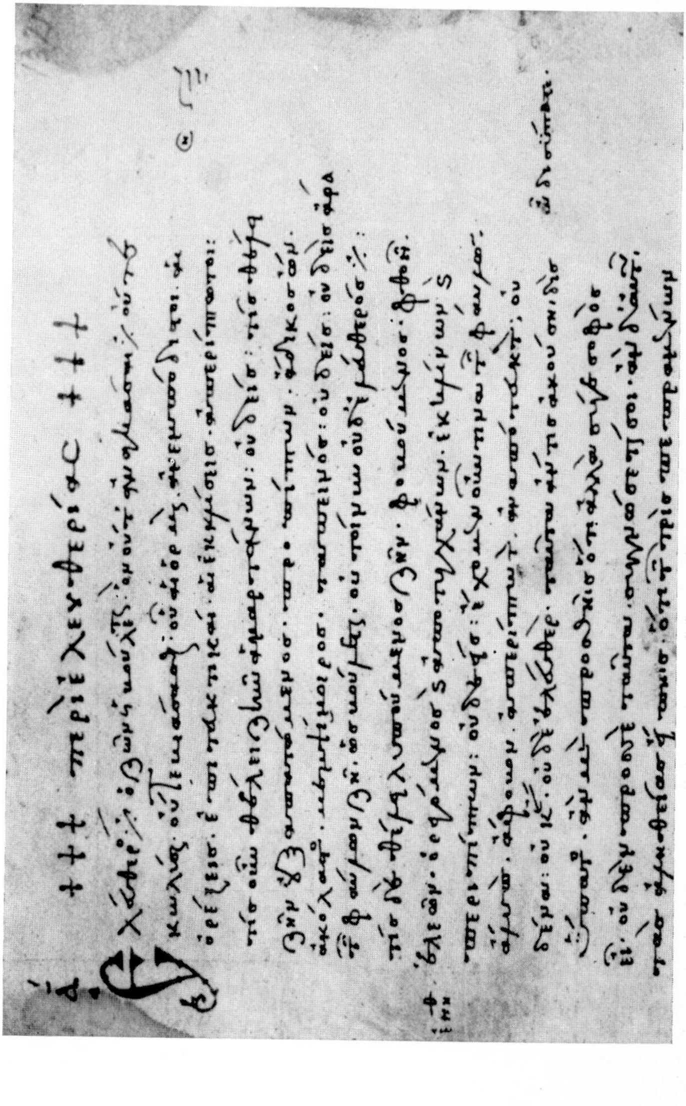

PLATE VI

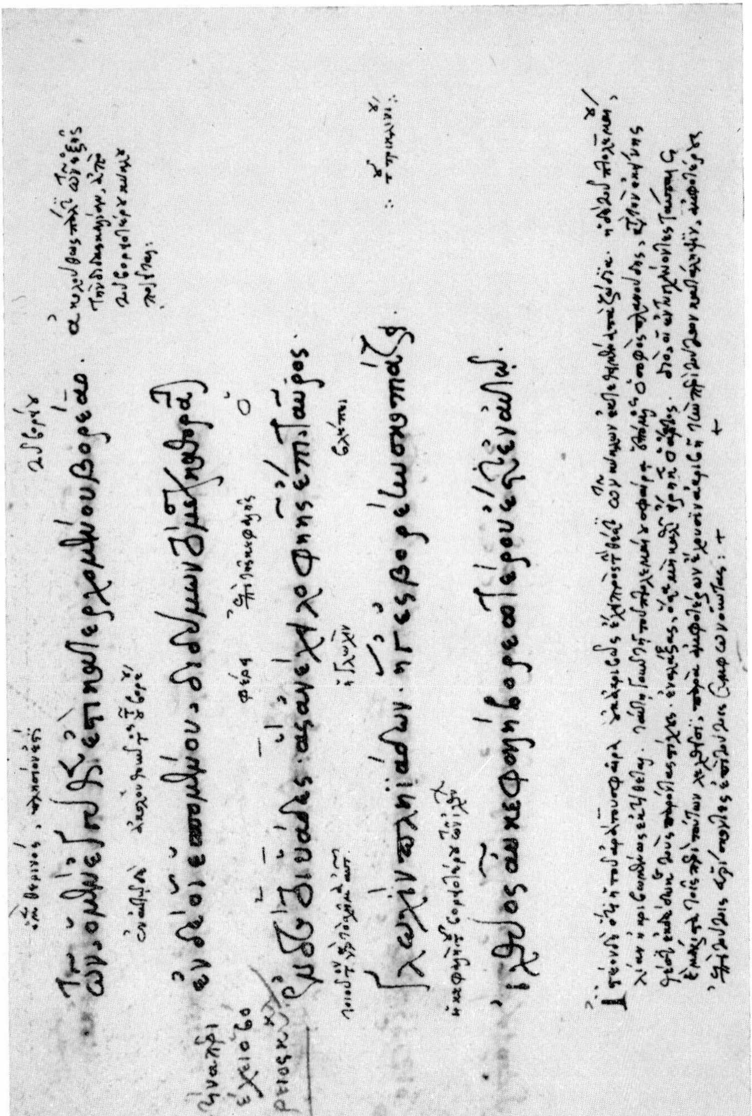

PLATE VII

PLATE VIII

PLATE IX

AUTDEUSILLEMALISHOMINUMMITESCEREDISCAT·
IAMNEQ·AMISSIDATADESERUSUANECCARMINANABIS
IPSAELACENTIPSAERUASUSAECONCIDITESILUAE
NONILLUMNOSTRIPOSSUNTMUTARELABORES
NECSITRIGORIB·MEDIISHEDRUMQ·BIBAMUS
SITHONIASQ·NIUESHIEMISSUDEAMUSAQUOSAE
NECSICUMMORIENSALTALIBERARETINULMO
AETHIOPUMUERSEMUSOUISSUBSIDERECANCRI
OMNIAUINCETAMORETNOSCIDAMUSAMORI
HAECSATERITDIUAEUESTRUMCECINISSEPOETAM
DUMSEDETETGRACILIFISCELLAMTEXITHIBISCO
PIERIDESUOSHAECFACIETISMAXIMAGALLO·
GALLOCUIUSAMOMANTUMMIHICRESCITINHORAS
QUANTUMUERENOUOUIRIDISSEUBIMALTHUS
SURGAMUSSOLETESSEGRAUISCANTANTIBUMBRA
IUNIPERIGRAUISUMBRANOCENTETFRUGIBUSUM
ITEDOMUMSATURAEUENITHESPERUSITECAPELLAE

TURCIUS RUFIUS APRONIANUS ASTERIUS UC ET INL EX COM ET DOM ES ET PRAEFECT VRB ET PATRICIUS
EX COMES DOM ET PATRICIUS ET CONSUL ORDIN LEGI ET DISTINXI CODICEM FRATRIS MACHARII UC
NON MEO SED EIUS STUDIO ET TABONIA SUMPTU UC IS ABBATIS ... BALEMA MONTE

P·   VIRGILII   MARONIS

BUCOLICON   LIBER   EXPLICIT

INCIPIT   GEORGICON

Note. The uncial script (Cicero) is written in two columns of which only the left is shown here. The Irish script is written across the width of the folio.

PLATE X

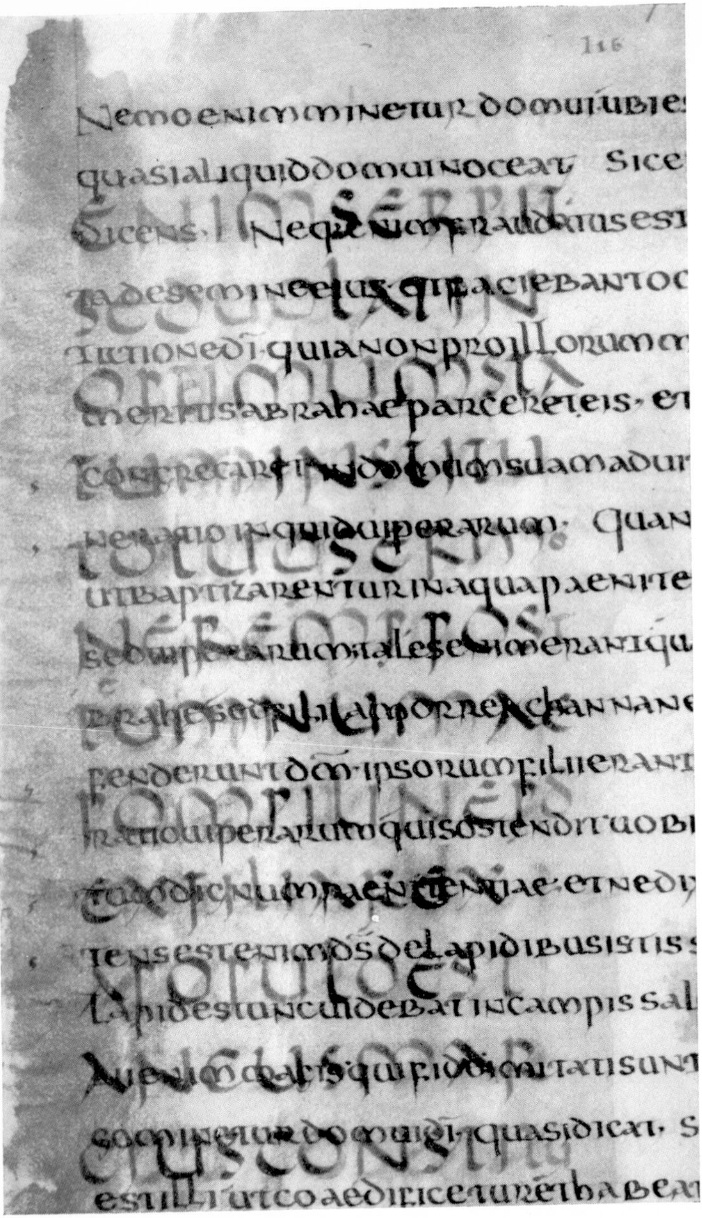

PLATE XI

hAECHANNIBALPOSTCAN
NENSEMPUGNAMCAPTA
ACDIREPTACONFESTIM
EXAPULIAINSAMNIUM
MOUERATACCITUSINHIR
PINOSASTATIOPOLICEN
TESSECOMPSXATRAQ·TU
TIAMCOMPSXNOSEXIT
TREBIUSNOBILISINTER
SUOSSOUIRENTENUM
MOPSIELLAIMPXETIUPX
MILINEPERGRATAMRO
MANXCIUITPOLICITUS
POSTXXIIIXATCAMPEO
SISPUGNXETIOLCASIUM
QUETREBISENATORIUS
ADUENTUMLXRGIOIBX
LISCOMCOMPSXANUA
BEOTEXCESSISSENTSI
NETARMXTIUELTXOT
TAMRPSTOENORPLLOSI
DICIMQ·NCCEPIUMERI
USBITRAEDXOMNINICH
IMPEDIMENTISKEUO
TISEXERCITUPXRTTO
MXCONEMPERTONIS

PLATE XII

TERTIVS EVRO
PE SINVS

tertius europe
sinus

a cenocenæ. unus incipit montib;
primum. helisponto complectitur.
præter. minores sinus xix xxii.
pæssuum meo eps posœ. cocrinœrnœ. creta
toliœ. phocis locris ceraiœ. messenia.
laconicœ. ariolicis megaris attice boetid.
itemum que. œbadio mari eaclem phocis
& locris donis phietis theseliœ. mag
nesiœ. mœcedoniœ. thrœciœ. omnisquieaq;
fœbulositœs. sicut & litterarum clari
tas exhoc. primum simi espulsit. quœ.
propter. parilum meo commorabimur.
Eps nos™unuersum œppellatœ. œcenœ.
unus incipit montibus ineœ. primi chœ.
ones œquibus choniœ. dentes prot i ceiti
tonenses locos hœornon & pestiferœ. œri
bus exœlatio. cestrum. per. œbi. quonum.
mons pi ndus cœssopœei. chuo pes sello.
epilopes molosi œpiri. quos dodonœei.

PLATE XIII

INCIPIT LIBER VICESIMUS TERTIUS·

Haec hannibal post cannensem pugnam capta ac direpta con-
festim ex apulia in samnium moverat accitus in hyrpinos a sta-
tio pollicentes se compsam traditurum Compsanus erat trebius nobilis inter-
suos sed premebat eum compsinorum factio romano
rum potens post fugam cannensis pugnae uolgata que trebi sermoni-
b; aduentu hannibalis cum compsam urbem excessissent fine certamine
tradita urbs poeno praesidium que acceptum est Ibi pdcomni atq; impedi
menta reliquas exercitu poeno magone regionis eius urbes diditque a defec-
enas a romanis accipere aut detractantes cogere ad defectionem iubet
ipse per agrum campanum ferum petit oppugnaturus nec potuit
urbem ea tramcam haberet Ubi si nes nec polanorum imminutu
nimdes paucam in nisidius et plerus que augustinius aut finus que occulta que
cum q; apte poterat disposuit alios praecatam praeda exagnis oftas

PLATE XIV

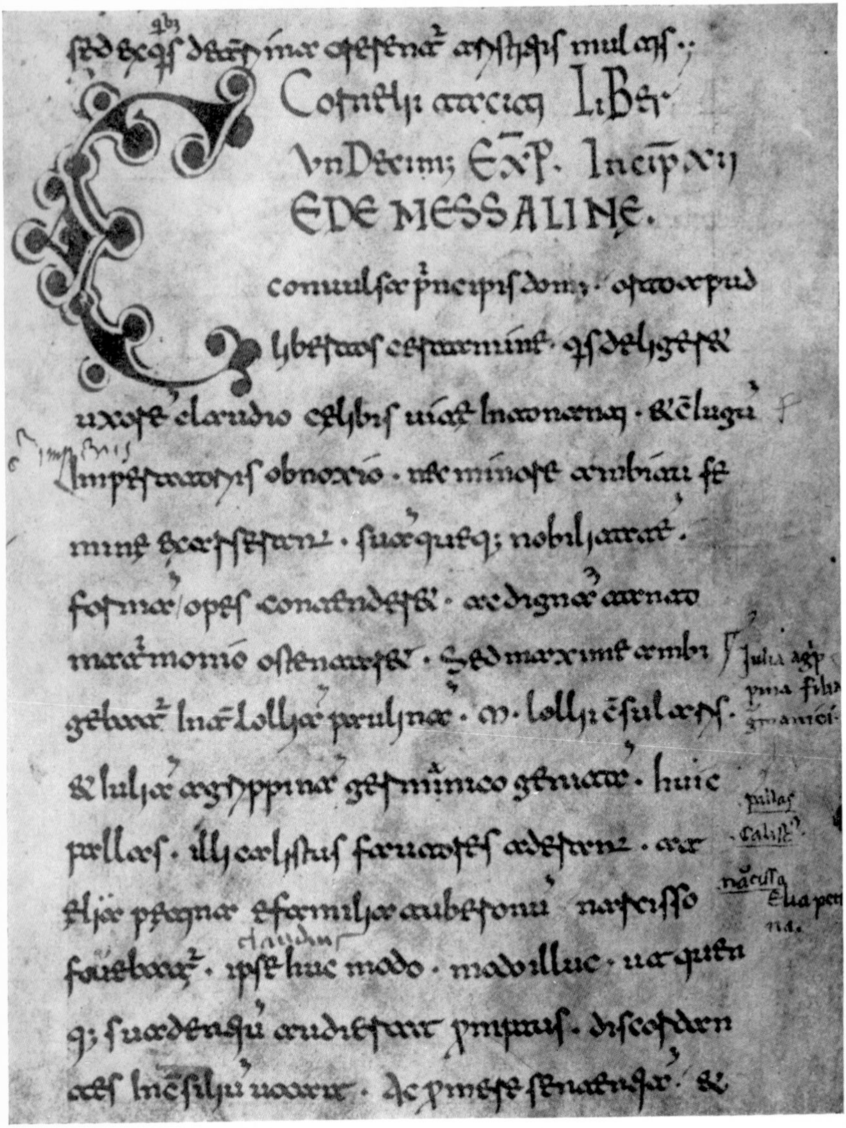